IN THE HANDS OF THE PEOPLE

Also by William L. Dwyer

THE GOLDMARK CASE: AN AMERICAN LIBEL TRIAL

IN THE
HANDS OF THE
PEOPLE

THE TRIAL JURY'S ORIGINS,

TRIUMPHS, TROUBLES, AND FUTURE

IN AMERICAN DEMOCRACY

William L. Dwyer

THOMAS DUNNE BOOKS

ST. MARTIN'S GRIFFIN ⚓ NEW YORK

THOMAS DUNNE BOOKS.
An imprint of St. Martin's Press.

www.stmartins.com

Library of Congress Cataloging-in-Publication Data

Excerpt from "Children in Exile" from *Children in Exile: Poems 1968–1984* by James Fenton. Copyright © 1985 by James Fenton. Reprinted by permission of Farrar, Straus and Giroux, LLC.

Dwyer, William L.
    In the hands of the people : the trial jury's origins, triumphs, troubles, and future in American democracy / William L. Dwyer.
        p. cm.
    Includes bibliographical references (p. 194) and index (p.229).
    ISBN 0-312-27812-8 (hc)
    ISBN 0-312-33094-4 (pbk)
    EAN 978-0312-33094-1
    1. Jury—United States. I. Title.

KF9680 .D89 2002
347.73'52—dc21   2001054756

First St. Martin's Griffin Edition: August 2004

10 9 8 7 6 5 4 3 2 1

FOR
VASILIKI

CONTENTS

ACKNOWLEDGMENTS

Years ago, although I was a trial lawyer and not an academic, the University of Washington School of Law invited me to teach a course on litigation—its history, current problems, and future prospects. I am grateful to the law school's deans, faculty, and librarians for getting me started on the road that led to this book, and for allowing a visitor to teach so challenging a subject.

At every stage of the writing, Fred Brack and Phyllis Hatfield gave encouragement and wise advice. Early drafts were read and helpfully criticized by Chris Addicott, Bernard V. Burke, Chris Goelz, Arthur W. Harrigan, Jr., Stewart Jay, Robert S. Lasnik, Cheryl McCall, Victor Ortiz de Montellano, Barbara Jacobs Rothstein, George Schatzki, Kristin Schumacher, Joanna Dwyer Tiffany, Fredric C. Tausend, and John L. Weinberg. None of these benefactors is responsible for the errors that undoubtedly remain.

For production and editing help I am indebted to Trish Graham and Shelley Hall. Jane Dystel, a paragon of literary agents, and Ruth Cavin, my good-humored and skillful editor at St. Martin's Press, made the publishing process a pleasure.

This book was written on weekend and holiday mornings while I was serving as a United States District Judge, a most demanding and time-consuming job. For putting up with that, and for too much else to recount here, I am grateful to Vasiliki Dwyer.

W.L.D.

When I walk into a courtroom, it is usually from the front, through the door that leads to the judge's bench, with the flag at one side and the seal of the federal court, featuring a splayed eagle, high on the wall behind where I sit. In the well just below, at floor level, are the clerk and court reporter; then the parties and their lawyers at tables; and, beyond them, the spectators. Along one side, near the judge's bench, is the jury box. On the first day of a trial it is occupied by twelve people who are strangers to one another, untrained in the law, and without knowledge of the case they will be asked to decide. They are new to all this, and some of them seem awed at first by their surroundings, but from past experience I know they will do well. Jurors have been my courtroom companions for a long time, and I like and respect them. They serve in a time-honored tradition that has contributed mightily to American liberty. Yet now there is a serious risk that they will disappear from our trials—not through any fault of theirs, but because of indifference, neglect, and misunderstanding about their work. That's why I have written this book.

To visitors from abroad—even to some Americans—the jury is a surprising invention. We enlist twelve citizens, chosen more or less at random, to hear evidence and arguments; we accept their verdict, ordinarily, as conclusive; and when their task is finished we send them back to their usual lives. Issues of nationwide importance, as well as routine disputes, are decided in this way. No other modern society has bet so heavily on the common man's and woman's good sense. Today's critics—they too are part of a long tradition—argue that a trial method dating back to medieval England cannot succeed in the world of the

Internet, genetic mapping, space travel, cellular telephones, rap and rock, an enormously complex economy, and still-unresolved racial divisions. As they see it, the jury has become too dim-witted, bias-prone, slow, and costly to be used in modern trials, and its death is imminent.

I think the critics are wrong. In hundreds of trials that I have had the good fortune to see as a lawyer and a judge, I have learned that the jury system works. Given a fair chance, it succeeds even in compli-cated, emotion-charged, highly publicized cases. What the jury needs is not abolition but firmer support from the public and better work by judges and lawyers. The old institution is in danger, but it can be saved; it will flourish or perish depending on how we treat it in the new century. The choice will be ours, and we should make it consciously, with knowledge of what is at stake.

These thoughts occurred to me often as I watched trials unfold before an ever-changing variety of men and women seated in the jury box. It seemed to me also that the work all of us do in the law is at the surfline of a deep sea of history that must be explored if we are to understand the tides and the breakers and the weather on shore. The story we need to know begins with prehistory, with our species' long tenure on earth before the arrival of agriculture, literacy, and industry, for it was then that our adversary system had its beginnings—and to understand the jury, or the daily happenings in American courts, we must first understand the adversary system with all its faults and virtues.

So my immediate concern over the jury's future tied into a long-standing interest in litigation history, a subject on which I had read at length and even had taught (with no surplus of credentials) at a law school. It is true everywhere, but nowhere more than in the law, that the past lives on in the present.

For that reason this book offers an overview of litigation's universe. The first half describes mankind's worldwide efforts to find ways to settle disputes without resorting to violence. It chronicles the rise of trial by jury in the thirteenth century, the unexpected and often heroic role of the jury in creating modern liberty, and the growth of rules of the game meant to assure fairness and accuracy in the process. These developments are illustrated by great cases of the past; I have used the original transcripts and other source documents whenever possible, and have quoted them verbatim except to modernize the spelling.

The second half of the book deals with what has gone wrong in American litigation, the controversy over the jury's competence and integrity, trial reforms that must be made, the need to bring fairness and economy into the battles that take place outside the courtroom (primarily discovery and settlement), and the changing shape of American litigation in the twenty-first century.

Scholars are cordially invited to read and criticize this book, but it is meant chiefly for those who know a little but not a lot about the legal system, and who care what happens to it. I do not claim to be neutral. Readers are entitled to full disclosure, and I admit at the start that my admiration for the jury, strong while I was a trial lawyer, has only deepened during my service as a judge. Imperfect and battle-scarred though it is, the jury, as I see it, still is able to reach fair and honest verdicts, to say "no" to official power when that small word must be uttered for the sake of freedom, and to legitimize hard decisions for a questioning public. It still "contributes most powerfully," as Tocqueville wrote a hundred and sixty-five years ago, "to form the judgment and to increase the natural intelligence of the people." And it sheds light on two other democratic institutions, the ballot box and the initiative and referendum. If jury trials as a rule produce sounder results than we can count on in elections—which I believe they do— one reason may be the quality of information given to the citizens who must decide. In contrast to the chaos and mendacity of much political campaigning, and to the scattergun delivery of thirty-second television commercials, a jury hears testimony that is kept to the point by an impartial referee, tested by cross-examination, and offered throughout a day. We should be able to learn something valuable from the differences in communication.

With about 1.5 million Americans serving in courtrooms each year, the trial jury achieves a unique dispersal of governmental power. Far from being obsolete, it gains importance as elected officials become more distant from those they represent. When the United States government began, there was one congressman for every 38,000 constituents. Due to population growth, there now is one for every 647,000, a seventeen-fold increase in remoteness; state legislatures have seen a similar change. The jury, by placing decisions directly in the hands of the people, bridges the widening gap between citizens and their government. Our challenge is not just to keep it, but to restore it to full health amid new and difficult conditions. In that we can succeed, and I think we will.

For those who want to read more, the main source documents, and a sampling of books and articles, are cited in the Notes. I have had the benefit of superb work by legal historians and other scholars, and I am grateful to the authors listed and to many others whose work has enriched the study of litigation.

Justice is probably the oldest and most universally professed value. Anthropologists and historians are hard put to name a healthy society that has not honored (or professed to honor) some variation of the idea. Nature is unjust, humans are often unjust, yet we refuse to live in a world without the idea of justice.

—John W. Gardner, *Morale*
(New York: W. W. Norton & Co., Inc., 1978)

[N]o tyrant could afford to leave a subject's freedom in the hands of twelve of his countrymen. So that trial by jury is more than an instrument of justice and more than one wheel of the constitution: it is the lamp that shows that freedom lives.

—Sir Patrick Devlin, "Trial by Jury,"
The Hamlyn Lectures (London:
Stevens & Sons Limited, 1956)

IN THE HANDS OF THE PEOPLE

The Endangered Jury

Trial by jury, enshrined in the United States Constitution and guaranteed by every state's laws, has deep roots in American life and at first glance might seem imperishable. But we could wake up one day to find that the great old tree has fallen. If that happens, the power to decide cases—to apply the law to flesh-and-blood people who are prosecuted or who bring their disputes to court—will fall exclusively into the hands of judges or other government officials. And if it happens the cause will be not a tyrant's ax but a long and scarcely noticed process of decay. Indifference, in the long run, is deadlier than any coup, and democratic institutions are easily lost through neglect followed by decline and abandonment. The trial jury, long neglected, is at the first stage and verging on the second. So far we have let it suffer without paying much heed, and we need to look at what is happening, and why, and what we stand to gain or lose.

The founders of the American republic would be surprised to learn that the jury's survival is in doubt. When they wrote the Constitution, trial by jury was widely seen as "the very palladium of free government," to use a phrase from *The Federalist Papers,* and would no more have been abandoned than would the ballot box. Thomas Jefferson, while serving as ambassador to France, wrote in a 1789 letter: "Were I called upon to decide whether the people had best be omitted in the Legislative or Judiciary department, I would say it is better to leave them out of the Legislative."

Today Jefferson's ranking is reversed: everyone understands that elections are vital in our republic, but many think the jury is expendable—"a howling anachronism," as one critic puts it.

Let's imagine that a group of eminent business leaders, public offi-cials, scholars, and journalists were to propose that the United States abandon elections and let panels of experts govern the country. "Elec-tions were fine when the Constitution was written," they might say, "but they have outlived their usefulness. Issues were simpler back then and nobody could vote except white male property owners. Now everybody can vote and the tasks of government are just too complex for ordinary people to understand. Often they get confused and elect the wrong candidates. They are easily swayed by irrational appeals to emotion and narrow self-interest. The voter-initiative process, in the states that have it, is distorted by money; in fact, campaign finance abuses corrupt the whole system. The public doesn't really care—only about half the eligible adults bother to vote in presidential contests and even fewer in other races. So let's drop the pretense. Let's get rid of elections and let the experts run the government with efficiency, econ-omy, and superior knowledge and judgment."

There would be an uproar. The promoters of this idea would be denounced as radical, even traitorous, and drummed out of the TV talking-head shows.

Yet a similar proposal, based on similar arguments, is being floated about trial by jury and is quietly gaining ground. Calls for jury aboli-tion are heard with increasing candor and frequency, even though the jury is as much an institution of self-government as is the election of our officials. To abolish the jury would be to take from the people one of their basic rights. There is no uproar—at least, not yet.

The late Warren Burger, Chief Justice of the Supreme Court, for example, recommended that we drop the civil jury in favor of bench trials, at least in complex cases. A bench trial is one decided entirely by the judge; there are no jurors in the box. In criminal cases, according to Michael Lind, a senior fellow at the New American Foundation and lecturer at Harvard Law School, "[t]he American jury system does not work to free the innocent and punish the guilty in an efficient and humane manner. It never has." Juries are "fundamentally dysfunctional," says Delaware judge John Babiarz, who led a state court task force on the subject.

Such critics maintain that the jury simply lacks competence and we should admit that, forgo sentimentality, and make the necessary changes.

Other experts do not call for abolition but see a crisis at hand. "I think the American jury is in serious trouble," says psychology professor Valerie Hans, a defender of the jury and a leading authority in the field. "Our democratic institutions are foundering, and the jury is among them," writes law professor Albert Alschuler. Federal appellate judge Richard Posner predicts that "in the long run the jury, or at least the civil jury, is probably doomed."

The signs of trouble appear throughout the country but most vividly in major cities. Public confidence in criminal prosecutions has been shaken by acquittals and hung juries in high-profile cases where, from a distance, the evidence seemed to many to be conclusive of guilt. There is a recurring demand—by California's former governor Pete Wilson, among others—that the unanimous verdict requirement be dropped to make convictions easier. Some observers propose the use of quotas to achieve racially balanced juries—a step that would admit defeat in our pursuit of justice without regard to race, creed, or economic condition. Juries of fewer than twelve, used in some jurisdictions, reduce both the reliability and the prestige of verdicts. Plea bargaining has replaced criminal trials so extensively that only 4.3 percent of federal criminal charges now end in jury verdicts, compared to 10.4 percent in 1988.

The criminal jury's future is far from certain, and the civil jury is even more clearly at risk. Some courts are overturning verdicts more freely than in the past—giving less weight, that is, to the jury's evaluation of the evidence. In Texas, for example, the state supreme court's reversals of verdicts awarding damages to injured claimants have caused dissenting judges to complain of "a steady erosion of our right to trial by jury."

In recent years some courts have removed whole areas from the civil jury and placed them in the judiciary's hands, including cases involving bankruptcy, employee benefits, the meaning of words in insurance policies, consumer protection, fraud, and the weighing of evidence to see whether it supports a plaintiff's verdict or is "equally balanced" so as to require a defense verdict. "There is absolutely a trend of taking issues away from the jury," says law professor Nancy King. These shifts of power from juries to judges are made, ordinarily, on statutory or constitutional grounds, but sometimes with an expressed skepticism about jury competence. The United States Supreme Court in 1996 sounded an ominous note in holding that the question of what a patent means must be kept from the jury and decided by the judge. This ruling was based largely on history—an attempt to discern what was intended in 1791, when the federal jury trial guarantee was adopted—but the Court added a functional reason: "[J]udges, not juries, are the better suited to find the acquired meaning of patent terms." That comment seemed to echo the attempt by several courts in the 1970s to carve out a "complexity exception" to the right to trial by jury—to let the judge decide that a case is too complicated for jurors to understand, and that a bench trial must be used.

Judges also are responsible for the expanded use of summary judgment, a type of order cutting short a civil case because the losing party has failed to show evidence that would raise a genuine question to decide. A case decided on summary judgment never gets to trial. The technique is legitimate but must be used with care; overloaded calendars can lead judges to convert what should be a scalpel into a meat ax. When that happens, trial by jury suffers.

Legislators in thirty-four states have set caps on damages that can be awarded. These changes in the law of remedies apply to bench trials as well, but are explained as curbs on "runaway juries." "Why have a jury at all?" asked one frustrated member of a jury whose punitive damage award to the family of a worker needlessly killed in a workplace explosion was drastically reduced under state law. And both state and federal legislators have chronically underfunded the courts, contributing to long delays that diminish the value of trials. Because of the slowness, expense, and risks of conventional litigation, business firms by the thousand are opting out of the court system by using agreements that require customers and employees to submit disputes to private arbitration. The jury suffers a loss of prestige—yet expense, slowness, and damages liability ordained by law are not of its making.

There are widespread beliefs, encouraged by media coverage and interest-group campaigning, that juries are easy marks for injured claimants and award excessive damages; that they cannot understand complex evidence; that they succumb to any appeal to sympathy and let off guilty defendants; and that they pay no attention to the judge's instructions on the law and do whatever they feel like doing. These beliefs are false, and ironically the same citizens who hold them, when they serve as jurors, prove they are false. But institutions held in low esteem can slip away more easily than those we revere. The low rate of response to jury summonses in many cities is worrisome because it shows a breach between citizens and a method of self-government that requires their participation. The jurors who show up do well, but the system needs a fuller response from the American public in all its diversity.

Our adversary system assumes that a spirited competition to persuade will best lead to justice and community satisfaction, and it gives the parties and their counsel unparalleled independence and freedom in conducting their cases.That has been the prime source of its strength over the centuries.

Today it has troubles, but they arise not from the jury but from the way we manage adversarial justice. We have problems of expense, delay, trial quality, and access to justice, but to treat these by abandoning the jury would be like amputating an arm to cure a case of influenza. The problems exist as well where there is no jury—in the thousands of bench trials held each year. If we held only bench trials— if the jury did not exist—we could make the needed improvements with a lower sense of urgency, secure in the knowledge that trials are bound to continue and judges, one way or another, will continue to preside over them. But we do have the jury, and the looming danger is that we will lose it if we move too slowly or incompetently to improve the system that surrounds it.

That is happening in England, birthplace of the jury, where decades of indifference, and a lack of constitutional protection, have driven the civil jury almost to extinction and reduced the criminal jury's scope and prestige. The English jury's decline continues; there is official pressure to take still more types of criminal cases away from it. The result, as one authority puts it, is "a different brand of justice altogether"—a brand that we should not accept unless we are sure we want it.

In the United States the jury's erosion is all the more dangerous for being largely unnoticed. "For the first time in our country's history, the future of the jury system is in serious jeopardy," says Ronald Jay Cohen, chairman of the American Bar Association's Litigation Section. "It's happening quietly in state after state, in court after court, and in several different areas of the law. But make no mistake, the right to trial by jury is slipping away."

We can reverse the trend, but first we must decide whether we want to. We need to step back, remember how we got our system and what it has achieved in the past, assess how it is working now, and understand how it brings benefits beyond merely placing verdicts in the court file. The debate over the jury is not just about current events but about the fate of an institution that has been with us throughout American history and that began centuries before European settlers reached this continent. What is it all about, this running battle of words that so intrigues us that every day's newspapers are filled with it? Why is it forever being re-created in novels, movies, and television shows? Why do we let ordinary citizens decide cases in the first place? Is what we have worth preserving? To answer, we must start at the beginning.

CIVILIZED FIGHTS

All litigation is personal. We see this easily where the case pits a man or woman openly against another—as in suits over divorce, bodily injury, libel, fraud, or breach of contract. But it is also true where the named parties are abstract entities such as governments or corporations. Behind *Brown v. Board of Education* were black children placed in segregated schools and, against them, legislators and school board members who were refusing to change an unjust system. An appeal for social security benefits is made against a bureaucracy, but the real contestants are the claimant and a living, breathing civil servant who has said no. In a robbery prosecution the state is the plaintiff, but the prosecutor is a person and she, in turn, speaks for the traumatized bank teller and the bank's shareholders whose money was stolen. The parties in a wildlife conservation case may be the Sierra Club and a loggers' association and a government department, but the struggle is among individual citizens who hike or work in the woods and a living person who happens to serve as a cabinet secretary. Even in a property forfeiture case—which might be called something like *United States v. One BMW Automobile*—there are people: the drug dealer whose profits bought the car, the addicts whom he supplied, the prosecutor and defense lawyer, the witnesses. However muted or sublimated or hemmed in by ritual, a lawsuit is a kind of civilized fight.

Reflecting this, our country since colonial days has had the adversary trial system. We are all accustomed to this word-based, impartially refereed battleground—so accustomed that we take it as a given, like the weather. But it is only one of countless ways humans have invented to resolve disputes, to order compensation or punishment or acquittal so that conflicts will end and peace be restored. Today our trial system needs repairs, but before we can fix it with confidence we need to see how it fits into the universal quest for justice. We may begin with a calamity that showed what can happen when communal dispute resolution fails to take control—the day the vice president of the United States shot and killed the nation's first secretary of the treasury.

At sunrise on July 11, 1804, Alexander Hamilton, accompanied by a doctor and a friend who would be his second, crossed the Hudson River in a skiff rowed by two oarsmen. In the cool of morning, Hamilton must have yearned to turn back to Manhattan. He was only forty-nine, he had a family to support, and, although in political decline, he dreamed of a triumphant return. He knew the peril he faced. His twenty-year-old son had been killed in a duel not long before, and Hamilton had condemned these affairs of honor as relics of "ignorance, superstition, and Gothic barbarism." Hamilton was a man of reason, and he knew this crossing was madness; yet he kept on toward the New Jersey shore.

Of course, he might yet survive this day. When the moment came and he stood facing his challenger, he would fire into the air. If the other man did the same, or simply missed, both could walk away with reputations intact.

The other man, unfortunately, was Aaron Burr, vice president of the United States. At forty-eight, Burr was a hot-tempered adventurer, a schemer thwarted in the pursuit of power, a rival avid for revenge. Burr saw in Hamilton the author of his frustration; he did not intend to miss.

For reasons still not entirely clear, a Burr-Hamilton enmity, surpassing even the harsh political rhetoric of the time, had been growing for years. Their similarities probably inflamed their rivalry. Both were New Yorkers; both were successful practicing lawyers (they had even tried a famous murder case as co-counsel); both were short, energetic, and passionate; both were renowned womanizers (Hamilton is thought to have been jealous of a mistress's attraction to Burr); and both were Machiavellian politicians. There were differences that grated as well: Burr was well-born, while Hamilton had begun life as a bastard; Hamilton's achievements in starting the republic were monumental, while Burr had accomplished little in public life. Hamilton habitually spoke ill of Burr, who returned the animosity in a crescendo of spite. Their hostility grew in 1800, when Burr and Thomas Jefferson finished in an electoral-vote tie for the presidency. The contest was thrown into the House of Representatives, where Hamilton, an opponent of both men, successfully urged Jefferson's election. An embittered Burr became vice president, a position then assigned to the runner-up. Four years later Burr ran for governor of New York. It was said that he wanted to form a northern confederacy, breaking up the Union. Hamilton, a power in New York politics, once more stood in the way, and Burr lost again.

In their political battles Hamilton had accused Burr of opportunism, demagoguery, and worse. Now a seething Burr had had enough. He seized on a press report that Hamilton, at a dinner party, had expressed a "despicable opinion" of him. Although Burr may have been as ignorant as we are of what Hamilton actually said, he sent a letter demanding a "prompt and unqualified acknowledgment or denial." Hamilton tried to answer in a way that salvaged honor while avoiding a duel. Such a vague report, he wrote back, did not require him to confirm or deny. "I trust on more reflection you will see the matter in the same light with me. If not, I can only regret the circumstances, and must abide the consequences."

Burr would have none of it. The answer gave him the opening he wanted, and he issued his challenge. Without losing face, Hamilton could not flee and could not say no; he could only accept.

At this point, with the use of deadly force imminent, many societies we tend to consider "primitive" would have stepped in to prevent disaster; elders, priests, or other authority figures would have taken control to assure that life was preserved. That did not happen in New York in 1804.

When Hamilton and his companions arrived on the New Jersey side they found Burr and his second already at the dueling ground, a partially wooded ledge easily reached from the riverbank. Soon all was ready, and the two men, armed with smooth-bore pistols, faced each other at a distance of ten paces as the morning sun began to burn away the haze.

A second called out the signal "Present!" What happened next has been obscured by the post-duel polemics of both sides' partisans and by the tradition that witnesses would turn their backs at the crucial moment so that they could deny having seen what was, despite its popularity, a crime. We know that two shots were fired a few seconds apart. Most probably, Hamilton fired first but deliberately sent his shot into a tree above and to the side of his opponent. Burr then raised his arm, took careful aim, and fired. The .54-caliber ball struck Hamilton just below his rib cage and he fell to the ground.

To the physician who rushed to his side, Hamilton managed to say, "This is a mortal wound, doctor," before he lost consciousness. The ball had passed through Hamilton's liver and lodged in his spine. His second and the doctor took him back across the river to a house in Manhattan. There, after thirty hours of agony, attended by his wife, their seven surviving children, and the Episcopal bishop of New York, he died.

Public opinion about the duel quickly coalesced in the dead man's favor, and Burr fled to the South to avoid prosecution. He lived through three more decades of misadventure, and expired, unrepentant, at eighty.

Alexander Hamilton could not afford to die when he did. Although an able lawyer, he had been so consumed by politics, so careless of his estate, that he left his wife and children deeply in debt. Friends, fortunately, paid off the debts, but no gesture of friendship could recoup the loss to the nation. Born out of wedlock in the British West Indies, Hamilton had come to New York at seventeen and had risen to become an officer in the Revolutionary War, a leading light at the Constitutional Convention of 1787, coauthor of *The Federalist Papers*, first secretary of the treasury, ghostwriter of Washington's famous

Farewell Address, early advocate of freeing the slaves, and foremost champion of a strong central government in the fractious United States. Adept at making enemies—both Jefferson and John Adams deplored him as a closet monarchist and a menace to the republic— Hamilton had scant regard for the common people and an excessive fondness for power. Yet his brilliance, his eloquence, and his devotion to public service led the French diplomat Talleyrand to call him the greatest of the "choice and master spirits of the age." Thanks to his youthful achievements and untimely death, he looks at us now from the face of every ten-dollar bill.

In the days before the duel Hamilton had gotten his business affairs in order, wound up as many cases as he could for his clients, and written his will. He had every reason to refuse to fight—but he could not. His self-regard, the esteem of his friends, even his political future, would be ruined if he shrank from Burr's challenge. And so he went to his early and unwanted end.

By 1804 the Age of Reason had long since arrived. The scientific method, the rights of man, and the rule of law had been proclaimed. How could such a man, in such a time, have perished so vainly? Both Hamilton and Burr were lawyers, and this country had libel suits to remedy slurs on reputation, a free press to publish denials and counter-charges, and statutes that outlawed dueling. Yet among the political gentry none of these was strong enough to fend off disaster if a gentleman insisted on a challenge. Alexander Hamilton died because he was trapped in a social class that lacked the subtlety and inventiveness of, say, the Greenland Inuit or the tribesmen of New Guinea.

To deal with raging quarrels—to stop anger from turning to murder, to prevent a homicide once committed from spiraling into general carnage, to avert feuds that spill the blood of generations—has been the first task of law. Men have always fought. They have battled over hunting and fishing territory, mating rights, land, possessions, office, insults real or imagined, or out of mere aggressiveness (often fueled by drink). The Book of Genesis tells us it all began in the second generation when

"Cain rose up against Abel his brother, and slew him." Cain is described as "a tiller of the ground," Abel as "a keeper of sheep." It was the first clash between farmers and ranchers. Cain avoided further trouble by moving east, but few societies can count on separation to end disputes. We must stay together and we must patch things up.

Every society has rules, although they may be unwritten and even unspoken, and every society has ways of settling disputes when rules are broken. We have learned that we must develop these ways. What happens if we don't is shown by international life today: conflicts spin out of control; fighting breaks out again and again; outrage and atrocity feed on each other. Rules of international law exist and are observed much of the time. But when they aren't—when one nation invades another with armed force, or terrorists blow an airplane out of the sky, or a dictator's police torture political prisoners—there is no reliable way to achieve justice. We should know better by now. Within each well-ordered society—in the intramural affairs of nations, tribes, and clans—we have known better for a long time.

Our forebears were hunters and gatherers and subsistence farmers, as some in the world still are. The people in such groups must work together to extract a living from the forest or sea or savannah or newly cleared field. They cannot afford to let an argument cause the death of a useful person, or a killing spread into a feud. So they have devised, since long before recorded history began, a marvelous variety of dispute-resolution methods—systems of justice—to give the group and the combatants an outcome all can accept. These methods have been chronicled by legal anthropologists, working mostly in the twentieth century but observing customs filled with the wisdom of untold ages. Traditional ways are fading as the postindustrial age envelops the globe, and I will use the past tense in describing them; but some of them still exist, and the past tense here includes the recent past.

The primeval step has been to draw a line between accepted killing and murder. Most societies have distinguished between death inflicted in a fair fight and killing by stealth or sneak attack, the latter being a likelier occasion for deadly revenge. To this small degree the Hamilton-Burr duel enjoyed the benefits of civilization. The duel, although barbarous, was a fair fight under the gentleman's code. The law forbade a cycle of revenge and reprisal, and there was none; later generations of Hamiltons and Burrs were spared the trouble of shooting at each other over an ancient grievance.

When the "fair fight" concept does not work, the loss of a life or body part calls irresistibly for action. To deal with this, to keep revenge within the bounds of poetic justice, a rule of equivalency has sprung up in many parts of the world. If you kill my brother, I may kill you or your brother—but no more; I may not kill your whole family—and once I have dispatched you or your equivalent relative, the affair is over.

A striking example is that of the Gisu in East Africa, among whom the kinsmen of a slain youth were required to wait until the killer's son reached the age of the departed, and then could take the young man's life.

The Bible's "an eye for an eye" is an equivalency rule—not just the cry for revenge it usually is taken to be, but a warning to let the response go no further than the provocation. If you take my eye, I may take yours—but not your life—and then we are even. There will be no escalation, no prolonging of the fight. This is found also in the Code of Hammurabi, a great codification of law written in Babylon about 1750 B.C.:

If a man destroy the eye of another man, they shall destroy his eye.

If he break a man's bone, they shall break his bone.

If a man knock out a tooth of a man of his own rank, they shall knock out his tooth.

But:

If he knock out a tooth of a common man, he shall pay one-third mana of silver.

"An eye for an eye" is always with us. It speaks to something deep in our souls and appears today in demands that murderers be killed or assailants whipped.

More sophisticated than eye-for-an-eye violence have been the ways found by preindustrial people to vent anger and aggression harmlessly without loss of face. In every part of the world, disputes have been channeled into physical contests that do not kill or maim but still produce a final result.

If Alexander Hamilton and Aaron Burr had been Inuit, for example, their quarrel could have been settled by a time-honored ritual. Custom would have required them to stand before a public gathering and deliver straight-arm blows to each other's head until one fell. Or they would have had to sit opposite each other and butt heads until one was unseated. Nothing more violent than the controlled fight would have been permitted by the group, and the outcome would have been accepted by the combatants and their kinsmen. Such was the rule of a society earning its living in the Arctic chill. The result, we must admit, would have been better than that of pistols at ten paces.

In the western highlands of New Guinea, equivalents of the Hamilton-Burr quarrel were defused through a ritual called the *tagba boz.* The antagonists and their relatives lined up, facing each other, arms clasped behind backs. They then kicked at each other's shins until one group withdrew. The fight impulse was satisfied without damage beyond what might be expected in a soccer game.

Controlled fighting often has been done by champions who represent the contending parties in a trial by battle. Among the Ifugao, in the Philippines, the boundaries of rice fields were perennially in doubt because of erosion in the rainy season followed by crumbling in the heat. The Ifugao learned to avoid letting boundary disputes become deadly. Invoking the blessings of their ancestors, each side picked a young man to engage in a ceremonial wrestling match. The two champions then wrestled in the mud and slime of the rice field, cheered on by their supporters, each trying to down the other so as to gain territory. The boundary points were determined, as firmly as we would treat an engineer's survey, by where the wrestlers fell. I must admit that occasionally, in property dispute cases, I have envied the Ifugao.

Many societies have had the wit to remove violence altogether and replace it with symbolic contests. So it was with the Inuit song competitions. The disputing parties met before the assembled community. One made up an insulting song and sang it as a verbal attack on the other. The other reciprocated, pouring out abuse in the cleverest form he could manage. There were replies and ripostes until the two were exhausted. The winner, at the end, was the singer who got more applause from the audience.

Among the Tongtong, in the Philippines, the quarreling parties were made to chew rice for the same length of time and then spit it out. The one with the better-masticated mouthful, as judged by the onlooking group, prevailed. A remarkably effective ritual fight was the competitive food exchange of the Trobriand Islanders in the South Pacific. When an exchange of insults risked a deadly struggle, a "big man" of the area would step in and direct that one man's village present all of its stored yams, as a gift, to the other man's village. The latter, by custom, had to reciprocate. Aggressive energies were diverted; the combatants and their allies exhausted themselves in days of counting, transporting, and delivering yams. When rough equality was achieved the argument was finished.

The Kwakiutl Indians of the Pacific Northwest devised the famous potlatch, a cousin of what came to be called, among the industrialized rich, conspicuous consumption. The adversaries threw their most valued possessions into a roaring bonfire. Each strove mightily to show he could afford to discard more than the other. Both suffered a loss of net worth, and the loser was shamed, but both lived to argue another day.

Custom may place the decision-making power in an outside judge. At first the judge is, most commonly, a god or a pantheon.

Since the gods are inscrutable, ways must be found to learn their judgment. The time-honored method is magic.

Australian aborigines, when a death was believed caused by sorcery, invoked the help of the victim himself. The corpse would be carried out on a bier among the tribespeople; when the procession came to the sorcerer, the deceased's spirit would cause the bier to move and touch him, as with a giant Ouija board. Punishment would follow.

In Burma, as late as the twentieth century, litigants were asked to light candles of the same length at the same moment. The one whose candle burned longer prevailed.

But the most widespread way of learning the judgment of the gods, the way used at some time or other in many parts of the world, has been the ordeal. A suspect was put to a test, often a very painful one. The outcome showed a divine judgment of guilt or innocence. Fire, hot water, cold water, and poison have all been used.

In the West African "trial by sasswood," the accused had to drink a liquid made from the toxic bark of the sasswood tree. If he vomited up the poison he was innocent and would live; if he kept it down he was guilty and would die—a neat coalescence of verdict and execution.

Among the Loma, in Liberia, a person accused of theft was made to pluck a brass anklet from the bottom of a pot of boiling oil. If he managed this without injury he was innocent; if noticeably burned, he was guilty.

This version—the use of hot water or hot iron, the suspect's skin tested later for peeling or blistering or festering, the outcome showing the verdict of the gods—was dominant in many places.

The cold-water ordeal, in contrast, was based on a river's or pond's treatment of the suspect's live body. It is found, among other places, in the Code of Hammurabi:

> If a man charge a man with sorcery, but cannot convict him, he who is charged with sorcery shall go to the sacred river, and he shall throw himself into the river; if the river overcome him, his prosecutor shall take to himself his house. If the river show that man to be

innocent and he come forth unharmed, he that charged him with sorcery shall be put to death.

Trial by ordeal has had a long and surprisingly successful run. In 1937 Margaret Hubbard, an American traveler in East Africa, described an ordeal she witnessed during a trek near the Zambezi River. Some of the brightly colored calico cloth with which the carriers were paid was stolen. The camp was searched in vain. If the theft went unsolved the remaining calico would probably vanish and the expedition would collapse. The Barotse tribesmen in the group proposed a trial by ordeal, and all of the sixty-odd natives agreed:

> There was a thief [wrote Ms. Hubbard] and the boiling water test was to be applied to find him. There was not one dissenting voice. All agreed it was a fair test, so a fire was built and on it settled a huge pot of water. Solemnly we watched it come to a boil, then boil furiously. A smaller pot of cold water was placed near the boiling pot, and when the water was turning over in huge violent rolls the tests began.
>
> Men, women, little children and big ones stepped forward one by one, each plunged his right arm into the cold water, then into the boiling pot to the elbow, and stepped into line on the other side of the fire. Everyone took the test without a murmur and when all was finished they were told to return at the same time the next afternoon. The one who, by that time, had lost some skin or showed a blister would be proved the thief.
>
> In single file they returned, every last one of them, passing before us, right arm bare and outstretched for an examination. Out of that small army one man alone showed blisters and peeling skin. No other had any sign of a burn. And he confessed to the crime and returned the calico!

As Ms. Hubbard's example shows, the gods of the ordeal sometimes got it right.

—

"Nothing makes us men, and no other means keeps us bound one to another, but our word," wrote Montaigne four centuries ago. Words may end as well as start a dispute, and the peace-restoring words may be uttered by a mediator who helps the parties reach agreement—as in the traditional Ashanti society of the African Gold Coast, where a respected elder would serve as conciliator—or by a judge. Words sustain the methods we deem civilized today, and words are the stock-in-trade of lawyers and judges.

This is not to say, of course, that every utterance from the bar is felicitous.

There was the lawyer in my court who became irritated at something his opponent had said in final argument, and rose to reply. "Your Honor," he said, "there is a red herring I would like to put to bed."

There was the criminal defense lawyer who insisted his client was being made an "escape goat"—"I mean," he corrected himself, "a scrape goat."

And there was the lawyer who invoked higher authority by saying, "If my old evidence professor were alive today, he'd be turning over in his grave."

There are enough courtroom malapropisms to brighten every judge's life—and yet to be a lawyer is to work in a tradition where language has been used as clearly, as pointedly, as beautifully as it ever has been used. Take, for example, the legal scholar James Madison. He wrote:

Congress shall make no law respecting an establishment of religion, or prohibiting the free exercise thereof; or abridging the freedom of speech or of the press. . . .

And so on through the lapidary Bill of Rights, the first ten amendments to our Constitution, written chiefly by Madison and adopted in 1791.

Or take the example of Justice Oliver Wendell Holmes, Jr. During World War I, a small group of anarchists had thrown leaflets out a third-floor window onto Broadway in New York City. Their message called on the workers of the country to wake up, stage a general strike, and force the government to stop intervening in newly revolutionary Russia. There was no chance that this scattering of leaflets would accomplish anything, but the anarchists were convicted under a sedition statute and sentenced to twenty years in prison.

One of them was a twenty-year-old girl. All of them were naive. Their convictions were affirmed in 1919 by the United States Supreme Court in *Abrams v. United States.* Justice Holmes, who was then seventy-eight years old, dissented. Several other justices felt so strongly about the case that they visited Holmes in his chambers and tried to persuade him to keep quiet, or to say no more than "I dissent." But on decision day Holmes read from the bench the most famous words ever written by a judge about freedom of speech:

> [W]hen men have realized that time has upset many fighting faiths, they may come to believe, even more than they believe the very foundations of their own conduct, that the ultimate good desired is better reached by a free trade in ideas—that the best test of truth is the power of the thought to get itself accepted in the competition of the market, and that truth is the only ground upon which their wishes safely can be carried out. That, at any rate, is the theory of our Constitution.

Notice that in this brief passage Holmes explained not only why we value free speech—it offers the best chance of arriving at truth—but why we value truth in the first place. Truth-telling is a moral imperative in our tradition, and we assume, with exceptions based on diplomacy or kindness, that knowing the truth is good in itself. That was not enough for the skeptical Holmes, who offered a pragmatic reason: truth is "the only ground upon which [our] wishes safely can be carried out." We get what we want, in other words—prosperity, safety, liberty, fulfillment—more surely by pursuing truth than by succumbing to falsehood or delusion.

Holmes expressed regret that he could not put his belief about the First Amendment "into more impressive words." Shakespeare could not have done better. Holmes lost in 1919, but since then he and his words have carried the day.

In today's world the word-based trial model is taken for granted. The courtroom puts even our most atrocious acts through the civilizing mill of evidence, analysis, and judgment. The claims and defenses of the parties are stated in advance—in the pleadings in a civil case, in the indictment and plea in a criminal prosecution. Proof of what happened is presented to a neutral decider, usually a judge or jury. The parties may have the help of skilled advocates. Once the evidence is in, the judge or jury decides what happened, applies the law, and enters judgment. An impartial search for the truth, and a faithful application of the law to the facts, are the heart of the process.

We admire this method for its appeal to reason, its fairness, and its fidelity to what has gone before. But these virtues are far from the whole story. Just as the impulse to fight is deep in our natures, so is the need to work out disputes, to resolve matters, to make peace. Disputes must be ended, but ended by a method that gives satisfaction. A trial is a civic function, but it is more than that; it is also a ceremony, a ritual, and an exorcism. The litigation process itself, with its evidence and arguments and reasoned decisions, is an important part of our lives. We do not go to a performance of *Hamlet* just to see the corpses strewn about the stage at the end; we do not hold court trials just to create papers called verdicts and judgments.

Mankind's myriad dispute resolution methods, however strange, fill universal needs. Aggressive impulses are vented; drama and catharsis are provided; conflicts are settled and the result accepted so life can go on; belief in the gods, or in a secular standard of justice, is vindicated. There are quick ways to achieve these goals, but there are no nonhuman ways. The need for drama in the process rises and falls with the emotions aroused by the case. Murders, assaults, rapes, and kidnappings are classically in need of dramatic resolution, but so are a surprising number of civil disputes, ranging from libel to divorces to breaches of contract to negligently inflicted injuries to complex commercial claims. This is not to say that every case needs to be tried; most can satisfactorily be settled. But it is to say that mechanical or lifelessly bureaucratic ways of resolving disputes serve us poorly.

"Life is painting a picture, not doing a sum," as Justice Holmes said, and the same is true of litigation. We are brothers and sisters of the Inuit, the Barotse, and the tribesmen of New Guinea. And our modern adversary system of justice, with its commitment to the truth, its logic and verbal trappings, its robed judges and elevated benches and incantations of "may it please the court," is a descendant of the ordeal, the magic contest, and the trial by battle. There is more to the law than syllogisms; to serve the living, the process must be filled with life.

FROM REVELATION TO VERDICT

The rise of trial by jury amid medieval superstition and violence is one of the great stories of human advancement. England is our legal parent, and to this day we are fascinated by her criminal trials: barristers in black robes and white wigs, clever cross-examinations, elegant closing arguments, Rumpole at the Old Bailey. It all seems like an especially civilized and witty version of our own courtroom scenes. But to understand where the American court system came from we must go back earlier—to Anglo-Saxon times, before the Norman Conquest, when England was an island of forests, bogs, and moors, when the wilderness pressed against rude farms, when roads were few and poor, literacy was almost unknown, and trial by persuasion was yet to be invented.

Imagine a summer day in Wessex in the year 1001. To the astonishment of some prophets, the millennium has recently come without bringing the end of the world, and the sun is shining on the fields and woods. A serf named Edric, twenty years old and in the prime of his strength, is working with others to clear a newly logged field of rocks and stumps, so that it can be ploughed. The men work shirtless in the heat.

A messenger arrives at the field. He is a helper of the priest, an errand-runner who escapes hard work by making himself useful. Edric does not like him.

The messenger approaches Edric and says, "You must come with me."

"Where?" asks Edric.

"To the village."

"Why? Why should I go to the village now? I have to work."

"There is a charge against you," says the messenger.

"What is it?"

"That you stole a calf of the thegn's herd. You and your friends butchered it in the forest and carried parts of it away."

"What calf? What friends?" asks Edric.

"I do not know."

"I did not do this."

"You must come."

The village is two miles away. Edric and the messenger walk in silence across the fields and then along a dusty road. Others follow to watch what will happen. Edric knows the penalty for stealing the thegn's livestock. Mutilation—the loss of a hand, perhaps—might be enough for lesser thefts, but he who steals a herd animal from the thegn will be hanged at once. He knows also that the farm and forest and he himself belong to his feudal lord the thegn, that unseen spirits and demons abound in the darkness, that God will send him to the torments of hell if he dies in sin, and that the priest is God's spokesman on earth. Edric cannot read or write. It does not occur to him that he might acquire these skills—not only because serfs and slaves never do, but because he has no idea that literacy could bring enlightenment. He has, in fact, no concept of enlightenment. His worldview is stark and simple. There are the earth, the summer of sweat and the winter of cold, the animals and plants and crops, the lords, the workers like himself, the occasional drunken festival, and the hereafter of longed-for reward or menacing damnation. And nothing more.

The village smells of manure and poultry and human habitation, alleviated by fresher odors from the fields. The square is an open space surrounded by the wooden house where the thegn and his family live, a smaller dwelling used by the reeve, who is the thegn's powerful steward, a chapel, a blacksmith's shed, a horse barn, and a scattering of huts. When Edric arrives the villagers have assembled to watch. As they part to let him through, Edric sees in their faces that some are with him, but others, leering, are eager for the spectacle of his punishment.

At the chapel entrance stand the priest and the reeve. Before them on a table are the mangled remains of a calf, missing both hindquarters, the tongue, and other choice parts.

The priest, portly, aged, intimidating, looks at Edric with eyes of ice. He says, "It is charged that you and other men with you did steal this calf from the thegn's herd, and did kill it and take of its meat in the forest. If this be true, I tell you on pain of eternal damnation to admit it now, that God be more merciful to your soul. Speak the truth, lest you carry into the next world the sins that beset you in this one."

Edric, in fear, glances at the old man's face and then lowers his eyes to the ground. "Father," he says, "I have not done it. I did not steal this calf."

"This knife known to be yours was found near the calf," says the priest, laying on the table a knife with a wooden handle, "and you were seen running with other young men from the glade where the calf was found."

"Father," says Edric, "I did not do it. I lost the knife last winter. I have not seen it since."

"Who were the other young men?"

"I do not know."

The questioning is finished. No witnesses will be called. There will be no trial committing Edric's guilt or innocence to human decision; a divine judgment will be sought. The priest and the reeve are the local court, but only as bailiffs for God.

The priest makes the sign of the cross and utters the words to turn bread into the Eucharist.

"I tell you," he says, "do not partake of the Body of Christ if you are guilty; but if you are innocent, come."

Edric goes to him, kneels, and receives the communion.

A fire has been set near the chapel door. The priest picks up an iron rod used for many ordeals in the past, and approaches the fire.

"O Lord God, bless this place," he says. "Bless this fire."

He places the iron in the fire and sprinkles it with holy water. "Lord

God, purify this metal that all falsehood and deceit be cast out of it and the truth of thy righteous judgment be opened."

The iron grows hot; the crucial time has come. "Upon this fire be the blessing of the Father, the Son, and the Holy Ghost," says the priest, "that it may be a sign to us of the judgment of God."

Edric picks up the burning iron in his right hand. He feels a searing pain but has to carry the iron for nine feet. He strides the full distance and then kneels and lays it on the ground.

He stands and chokes back a sob as the crowd surges around to watch the bandaging. The priest wraps the burned hand in linen and seals the cloth with the wax signet of the church. The judgment will come when the bandage is removed after three days: guilty if a festering wound appears, innocent if it does not. The priest utters a few more ritual words and the crowd disperses.

Edric walks slowly away. He has a sixteen-year-old wife, a toothless old father, aged forty-five, and two younger sisters. Edric finds all of them in the village and tells them he is innocent and God will save him. But he cannot convince himself. He walks alone, across a field, through a patch of woods and along a creek. He longs to put his burned hand into the cool water, but that is forbidden.

The next day, and the day after, Edric works with one hand. He asks other serfs to say who accused him. No one knows, but all know that the "other young men" seen running from the forest glade got away unrecognized. Edric will never learn who his accuser was. It matters little; his fate will be decided not by any man's word, but by the ordeal. "Dear God, save me," he prays. He can think of no more elaborate prayer.

On the late afternoon of the third day Edric goes to the chapel door and waits. His hand still hurts and he fears it will betray him. The men, women, and children of the village gather for one of the few moments of high drama in their lives.

The priest and the reeve come out of the chapel. Edric stands before them. The priest makes the sign of the cross and says, "Lord God, give us thy blessed sign that we may do justice in Thy name."

He breaks the seal on the linen and slowly unwinds the bandage. Then he takes Edric's right hand in his and looks at it long and thoughtfully. The crowd stirs and waits. Edric sees a red mark running across his palm. Fear seizes him; he will be put to death, and then will come damnation.

The priest puts down Edric's hand and turns to the crowd. He waits for quiet. Then he says: "This man did not steal the calf. The wound has not festered. It is not flaming. The hand bears only the mark of innocence." He makes the sign of the cross again. "In the name of the Father, the Son, and the Holy Spirit. Amen." He turns and goes back into the chapel.

There is a moment of silence. Some in the crowd turn away, muttering their disappointment. Then a shout goes up from Edric's friends; his wife and sisters rush up and embrace him, his old father grins, and Edric looks up at the blue sky and weeps.

At his prayers that night the priest is visited by the thought that Edric's case had been close. Had he been right in reading the Lord's sign? It is not a question to tarry over. Doubt is not in his repertoire of thoughts. Yet it would have been a pity to send a strong young man to his death. He will tell the thegn what happened. The thegn's displeasure that the thieves escaped will be offset by his satisfaction that Edric, a good worker, has been saved. There will be no trouble. The priest thanks the Lord for all blessings and prays for salvation for his flock and himself.

The case of Edric is made up—it has to be, since the England of 1001 did not have trial transcripts. We know the methods used, but the words that were spoken have vanished.

In constructing a case we have to use English, not the blunt tongue of the Anglo-Saxons. An idea of their language can be gained by sampling the prose of Abbot Ælfric, who lived in Wessex from about 955 to 1010: *Thā heofonlican æhta sind ūs eallum gemæne. Nacode wē wæron ācennede, and nacode wē gewitath.* " This meant, "Heavenly possessions are common to us all. Naked we were born, and naked we depart." (Ælfric's homilies were widely ignored in his lifetime, as now.)

We are handicapped most of all, in looking back a thousand years, by modern sensibilities. We can envision what happened, but to enter fully into our forebears' state of mind is beyond us. Old England's countryside was green and unspoiled, but our ancestors of the Dark Ages and early Middle Ages were semibarbarous and primitive farmers with a bent for violence. To be killed in a sword-fight, to have a limb hacked off by an ax or an eye put out by a knife, were common fates, met with a fortitude now alien to us. Even in peace the conditions of life were harsh. A short harvest in the fall could mean starvation, and every winter brought a siege of cold and isolation. The uncut wilderness was an adversary in the struggle for life. Men hunted out of necessity—to destroy livestock-killing wolves and foxes, and to bring deer, rabbits, and birds to the table.

Serfs and slaves were owned as property; women were child-bearers and drudges; all were bound by the unbreakable ties of feudal society, the freeman in thrall to the thegn, the thegn to the king.

In this society of vertical allegiance, a "lordless man" was an outlaw and anyone from parts unknown a suspect. Fragments of Anglo-Saxon law have come down to us. One of them, from Wessex, says:

> If a man from afar or a foreigner fares through the wood off the highway and neither hollas nor blows a horn, he shall be counted a thief and may be slain or put to ransom.

The church, in whose doctrines all believed, was immensely powerful as landowner and keeper of the keys to salvation. Blue laws existed with a vengeance. "If a slave works on Sunday by his lord's command," one provided, "he shall become free. . . . If, however, a freeman works on that day, except by his lord's command, he shall be reduced to slavery."

There was no clear distinction between church and state; power was shared by lay and ecclesiastical lords. There was, in fact, no state in the modern sense. An Anglo-Saxon kingdom existed but lacked central authority; a man looked to his local lord for protection and justice.

The legacy of ancient Greece and Rome—science, the arts, law— had been lost except for the Latin used by clergymen. There were no police, no lawyers, no professional judges. Laws existed, mostly in the form of custom, sometimes committed to writing; but to gain compliance was a fierce and uneven struggle.

The struggle was waged in the beginning through self-help. The "hue and cry"—a phrase now applied to gentler activities—would spring into use if someone was seen committing a crime. Anyone who witnessed a theft, for example, was duty-bound to raise a shout; the suspect, predictably, would flee; all who heard the commotion would join in the chase, like a pack of baying hounds; and the suspect, when captured, would be hanged on the spot. There must have been hangings of innocent people who fled out of fear. There was plenty to be afraid of, once the shouting began.

Homicide was dealt with privately by the blood feud. A slain man's kinsmen were expected to take revenge in kind—leading, of course, to counterrevenge and a cycle of deadly violence. An early effort to stop the blood feuds was the *wergeld,* which substituted payment for life-taking. Each rank of man, each body part, had its fixed price. "If one man slays another, one hundred shillings wergeld," says a surviving text; "if a bone is laid bare, three shillings; if an ear is struck off, twelve shillings."

The hue and cry and the blood feud entailed no process and no judgment. Carnage was unaccompanied by thought. In comparison, the ordeals that came to dominate justice in England represented an advance: irrational process replaced no process at all. Grounded in superstition, they nevertheless marked a shift from lynchings and private feuds to communal decision-making and public penalties. The difference might be marginal for the accused, but a hanging after a trial is much better for the community than a hanging without one. To get law onto a public footing was a long and hard struggle in which the hot iron played an honorable, if painful, part.

There were other Anglo-Saxon trial methods. In the ordeal by cold water, the accused was bound, hands beneath knees, and lowered at the end of a rope into a pond sanctified for the purpose. If he floated he was guilty; the water had rejected him, and execution or mutilation would follow. If he sank he was innocent, as shown by the pond's acceptance of his body. The innocent, if lucky enough, would be fished out in time to avoid drowning.

In the class structure of medieval England the ordeals were chiefly for the lower orders, among whom the most popular offenses were theft, robbery, assault, and murder. For the nobility a different method came into use. The upper classes committed felonies too, but their most rampant disputes were about land ownership. Land was the source of wealth and power, and they fought over it by means ranging from armed combat to strategic marriages to litigation. Compurgation, a kind of oath-testing, became their trial method of choice. A man swore to his own right to the land, or innocence of the charge. He brought to the trial six to twelve compurgators—oath-helpers—to swear that his oath was valid. The oath-helpers were not witnesses; they said nothing about the facts of the case, and spoke only to the quality of their party's oath. They had to stick to a precise verbal formula; if a wrong word slipped in, the oath would "burst" and the cause would be lost.

Did the Anglo-Saxons really believe in trial by ordeal and compurgation? They did indeed. These methods held sway for centuries and the church collected fees for administering them. Our forebears were not demented; they simply had a worldview weaker in reason, but stronger in religious conviction, than ours. Salvation and damnation were real and imminent, with no middle ground. Truth was absolute—not shaded, not relative, not subject to doubt or skepticism—and was authoritatively revealed, not found by rational inquiry. As God not only created but supervised the earth, His judgment must settle issues of guilt and deadly quarrels. The hunger for certainty, for indisputable answers, was satisfied by the belief that the judgments came from above. The need to deflect blame from human judges was served as well. If a festering hand showed guilt, or a body's descent into the depths proved innocence, that was not the judges' doing. If a compurgator's tongue became twisted and his party's oath collapsed, the judgment was divine, not human.

The old trial methods owed their long run in part to their entertainment value. Suspense over the outcome, the thrill of the contest, drew crowds. Many came not just for drama but for an enjoyable bout of sadism. The records of some times and places in old England show a disproportionate number of women put through ordeals—due, in all likelihood, to sadism masquerading as justice. As the ordeals were legally sanctioned, and the accused had a chance to get off, onlookers could relish the spectacle without pangs of guilt. If a hanging followed immediately, so much the better; the children would learn from it.

The oath-contest called compurgation depended on a magical connection between words and the subjects they described. If the ritual words could be uttered successfully, the oath must be true; falsity would shatter the formula in the speaker's mouth. And it was known that hell's flames awaited the perjurer—a thought that every modern judge, at times, would like to see reawakened.

When William the Conqueror and his Norman-speaking knights occupied England in 1066, they brought with them a trial method which added a note of chivalry, if not of logic. This was trial by battle, long a tradition in continental Europe. It was quick and simple. The contending parties would fight with archaic weapons, blessed for the occasion. Or, if rich enough, they would hire champions to fight in their place. The winner in the clash of arms would prevail in the lawsuit. No breath was wasted in arguing about the merits.

Trial by battle never gained popularity among the native English. The ruling Normans practiced it among themselves, while retaining the Anglo-Saxon methods of ordeal and compurgation for general use.

So matters stood well into the reigns of William's successors. All of the trial methods used in England sought divine judgments; all, by our lights, were irrational.

The change from revelation to verdict took about two hundred years. The records are not copious, but are enough to tell us what happened.

There was a gradual ebbing of belief in the old methods. There was, at the same time, a growing use of small groups of "lawful men" summoned and sworn to pronounce the truth about something the king needed to know. By fits and starts, amid doubt and confusion and backsliding, the unmet need left by the demise of an old institution was filled by the birth of a new one. The result was as momentous, as vital to modern life, as anything that happened in the Renaissance. Human judgment replaced divine; men took on, at last, the burden and the glory of deciding for themselves. It was a change that took place, with differing outcomes but the same thrust, everywhere in the Western world.

Juries, in their first incarnation in England, had nothing to do with trials. The Norman kings were out to bring the chaotic island, and its tax base, under central control. To get a grip on things they summoned local noblemen to assizes—court sessions—to describe on oath every manor in their area: who owned it, what properties and people it contained, and how much it was worth. The sworn informants were a kind of jury. The nationwide results were first published in 1086, in the famous Domesday Book.

Controlling crime, making houses and highways safe, was a royal interest, then as now. "Presenting" juries—what we would call grand juries—gradually came into use to deal with crime. The royal judges would look to a panel of reputable men to state on oath who was suspected. Those accused would then be tried—but the trials were still conducted by the old methods.

By the twelfth century compurgation—trial by oath-contest—was waning because of its manifest unreliability. Perjury, even bribery, in its use had become a frequent scandal. And what if both sides' oath-helpers recited the magic formulae correctly? The tie was broken in some cases, unsatisfactorily, by awarding judgment to the party who had more oath-helpers.

As for the ordeals, even the most devout began to feel skeptical when divine signs clashed with firsthand knowledge. A recognition grew that the outcomes could be wrong—the innocent hanged, or the guilty freed, as the cases were seen by human reason. The sense of injustice, a sometimes dormant part of our mental equipment, was awakening.

There was, in addition, friction between church and crown. Priests who administered the ordeals might skew the results out of sympathy or prejudice, and royal officials could do nothing about it. As early as 1100, the Conqueror's son William Rufus was vexed when fifty men charged with breaking the forest laws were sent to the hot iron ordeal and all fifty were found innocent—the doing, William Rufus understandably thought, of a meddlesome and soft-headed clergy.

Henry II—brilliant, dynamic, tireless, versed in languages, uniquely literate among English kings since the Conquest—came to the throne in 1154 and ruled for thirty-five years. He lives in popular memory because his running quarrel with Archbishop Thomas à Becket, an erstwhile friend and drinking companion, led to Thomas's murder in Canterbury Cathedral at the hands of four knights incited by the king's anger. But Henry deserves to be remembered for more than that. He was a lawgiver. He, more than anyone else, established English royal justice.

Henry's aim was to curb outbreaks of crime and usurpations of land, which had been inadequately dealt with by the local lords and their courts. He was not being entirely magnanimous; better justice would enhance the power of the crown.

In 1166 his government systematized the grand jury. Jurors in each locality were to give the sheriff or royal judge, periodically, a list of notorious criminals. The accused were then put to the ordeal. A regular roundup of lawbreakers came to be expected.

Although the ordeals were still in use, Henry had little faith in them. He ordered that anyone accused of a serious crime but acquitted in the ordeal of water be banished from the realm if enough "lawful men" of the community declared him to be of bad repute. The decree quietly shifted part of the case-deciding responsibility from God to the "lawful men."

Henry also established new remedies for landholders. A man ousted from possession of his fields, or challenged in his title, could buy a writ directing the sheriff to summon a jury. The jurors, local landholders themselves, would use their own knowledge of every hedge and furrow in the neighborhood to decide the case. For knights unenthused about trial by battle, the change must have been a welcome relief.

Henry's reforms brought the jury, and the nascent legal profession, closer to roles we would recognize. Yet trial by ordeal endured through his reign and for years afterward. There was a profound reluctance to let go of it. And there was a practical problem: if the ordeals were abandoned, how would the cases be decided?

The final blow came from the church. For years thoughtful clergymen had said that it was "tempting God" to demand one miraculous revelation after another; God might be omnipotent, but His patience had limits. At last, in 1215, the church at Rome denounced the ordeals. Priests could no longer take part in them. What had been accepted for centuries was suddenly forbidden as barbaric.

The church's withdrawal left a gaping void in English law. The ordeals were gone, but nothing was at hand to take their place. Magna Carta, also signed in 1215, confirmed important rights of English subjects against their king, but trial by jury was not one of them. The great charter assumed that the old trial methods would continue.

The royal judges were left in confusion. Those going on circuit were told to imprison persons accused of grave crimes "yet so that they do not incur danger of life or limb by reason of our prison"; to allow those accused of middling crimes to leave the realm; and to take security for good behavior from minor offenders. No criminal trials were held because no one, for the moment, knew how to conduct one.

Such a vacuum must be filled quickly, and this one was. With capital punishment for felonies still linked to eternal damnation, with life-or-death importance given to land disputes, judges were loath to seize for themselves the case-deciding power and the risks of blame and downfall that would come with it. They lacked the knowledge to decide the cases in the first place, and there was no system of evidence-gathering to help them. There was also no popular demand that judges take the place of God. So they turned to a solution at hand—to the jury, which already existed for other purposes.

In the thirteenth century, trial by jury became the dominant method of trial in England. Local juries of twelve were sworn to decide cases based on their own knowledge of the facts and the litigants. Each juror took an oath to speak the truth in the *verdict,* which means "true saying." Juries would decide using their knowledge and common sense; judges would enjoy a buffer against unpopular decisions; justice would be done.

The solution was so apt and timely that trial by jury outpaced any legal underpinning it might claim. No law authorized its use in criminal cases. The judges decided they could not force an accused to undergo jury trial if he did not agree to it, leaving an awkward question of what to do with those who balked. Some who refused to enter a plea were simply banished from the realm, without trial. In 1275 a statute directed that accused persons who refused to submit to jury trial be jailed under harsh conditions until they gave in. The practice was soon transformed into a kind of torture. An accused who rejected trial by jury was placed between two planks and heavy stones were piled on the top one until he changed his mind or was crushed to death. A few chose to die, inspired by the knowledge that a convicted felon would forfeit his property to the crown but one who perished under the heavy stones, never having been found guilty, would leave his estate to his heirs. Acceptance of trial by jury became nearly universal, most felony defendants having no property to worry about. Oddly, not until 1772 was an accused's refusal to submit to trial simply considered a plea—a plea of guilty, at first, and then, after another half-century, a plea of not guilty, as it is today.

The trial jurors in a criminal case were at first chosen from the presenting jury. Having issued the charge, they presumably would know enough to decide guilt or innocence. But there was an obvious drawback: men were unlikely to return a not-guilty verdict showing their own accusation to be false. Outside jurors began to be brought in, and by the mid-fourteenth century the two juries were separate and distinct: the grand jury, which brought the charge, and the freshly constituted trial jury, which decided it.

For a long time the trial jury remained self-informing; it relied on the knowledge it already had. As communities grew, as jurors needed more information, witnesses were sometimes called to testify. The door through which the trial lawyer would eventually walk was opened. The assumption that the jury would know enough to decide without help gave way gradually to the assumption that it would need to hear evidence. Many cases were decided on a combination of what the jurors knew at the start and what they learned in court. By the end of the seventeenth century the law required that the verdict be based *solely* on the evidence received in court. It was seen that fairness and impartiality are served by lack of foreknowledge. We had moved from requiring that a juror know about the case, to assuming that he would not know enough, to requiring that he know as little as possible.

The arrival of trial by jury was not a burst of light banishing all darkness. For a long time, trials were rough-and-tumble: jurors wrangled with defendants and witnesses, rules of procedure were loose, felony defendants could not have counsel, instructions on the law were vague or manipulative, judges coerced verdicts by locking jurors up or having them dragged through the streets in a cart until they agreed. Many cases continued to be tried by local courts operated by the landed gentry, rather than the crown, with major variations in quality.

But a giant step had been taken. We had moved, after centuries, from magic to reason. Trial by revelation gave way to trial by persuasion. Men relieved the deity, at last, of the burden of deciding their earthly disputes.

Yet in making this change we did not shed every vestige of the past. Trial by jury succeeded in part because it appealed to the same irrational values that were served so well by the old methods. And it still does. Drama and catharsis are provided on a scale rivaling that of team sports. The adversary system pits one party against the other. Trial by battle lives on in the contest between hired champions called lawyers. Oath-helpers are no longer around, but character witnesses sometimes play a similar role. The requirement that the verdict be unanimous—originally adopted on the premise that the outcome must reflect the unambiguous will of God—now serves a different goal: that of making the jury listen carefully to the views of all of its members.

And still, committed though we are to rationality, we are sometimes brought up against its limits. Despite centuries of accumulated knowledge and wisdom and precedents, there are still cases so difficult, so challenging to our moral sense, so unanswerable by legal reasoning, that we yearn for a divine sign telling us what to do. In those cases, the jury has a special advantage: it does not have to explain.

The old sailing yacht *Mignonette,* a fifty-two-foot wooden yacht, was en route from England to Australia, where her new owner wanted to keep her. Aboard was a crew hired for the long voyage down the coast of Africa, around the Cape of Good Hope, and across the Indian Ocean. The sailors were Thomas Dudley, captain; Edwin Stephens, mate; Edmund Brooks, able seaman; and Richard Parker, a boy of seventeen, ordinary seaman.

Off the west coast of Africa, south of the equator, the yacht was caught in a raging storm. A wave stove in her topside and she sank in five minutes. Through luck and Captain Dudley's skill and coolness, the four men escaped in a dinghy. Using materials salvaged from the wreck, Dudley improvised a sea anchor which kept them from capsizing in the gale.

It was July 5, 1884. The men rode out the storm. But the nearest land, hundreds of miles distant, could never be reached; the prevailing easterlies would carry them toward South America, at least two thousand miles away.

The crew of the *Mignonete* had no fresh water in the tiny boat and no food but two cans of turnips. As the days wore on they were blistered by the sun and tortured by thirst. They made a sail of their shirts.

They caught a small turtle and ate it but could find no other suste-
nance. Sinking into weakness and dehydration, they began to drink
their own urine.

They saw death coming near for all of them. Dudley wrote a note to
his wife in the frail hope that she might some day see it:

We have been here 17 days; have no food, we are all four living,
hoping to get a passing ship. If not we must soon die. Mr. Thompson will put everything right if you go to him, and I am sorry, dear,
I ever started on such a trip, but I was doing it for our best. You
know, dear, I should so like to be spared. You would find I should
live a Christian life for the rest of my days. If ever this note reaches
your hands, you know the last of your Tom and loving husband. . . .
Goodbye and God bless you all, and may life provide for you.

There was talk of drawing lots to see who would be killed and eaten
by the others, but the subject was dropped. Then nature presented a
candidate. The boy Richard Parker, who had become violently ill from
drinking seawater, weakened rapidly and lay semiconscious in the bottom of the boat. Dudley and Stephens, the mate, saw that Richard was
about to die. On the twentieth day, they decided that his death must
be hastened or all four would perish. Dudley cut Richard's jugular vein
with a knife.

For the next four days the three men lived on Richard Parker's blood
and flesh. On the twenty-fourth day they saw a sail. Dudley would say
later, in an unfortunate choice of words, that "their hearts were in their
mouths" for fear of being passed by unseen. But seen they were, and the
German sailing barque *Moctezuma,* en route from South America to
Hamburg, picked them up. Dudley and Stephens were so weak they
had to be lifted to the deck by ropes; Brooks managed to climb aboard.
The dinghy had sailed and drifted more than a thousand miles, and was
about 990 miles east of Rio de Janeiro. The last remnants of poor
Richard Parker's body still in the boat—a rib and a few shreds of
flesh—were thrown overboard on orders of the *Moctezuma*'s captain.

The *Moctezuma* detoured to England to deliver the emaciated survivors. Put ashore at Falmouth, Dudley and Stephens were forthright about what had happened. They had no idea that they would be prosecuted. Cannibalism had been resorted to often before by desperate shipwrecked sailors. Walt Whitman, in America, had spoken of such disasters in *Leaves of Grass:*

> *I sit and look out upon all the sorrows of the world . . .*
> *I observe a famine at sea, I observe the sailors casting lots who shall be*
>   *kill'd to preserve the lives of the rest . . .*

The captain and mate were reputable men; Dudley, a devout Anglican, had conducted services aboard the *Mignonette* every Sunday, and had tutored young Richard Parker in religion.

Dudley gave a deposition. "[O]n the twentieth day," he said, "the lad Richard Parker was very weak through drinking salt water. Deponent, with the assistance of the mate Stephens, killed him to sustain the existence of those remaining, they being all agreed the act was absolutely necessary."

Stephens said he had "agreed with the Master that it was absolutely necessary that one should be sacrificed to save the rest, and the Master selected Richard Parker boy as being the weakest. Deponent agreed to this and the Master accordingly killed the lad."

There was a public furor over what to do. Editorial writers who had never been to sea, and seldom missed a meal, demanded justice. The crown vacillated, then came down firmly on the side of discipline: British seamen must not assume they could eat one another when supplies ran out. Dudley and Stephens were charged with murder. If convicted they would be hanged.

The defense at trial was necessity: these men were at the brink of death, and had had no choice. Yet there was no such defense—the law made no provision for taking another's life, even an ebbing life, to save one's own. Nor did the law speak clearly to the other questions raised by the case: did English law apply in the first place? Or should these wretched men in their cramped dinghy in mid-Atlantic be allowed a polity of their own? In that dire setting, could the need to save three lives justify taking one? Could practical reasons—the boy's impending death from natural causes, or Dudley's and Stephens's duty to provide for wives and children back home—justify selecting one to be killed rather than another? Or should lots be drawn by agreement? If the choice were left to fate, what if the loser in the lottery changed his mind and resisted being put to death? Was there any legal solution? Or did the law give the men no choice but starvation or the gallows?

At the trial, Brooks, the one survivor against whom charges had been dropped, testified for the prosecution but helped the defense on a key point: without the cannibalism, none would have survived.

DEFENSE COUNSEL: And for those four days was life kept in you by this unfortunate boy's body?
BROOKS: Yes, no doubt, it was Sir, I believe so.

The trial judge, Baron Huddleston, was determined not to let public sympathy for Dudley and Stephens weaken the mandates of English law. There must be a verdict of guilty of murder. But how to prevent the jurors from convicting the men only of manslaughter, or, worse yet, acquitting them? Huddleston hit on a clever, if dubious, tactic: he would ask the jury to find only the facts and to leave guilt or innocence to the court. He wrote a narrative of what he thought the evidence showed and, when both sides had rested, read it to the jurors. Did they agree?

The jurors accepted the judge's narrative, with a few amendments. They insisted that the findings include the fact of necessity: "That if the men had not fed upon the body of the boy, they would probably not have survived . . . but would within the four days have died of famine." As the judge desired, the verdict left guilt or innocence to the professionals: "But whether upon the whole matter the prisoners were and are guilty of murder the Jury are ignorant and refer to the court." The jury recommended mercy.

Now the bench faced a dilemma of its own making. The jury could have reached a decision without having to state its reasons, but the dignitaries in robes and wigs were bound to explain their ruling in a case where logic was not up to the job. Argument was held before five judges of the High Court of Justice, Queen's Bench Division. Brushing aside contentions that Huddleston's procedure illegally took away the jury's right to decide the case, the judges found Dudley and Stephens guilty of murder. To justify the decision they resorted to an absurdity: the law, they said, was entitled to demand more than mortals could endure. "We are often compelled to set up standards we cannot reach ourselves, and to lay down rules which we could not ourselves satisfy."

Thus the law's majesty was safeguarded from human frailty. Dudley and Stephens were sentenced to death.

Many had expected the crown to grant clemency if the shipwrecked sailors were convicted. But would it? Weeks passed, letters poured in, while royal officials hesitated. At last word came from the home secretary: Queen Victoria would pardon the men on condition that they serve six months in prison. There would be no outright reprieve, but also no hanging.

Through tortured contrivances, the government finally had reached a tolerable outcome. Although the jury could have achieved one sooner and without an illegal trial procedure or a fractured judicial opinion, the court had kept the sailors' fate out of the jury's hands and in its own. The result was an awkward embarrassment. Justice would have been better served, as it usually is, by letting the jury decide the case.

Dudley and Stephens served their time, were released, and went on with their lives. Their prosecution is a reminder that in the modern era no signs from the gods are forthcoming. Having accepted the responsibility to decide for ourselves, we cannot shed it in a hard case. We must do our best with what we have. Some judges pray for divine guidance; but does anyone want to appear before a judge who really thinks he has it?

The Jury Breaks Free

The kings and lords who adopted the jury saw it as a way to keep order in a realm plagued by strife and lawlessness. They had not the slightest thought of expanding citizens' rights; what mattered to them was simply that the jury system worked. Disputes over land ownership, the prime source of medieval civil cases, moved from the dubious and deadly field of battle to the courts. Among contending landowners, violence gave way to litigiousness. Criminal cases were tried, under a judge's watchful eye, by jurors who knew the neighborhood, the accused, and the victim. Justice was rough but better than Englishmen had known before—and so the new system buttressed the crown's power.

But the jury, like many other children, soon surprised its parents. It became not just a tool of government but a welling up, a resistance, a brake on cruelty and excess, a force for reason and common sense and mercy. To play that role in full it had to win its own freedom—its right to decide cases without fear of reprisal by the king or the judge or the local lord. The culminating case brought the scion of one of England's great families into the criminal dock.

Admiral Sir William Penn was a lion of the seventeenth-century establishment. He had fought in naval wars against the Dutch, taken Jamaica for the crown, won a knighthood, and written the British navy's tactical handbook. He was the wealthy owner of estates in England and Ireland. His was a life of scope and command—except that he could not, no matter what he did, control his son and namesake.

The younger William Penn was bright, high-spirited, and potential heir to a fortune. Yet somehow—just how, the admiral could not fathom—he had become a religious dissenter while still a schoolboy. Delivered to Oxford at age sixteen for a gentleman's education, William had lasted only a year before being sent down for nonconformity. Everything the admiral had done for him since—a sojourn in France, a tour of duty managing the family estates in Ireland—seemed only to strengthen the boy's pigheaded convictions. By his early twenties, William had become a Quaker, and, worse yet, a spokesman and pamphleteer for his new faith.

The admiral was apoplectic. Of all the dissenters, the Quakers—the Society of Friends—were among the most despised. They were pacifist, virtuous, independent, and serenely confident. They called everybody "thou" regardless of rank. They refused to take oaths—a serious offense when oath-swearing was a test of loyalty. They were so nettlesome that more than three thousand of them were imprisoned in the first two years of the Restoration.

The admiral cursed and threatened to disinherit his son. But William was deaf to threats; he heard only the quiet voice of the Quaker conscience. And in him the Friends had found an ideal champion: a young man not only brave and charismatic but, as it happened, an aristocrat.

Penn wrote pamphlets attacking Anglican Church doctrines. The authorities locked him up in the Tower of London, which of course only fueled his fire. Although dissenters in that age were jailed on the flimsiest grounds, they were allowed to pass the time by writing. Penn, in the Tower, wrote a classic of prison literature: *No Cross, No Crown,* a book expounding the Friends' morality with eloquence and good humor. The Quakers hoped not just to reach heaven but to change the world. "True Godliness," wrote Penn, "don't turn men out of the world, but enables them to live better in it, and excites their endeavors to mend it."

In the summer of 1670 William Penn, released, was again at large in London. He was now twenty-six and filled with self-assurance.

On Sunday, August 14, he wanted to give a sermon, but found that the city authorities, struggling to silence Quaker preachers, had pad-

locked the Friends' meetinghouse in Gracechurch Street. Barred from
his church, Penn spoke in the street. A crowd of several hundred gathered—bustling, listening, talking among themselves. Penn was assisted
by William Mead, a forty-two-year-old linen draper, who stood nearby.

As Penn was speaking, constables forced their way through the
crowd. Armed with warrants, they arrested Penn and Mead and took
them to Newgate Prison. An indictment charged both men with
unlawfully assembling and disturbing the peace. Penn, it alleged, "by
abetment of . . . Mead . . . did preach and speak," and as a result "a
great concourse and tumult of people in the street . . . a long time did
remain and continue, in contempt of . . . the King, and of his law, to
the great disturbance of his peace."

This was a serious charge, a felony akin to insurrection or rebellion.
Penn and Mead, if convicted, would face heavy penalties. They knew
this and were ready for it. "And now, dear father," Penn wrote to the
admiral, "be not displeased or grieved. What if this be designed of the
Lord for an exercise of our patience?" The accused men's earthly hope
would be the jury, an institution that was, by this time, four centuries
old but still evolving.

Jury trials in the beginning were simple and direct. Yeomen of the
vicinity were summoned to serve, and when twelve were chosen the
trial went forward speedily. The jurors were sworn to give a true verdict based on what they knew of the parties and the facts; as time went
on, and communities grew, the testimony of witnesses was brought in.

In civil cases a highly technical system of written pleadings came into
being. The documents, written in a bastardized tongue called Law
French, had to meet rigid requirements in stating the claims and
defenses. An error of form could lose the case; counsel's verbal dexterity
replaced the client's broadsword. Trial, when it occurred, was by jury.

Criminal cases were simpler, shorter, and almost entirely concerned
with the fates of lower-class people. It was here that juries began to disagree at times with official mandates, and to say a muted "no." In the
Middle Ages, as now, the judge and jury usually agreed on the out-

come, although the judge's agreement was seldom voiced. But what happened—what should happen—when the judge and jury disagreed? When the judge believed firmly that the jury was letting off a guilty man? When that guilty man posed a threat to the very crown that appointed the judge and kept him in red robes and full-bottomed wig?

The struggle over who would have the last word—the judge or the jury—began in medieval criminal trials. There were no trial lawyers in these cases; the judges ran the proceedings, questioned the witnesses, instructed the jury. The accused was not presumed innocent. He had no right to counsel, nor to remain silent, nor to subpoena witnesses, nor to appeal. He could defend himself by speaking in answer to the proof against him. The theory was that an innocent man's spontaneous reaction to the charge would be an ample defense. "[I]t requires no manner of skill," said a defender of the system, "to make a plain and honest defense, which in cases of this kind is always the best."

Records predating the sixteenth century are scant, but Sir Thomas Smith's observations, written when Elizabeth I was a young queen in 1562, probably describe what had been practiced for many years. Sir Thomas, a careful scholar, gives us a vivid glimpse of the law courts that swiftly sent men and women to the gallows, or branded them, or turned them free.

There were tiered benches for the traveling royal judges, for local justices of the peace "according to their estate and degree," and for the staff and clerks. The prisoners, charged by a grand jury, were brought in "all chained to one another."

> Then the crier crieth, and commandeth silence. One of the judges briefly telleth the cause of their coming, and giveth a good lesson to the people. Then the prisoners are called for by name, and bidden to answer to their names.

The clerk read the charge against each defendant and asked for his plea. The ritual answer was "by God and country"—which meant trial by jury.

Jurors, "substantial yeomen, that dwell about the place, or at the least in the hundred, or near where the felony is supposed to be committed," were called to fill the box. A defendant could object that a juror was biased, and might succeed in getting a challenge upheld. When a jury of twelve was ready the court called for witnesses.

By the time Smith wrote, juries relied on evidence presented to them. If no witness showed up, the accused was released. But "this doth seldom chance," according to Sir Thomas, "except it be in small matters."

The witnesses were sworn and the first one, usually the victim of the crime, was asked if he knew the prisoner. "He saith yea, the prisoner sometime saith nay." Often there were arguments between the witness and the man or woman in the dock:

I know thee well enough, thou robbest me in such a place, thou beatest me, thou tookest my horse from me, and my purse, thou hadst then such a coat and such a man in thy company: the thief will say no, and so they stand a while in altercation, then he telleth all that he can say: after him likewise all those who were at the apprehension of the prisoner, or who can give any *indices* or tokens which we call in our language evidence against the malefactor.

There were arguments, too, between jurors and defendants; unlike today's passive listeners, jurors often jumped into the fray.

When the evidence was in the judge instructed the jury:

Good men (saith he), ye of the inquest, ye have heard what these men say against the prisoner, ye have also heard what the prisoner can say for himself, have an eye to your oath, and to your duty, and do that which God shall put in your minds to the discharge of your consciences, and mark well what is said.

Little else was said about the law; no elements of the offense were laid out, no burden of proof defined.

When the first case was submitted, the jury usually stayed in the box and listened to the evidence in the next case, and the next. At last, overtaxed, the jurors might ask for mercy: "My Lord, we pray you charge us with no more, it is enough for our memory."

With several cases to decide, the jury would be sent out to deliberate. When it came back the foreman was asked to state the verdict on each defendant:

[W]hat say you? Is he guilty or not guilty? The foreman maketh answer in one word, guilty, or in two, not guilty: the one is deadly, the other acquiteth the prisoner.

A man who showed that he could read, who had not been convicted before, and who stood convicted of a "clergyable" offense (depending on the time and place, this might be simple theft, or poaching, or any felony other than murder or highway robbery), could demand the right of clergy. A bishop's delegate was present to answer the court's question: *Legit* or *non-legit?* If the word *legit* come in reply, the defendant would escape the death penalty and be "burned forthwith in the presence of the judges in the brand of his hand with a hot iron marked with the letter *T* for a thief, or M for a manslayer." The brand would guarantee hanging for a second felony.

If the clergyman said *"non-legit"* the accused was left among the great majority of those found guilty. For most defendants, poor and illiterate, the first felony conviction was the last. There would be no benefit of clergy. The judge would say:

[T]hey have found thee guilty, thou hast nothing to say for thyself, the law is, thou shalt first return to the place from whence thou camest, from thence thou shalt go to the place of execution, there thou shalt hang till thou be dead.

A few days later the prisoner would be hanged before a crowd of onlookers. There was no appeal. As Sir Thomas wrote: "[N]either judge nor justice hath to do, or can reverse, alter or change that matter, if [the jury] say guilty."

Death was the punishment for all felonies, from theft to murder.

The records that have come down to us show that in the thirteenth and fourteenth centuries a high proportion of felony defendants—perhaps a majority—were acquitted. Some acquittals were no doubt due to failure of proof; medieval charging methods left plenty of room for accusations never borne out. Others must have resulted from jurors being bribed, or from their fearing revenge by a defendant's allies and relatives. But it is clear that juries in many cases voted to acquit simply because they believed the defendant should not be put to death. So it was that the death penalty played an unexpected role in creating modern liberty—it strengthened the trial jury's independence.

Faced with medieval laws that condemned all felons to the gallows, and that recognized no degrees of homicide, jurors who thought mercy was called for worked around the law by finding self-defense, or accident, or some other justification. Their common sense brought flexibility to harsh and rigid laws. They proved what today's trial lawyers know: Juries do not just "find facts," they decide whole cases. As law professor Thomas Green has written, the work of early juries:

> involved an assessment of personal worth: Was the suspect the sort of person likely to have committed a certain act with malice? And almost inevitably trial jury verdicts came to be judgments about who ought to live and who ought to die, not merely determinations regarding who did what to whom and with what intent.

As long as jurors relied on their own knowledge of the facts, the judge was ill equipped to dispute the verdict; he did not know the evidence. But as witnesses were brought in, as trials began to turn on proof received in open court, a tension developed: the judge had heard the evidence too; what if he thought the jury was wrong?

We are accustomed to juries doing their work without fear. Whatever their verdict may have been, today's jurors leave the courthouse immune to official reprisals and even to questions about how they reached their decision. (That some jurors choose to give press interviews or appear on talk shows is beside the point.) These rights of jurors did not fall from the sky; they were hard-won against a determined government.

Anyone who resents jury service as an inconvenience might ponder what it was like five hundred years ago. To be summoned was to be dragged into harm's way. Jurors were expected to reach a verdict that was not just honest but *true*—failing which they could be punished. If the judge or another high personage disagreed with the outcome, a writ of attaint could issue. A new jury of twenty-four would be sworn to try the original jurors for perjury. If the second jury decided the first had reached a false verdict, then, as an observer wrote in 1470: "All of the first jury shall be committed to the King's prison, their goods shall be confiscated, their possessions seized into the King's hands, their habitations and houses shall be pulled down, their woodland shall be felled, their meadows shall be plowed up and they themselves forever thenceforward be esteemed in the eye of the law infamous."

Given this prospect, many a jury was loath to reach a verdict at all. Coercion was the bench's frequent response. Jurors were routinely denied food and water while they deliberated. If they were obdurate the judge might have them hauled through the town in open carts until they came to their senses. If they returned a verdict the judge thought wrong, they might be harangued and sent back to reconsider—often with a reminder of the peril they faced. That peril grew to include sanctions faster and surer than the cumbersome writ of attaint. The judge, displeased by a verdict contrary to his advice, might fine the jurors on the spot, with imprisonment until they paid. Some jurors paid; others gave in to the pressure by changing their verdict.

As the Middle Ages gave way to the Renaissance, conviction rates went up—due in part, it appears, to judicial pressure tactics. But still jurors resisted, in many cases, when their sense of justice told them to.

The crisis came in the seventeenth century—in Restoration England, a time of celebration among the gentry, high comedy in the theaters, and persecution of religious minorities in the streets and courts. Charles II, called to the throne from exile after a chaotic civil war, was not the kind to hold a grudge. Nor did he take too seriously the demands of religion. He had developed, while on the Continent, a taste for entertainments and mistresses, which he continued to indulge while king. He agreed to share power with Parliament. Revenge would be kept to a minimum; only a dozen men held responsible for the beheading of Charles's father, eleven years earlier, would be hanged. One of these public executions was described by Samuel Pepys, then a young clerk in the Royal Navy's administrative office, in his diary entry for October 13, 1660:

> I went out to Charing Cross to see Major-General Harrison hanged, drawn, and quartered—which was done there—he looking as cheerfully as any man could do in that condition. He was presently cut down and his head and his heart shown to the people, at which there was great shouts of joy.

Consistent with his friendly and easygoing nature, Charles II had little interest in persecuting religious dissenters; he was even suspected of Catholic sympathies. But the gentry-dominated Cavalier Parliament did not share the king's laxity. The Church of England was restored as the realm's official faith. In an age of endemic persecution, Parliament saw no reason to tolerate dissenters who had been on the Puritan side in the civil war, whose rejection of ecclesiastical authority threatened the establishment, and whose insistence on spiritual freedom might unwittingly open the door to the dreaded Catholics. It passed laws cracking down on nonconformists. In the Conventicle Act of 1664, Parliament made it a crime to conduct or attend any religious service that did not use the Anglican liturgy. The Quakers were a prime target of this legislation, and of the laws prohibiting unlawful assembly and breach of the peace.

—

By the time their trial began on September 1, 1670, William Penn and William Mead had been in jail for sixteen days. They were brought before the London Court of Sessions. Presiding were the lord mayor of the city, the recorder (the city's chief criminal judge), and five aldermen. A jury of twelve was sworn to "well and truly try, and true deliverance make betwixt our Sovereign Lord the King, and the prisoners at the bar."

Penn's account of the trial, written shortly afterward, has come down to us; most of it is uncontradicted by the lord mayor, who also wrote a post-trial narrative.

The lord mayor began by trapping Penn and Mead on a point of Quaker belief. The Friends habitually kept on their wide-brimmed hats in the presence of officials; doffing their hats, they believed, would pay undue homage to earthly powers. Yet Penn and Mead came into court bareheaded.

"Sirrah, who bid you put off their hats?" said the lord mayor to a bailiff. "Put on their hats again."

A court officer carried out this order and the two men were brought to the bar with their hats on.

"Do you not know that there is respect due to the court?" the recorder asked them.

"Yes," said Penn.

"Why do you not pay it then?"

"I do so," said Penn.

"Why do you not pull off your hat then?"

"Because I do not believe that to be any respect," Penn answered.

The recorder pounced on this: "Well, the court sets forty marks apiece upon your heads as a fine for your contempt of the court."

The evidence had not begun and already the defendants had been fined. In reply Penn showed his courage and wit: "I desire it might be observed, that we came into the court with our hats off, and if they have been put on since, it was by order from the Bench; and therefore not we, but the Bench should be fined."

The gallery could see already that this trial would provide high entertainment. The defendants were fearless and the lord mayor and recorder were going to bait them.

The crown called as witnesses three men who had seen Penn preaching in Gracechurch Street. Questioned by the bench, they said that because of crowd noise they had been unable to hear Penn's words. It did not matter; far from denying that Penn had preached, the defendants gloried in what they had done. Penn said: "We confess ourselves to be so far from recanting, or declining to vindicate the assembling of ourselves to preach, pray, or worship the Eternal, Holy, Just God, that we declare to all the world, that we do believe it to be our indispensable duty."

The defendants demanded to know upon what law the indictment was based. "Upon the common law," answered the recorder. He refused to be more specific. If the law "be common," said Penn, "it should not be so hard to produce." Penn challenged the legality of the charge. "The question is not whether I am guilty of this indictment, but whether this indictment be legal."

The court's patience was quickly exhausted. "Take him away," said the recorder. "My Lord, if you take not some course with this pestilent fellow, to stop his mouth, we shall not be able to do anything tonight."

The lord mayor agreed. "Take him away, take him away," he said. "Turn him into the bale-dock."

As Penn was led away he called out to the jury: "Must I therefore be taken away because I plead for the fundamental laws of England? However, this I leave upon your consciences, who are of the jury. . . ."

The bailiffs confined Penn to the bale-dock, a corner of the room enclosed by partitions that did not reach the ceiling. Penn and the jury could no longer see each other.

William Mead, questioned next, told the jury he was a peaceable man and the indictment was riddled with lies. "The lord Coke tells us," he said, "what makes a riot, a rout and an unlawful assembly."

"You deserve to have your tongue cut out," the lord mayor answered Mead.

"Thou didst promise me," said Mead, "I should have fair liberty to be heard; why may I not have the privilege of an Englishman? I am an Englishman, and you might be ashamed of this dealing."

"I look upon you to be an enemy of the laws of England," said the recorder, ". . . nor are you worthy of such privilege, as others have."

"The Lord is judge between me and thee in this matter," said Mead. He too was hauled away to the bale-dock.

The recorder then instructed the jury:

You have heard what the indictment is, it is for preaching to the people, and drawing a tumultuous company after them, and Mr. Penn was speaking; if they [the Quakers] should not be disturbed, you see they will go on; there are three or four witnesses that have proved this, that he did preach there; that Mr. Mead did allow of it: after this, you have heard by substantial witnesses what is said against them: Now we are upon the matter of fact, which you are to keep to, and observe, as what has been fully sworn, at your peril.

In other words, the jury should decide only whether Penn preached and Mead abetted him; the evidence showed these things had been done; and a verdict other than "guilty" could bring down punishment on the jurors' heads—the verdict was "at your peril."

At this point Penn climbed to the top of the bale-dock wall and called out: "I appeal to the jurors who are my judges, and this great assembly, whether the proceedings of the court are not most arbitrary, and void of all law, in offering to give the jury their charge in the absence of the prisoners. . . ."

"Pull that fellow down, pull him down," said the recorder.

Mead then appeared at the top of the wall and said: "Are these according to the rights and privileges of Englishmen, that we should not be heard, but turned into the bale-dock, for making our defense. . . ."

"Take them away into the Hole," the recorder said.

The prisoners were taken downstairs to a place called "the stinking hole."

After an hour and a half the jurors reported that they stood eight to four for conviction. One of the aldermen knew a juror, Edward Bushel, and suspected he was a holdout. "Mr. Bushel," said the alderman, "you have thrust yourself upon this jury. . . . You deserve to be indicted more than any man that hath been brought to the bar this day."

Bushel protested: "No, Sir John, there were three-score before me, and I would willingly have got off, but could not."

The lord mayor threatened Bushel with branding: "Sirrah, you are an impudent fellow. I will put a mark upon you."

Sent out to deliberate again, the jury soon came back with a verdict. The prisoners were brought in and the clerk asked: "Was William Penn guilty or not guilty?"

"Guilty of speaking in Gracechurch Street," said the foreman.

The recorder was incensed. "You had as good say nothing."

The lord mayor demanded: "Was it not an unlawful assembly? You mean he was speaking to a tumult of people there?"

On one side were the robed officials at their elevated bench, the bailiffs and guards, and behind them all the force and majesty of the state. On the other were twelve ordinary men in the jury box, powerless as individuals, unschooled in the law. At the lord mayor's demand some of the jurors "seemed to buckle," but others stood firm. The foreman said, "My Lord, this was all I had in commission." The court told the jurors they would not be released until they had reached a verdict, and sent them out again.

Half an hour later the jury was back. The verdict on Penn was the same: "Guilty of speaking in Gracechurch Street." The verdict on Mead was new: "Not guilty."

The lord mayor was enraged: "What, will you be led by such a silly fellow as Bushel?" The recorder joined in: "Gentlemen, you shall not be dismissed, till we have a verdict that the court will accept; and you shall be locked up, without meat, drink, fire and tobacco; you shall not . . . abuse the court, we will have a verdict by the help of God, or you shall starve for it."

Penn protested: "My jury, who are my judges, ought not to be thus menaced; their verdict should be free, and not compelled."

"Stop that prating fellow's mouth, or put him out of the court," said the recorder.

Penn at this point showed that he was a born advocate, even though not a lawyer. The battle so far had consisted of the court officials insisting that Penn had preached to a tumult and the defendants arguing that the proceedings were unjust. Penn now managed to get a defense on the merits—on the facts of the case—before the jury for the first time. "[T]he jury cannot be so ignorant," he said, "as to think, that we met there, with a design to disturb the civil peace, since (first) we were by force of arms kept out of our lawful house, and met as near it in the street, as their soldiers would give us leave; and (secondly) because it was no new thing . . . but what was usual and customary with us; 'tis very well known that we are a peaceable people, and cannot offer violence to any man."

He turned to the jury: "You are Englishmen, mind your privilege, give not away your right."

"Nor will we ever do it," came an answer from the jury box.

Out again went the jurors. They were kept "all night without meat, drink, fire, or . . . so much as a chamber pot though desired." At seven the next morning, Sunday, they repeated their verdict: "Guilty of speaking in Gracechurch Street."

"To an unlawful assembly?" demanded the lord mayor.

"No, my Lord," answered Edward Bushel.

"You are a factious fellow," said the lord mayor. "I'll take a course with you. . . ."

Bushel answered calmly: "Sir Thomas, I have done according to my conscience."

"That conscience of yours would cut my throat," said the lord mayor. ". . . I will cut yours as soon as I can."

Twice more the jury went out and twice it came back, its verdict unchanged. "Have you no more wit," said the mayor, referring to Bushel, "than to be led by such a pitiful fellow? I will cut his nose."

"It is intolerable that my jury should be thus menaced," said Penn. "Is this according to the fundamental laws? Are not they my proper judges by the Great Charter of England?"

"My Lord," said the recorder, "You must take a course with that same fellow."

"Stop his mouth, gaoler, bring fetters, and stake him to the ground," demanded the lord mayor.

The recorder was now ready to throw out English liberty: " 'Til now I never understood the reason of the policy and prudence of the Spaniards, in suffering the Inquisition among them," he said. "And certainly it will never be well with us, until something like unto the Spanish Inquisition be in England."

The jurors were weary after days of verbal violence. Ordered to go out again, they at first refused. "We have given our verdict," said the foreman, "and all agreed to it; and if we give in another, it will be a force upon us to save our lives." But they decided to try again, and after another long night came back with a final verdict: William Penn, "Not Guilty." William Mead, "Not Guilty."

The presiding officials were furious. Each juror was asked to state his name and verdict separately—"which they unanimously did, in saying, not guilty, to the great satisfaction of the assembly."

The officials had to accept the verdict, but still had the power to punish the jurors for deciding the case wrongly. "God keep my life out of your hands," the recorder told the jury, "but for this the Court fines you forty marks a man; and imprisonment till paid."

Penn, acquitted, stepped up to the bench and demanded his liberty. The court refused; the defendants were to be jailed for nonpayment of the contempt fines imposed at the start. What about the rights secured by Magna Carta? Penn demanded. "Take him away," said the recorder.

And all of them—Penn, Mead, and the twelve jurors—were locked up in Newgate Prison.

—

Penn by now was no stranger to prison life. He wrote to his father: "I desire thee not to be troubled at my present confinement; I could scarce suffer on a better account, nor by a worse hand, and the will of God be done."

But the admiral, gravely ill, wanted to see his son; he paid the fines for Penn and Mead and secured their release.

Eight of the jurors soon grew tired of confinement and their fines were paid as well. But Edward Bushel and three others stood their ground. They retained counsel and sued in the Court of Common Pleas for their freedom and remission of their fines. Released on bail, they still pursued their case.

The decision in *Bushel's Case* came in 1671, a year after the trial of Penn and Mead. The jurors had been fined and imprisoned for refusing to reach a verdict "according to the direction of the court in matters of law." Chief Justice Vaughan wrote a commonsense opinion that avoided any mention of the struggle between the government and the Quakers. Vaughan believed firmly that the law was the judge's province, not the jury's. But he saw also that to return the verdict demanded, the jurors would have had to accept the bench's version of the facts—and they, not the presiding officials, were empowered by the common law to find the facts. The judge, wrote Vaughan, "can never know what evidence the jury have"—a statement reflecting the ancient concept that jurors could consider what they knew from sources outside the trial. And even if all the proof were presented in open court, "the judge and jury might honestly differ in the result from the evidence, as well as two judges may, which often happens."

The modern view that all men are fallible, and that official truth therefore should not be imposed, is implied in Vaughan's opinion: "A man cannot see by another's eye, nor hear by another's ear, no more can a man conclude or infer the thing to be resolved by another's understanding or reasoning."

Jurors sworn to find a true verdict according to the evidence should not be forced to violate their oaths by returning a verdict against the

evidence as they understand it. It follows that no juror should be punished for reaching a verdict deemed wrong by the judge. The writ was
granted.

Edward Bushel and his brave fellow jurors had won—not just for
themselves, but for all inheritors of Anglo-American law. Judges would
harangue juries again, jurors at times would yield to official pressure,
the jury system like any other would have its failures. Yet a great principle had been founded: the jurors, not the judge, decide the verdict;
they must never be coerced; and they are immune to punishment over
a verdict honestly reached, however wrong the judge might think it.
Within the boundaries of the law, the people and not their officials
would have the last word on guilt or innocence. There has been no
greater victory for justice in the courts.

Reconciled at last to his son's Quakerism, Admiral Sir William Penn
dropped the threat to change his will, and died soon after the 1670 trial.

Young William inherited the family estates and went on to a famous
life. Rash and fearless in his early years, willing to spend months in vile
prisons to secure liberty of conscience, Penn became over time a more
cautious and prudent man, versed in the subtleties of politics. He even
became, while keeping his faith, a friend of King Charles II and his
brother James. Penn married twice and fathered fifteen children; wrote
more than a hundred works, ranging from broadsheets to books, in
support of his religion; and obtained from the king, in satisfaction of a
royal debt owed to the admiral, a huge grant of land on the west bank
of the Delaware River in America. There, in 1681, he founded a
colony named Pennsylvania in honor of the admiral. It was to be a
refuge for the persecuted, a community of brotherly love. Penn drew
up a charter of government for this new land. It provided: "[A]ll trials
shall be by twelve men, and as near as may be, peers or equals, and of
the neighborhood, and men without just exception." All thirteen
American colonies adopted trial by jury, but in Pennsylvania there was
a special resonance: the great Quaker had not forgotten his trial by the
jurors of London.

V

JURIES AND LIBERTY IN THE UNITED STATES

Jurors in this country are told to use their own good sense in "finding the facts"—in deciding who is telling the truth, what evidence to believe, what happened on the day in question—but to take as gospel the judge's statement of the law. Typical is this jury instruction recommended by the Federal Judicial Center for use in criminal trials:

> Members of the jury, it will be your duty to find from the evidence what the facts are. You and you alone will be the judges of the facts. You will then have to apply to those facts the law as the court will give it to you. *You must follow that law whether you agree with it or not.* [My emphasis]

This tells the jurors to decide the case by a formula: facts (found by the jury) × law (laid down by the judge) = verdict. The outcome, says the usual instruction, "must not be influenced by any personal likes or dislikes, opinions, prejudices, or sympathy." The jury is to accept the major premise from the judge, fill in the minor premise, and, like a computer, turn out a logical conclusion, the verdict.

This formula describes only a fraction of what goes on—jury work, far from being mechanical, is filled with discretion and value judgments—but it does channel the deliberations, and today it is stridently opposed by a protest movement. In the name of traditional American liberty, the Fully Informed Jury Association (FIJA) and similar organizations lobby for laws requiring that juries be told they can "nullify" the judge's instructions if they disagree with them—in other words, can decide the law for themselves. Law-resisters across the political spectrum—advocates of unrestricted handgun-carrying, or marijuana legalization, or income tax abolition, or the right to blockade abortion clinics—support this view. Jurors are urged, outside the courtroom, to rise against judicial domination for the sake of higher justice.

In a California abortion protesters' trial (the defendants were charged with trespass and resisting arrest), a newspaper ad asked jurors not only to reject the judge's instructions but to lie about their intention to do so: "[D]on't let the judge and prosecutor know that you know about this right." Word is gotten to jurors in some drug-dealer prosecutions that the penalties are so draconian they should acquit whether the defendants are guilty or not. The FIJA sends out "jury power information kits" telling potential jurors that "no juror's oath is enforceable." A recent letter to the editor in Seattle argued that the jury "can decline to convict, in the face of the facts, if it feels the prosecution is unwarranted, the accused has suffered enough, the likely penalty is too severe, or the law itself is wrong, misapplied, or vague."

Few citizens and no judges would agree that oaths are unenforceable or that jurors should lie about their intentions. But the protest movement is no crackpot aberration; it is, rather, the latest chapter in a struggle over the jury's role that goes back to our country's origins. It revives a question that has been with us, off and on, from the beginning: what division of courtroom power among the judge, the lawyers, and the jury will serve both justice and liberty?

In eighteenth-century America, the transplanted jury took root and flourished as never before. Lay citizens' common sense was exalted over the specialized knowledge of judges and lawyers; jury independence became an article of faith. The jury gained, and then held for more than a century, the right to decide what the law was, even if the judge thought differently. In criminal cases the jury's right to acquit on grounds of conscience became firm. Although these two threads of jury power are often tangled under the label "jury nullification," they are distinct and have met different fates. Law-defining by juries is no more, but the jury's right to acquit for conscience's sake lives on. And jury discretion—the ability to make the law make sense, to temper the law's iron logic with fairness, moderation, and mercy—endures and thrives. To understand how we reached this compromise—and to see where the current dispute over the jury's role may lead us—we should look first at a great case in which the jurors did very well but the crucial difference was made by one man, a trial lawyer.

William Cosby, installed by King George III as royal governor of New York, lost no time in proving himself arrogant, greedy, and corrupt. He profited shamelessly from his position, silenced any opposition, and removed from office a colonial chief justice who dared stand up to him. Under the law of the time, to criticize a public official, in any public way, was to commit the crime of seditious libel. The thought of jail—even less attractive in the eighteenth century than now—gave pause to most dissenters. A group of wealthy New Yorkers decided to resist Cosby, in a reasonably safe way, by sponsoring a newspaper. The printer's neck, more than their own, would be on the line. They could not do business with the colony's official printer, whose livelihood depended on the governor's patronage. So they turned to John Peter Zenger, a German immigrant who scratched out a living printing religious tracts and playing the organ in church. If the wealthy gentlemen put up the money, would Zenger publish a newspaper? He would. The *New York Weekly Journal*, edited and printed by Zenger, first appeared in March 1733.

The *Journal*, issue after issue, carried sharp, satirical articles on the Cosby regime. These were written not by Zenger but by the governor's leading opponents, who prudently refrained from signing their names. One article described a Cosby sycophant as a dog "lately strayed from his kennel with his mouth full of fulsome panegyrics." Another referred to the sheriff as a monkey "lately broke from his chain and run into the country." The Cosby crowd were called "petty-fogging knaves [who] deny us the rights of Englishmen."

As Cosby was repeatedly (and justly) accused of malfeasance in office, a growing demand for his ouster spread from a few discontented aristocrats to the public at large. Cosby fought back with a tactic used many times before and since: to silence his critics, he invoked the criminal law. In November 1734 Cosby ordered that four issues of Zenger's newspaper be seized and burned by the common hangman. The hangman gained a small niche in history by refusing. The sheriff then had his servant carry out the order. Not content with burning the printed word, Cosby ordered an arrest—not of the *Journal*'s prosperous backers, but of its impecunious printer. Zenger was charged with "presenting and publishing several seditious libels . . . influencing [the people's] Minds with Contempt of His Majesty's Governor."

Zenger was clapped into jail and held on £400 bail. The amount was high enough to guarantee that he would stay locked up until trial.

Eight months went by. Zenger, from his pretrial dungeon, gave his wife directions for the *Journal*'s ongoing publication. The paper kept appearing; only one issue was missed.

To hamstring the defense, the governor disbarred two lawyers who had agreed to represent Zenger and appointed a Cosby loyalist, John Chambers, to replace them. As the trial approached the case appeared hopeless. Zenger had unquestionably published the offending articles. Under standard procedure, the jury would be allowed to decide only the fact of publication, which was obvious; the judge would rule that the printed words amounted to seditious libel; and Zenger would be found guilty and sentenced.

But the governor had not reckoned with the difference a great lawyer can make. When the trial opened a stranger rose and introduced himself. He was Andrew Hamilton, age sixty, of Philadelphia, who had come north at the request of Zenger's influential friends to defend the prisoner. Hamilton (no relation to the later Alexander) was the most famous advocate in the colonies. The appointed lawyer, Chambers, stepped aside, no doubt with a feeling of relief, and Hamilton took over the defense.

The trial record we have was written by an anti-Cosby lawyer who watched from the gallery, but there is no reason to doubt its essential accuracy. A jury of twelve was sworn. Hamilton immediately shifted the focus of the case: the prosecution, he said, need not bother proving that Zenger had published the articles; this was readily admitted, and the witnesses on hand to prove publication could go home.

The question for the jury, Hamilton went on, would be whether the two articles charged against Zenger were libelous. One article had argued that the "LIBERTIES and PROPERTIES [of New York's people] are precarious, and that SLAVERY is like to be entailed on them and their posterity. . . ." The other said, "WE SEE MEN'S DEEDS DESTROYED, JUDGES ARBITRARILY DISPLACED, . . . TRIALS BY JURIES ARE TAKEN AWAY WHEN A GOVERNOR PLEASES . . . MEN OF KNOWN ESTATES DENIED THEIR VOTES CONTRARY TO THE RECEIVED PRACTICE. . . ." If these words were true, Hamilton argued, they could not be a libel—and the jury should decide whether they were true or not.

No, said the judge, counsel is wrong on both points. Truth is no defense in a seditious libel case. In fact, "the greater appearance there is of truth in any malicious invective, so much the more provoking it is." And whether the words were libelous—that is, criminal—would be determined by the judge; the jury would decide only whether the defendant published them. This, too, reflected the prevailing law.

These rulings by the court blocked the defense from presenting evidence that the articles were true. Hamilton had only one weapon left: argument to the jury. And he gave an argument so compelling that it still resounds today. To this great summation we owe the saying, "You'd better get a Philadelphia lawyer."

"[I]t is to you," Hamilton told the jury, "we must now appeal for witnesses to the truth of the facts we have offered and are denied the liberty to prove. . . . You are citizens of New York; you are really what the law supposes you to be, honest and lawful men; and, according to my brief, the facts which we offer to prove were not committed in a corner; they are notoriously known to be true; and therefore in your justice lies our safety."

Wouldn't a libel, Hamilton asked, depend on how the words were understood by those who heard or read them? He drew a favorable response from the bench:

JUDGE: That is certain. All words are libelous or not, as they are *understood.* Those who are to judge of the words must judge whether they *are scandalous* or *ironical, tend to the breach of peace,* or are *seditious:* There can be no doubt of it.

HAMILTON: I thank Your Honor; I am glad to find the Court of this opinion. Then it follows that those twelve men must *understand* the words in the information to be *scandalous,* that is to say *false;* for I think it is not pretended they are of the *ironical* sort; and when they understand the words to be so, they will say we are guilty of publishing a *false libel,* and not otherwise.

JUDGE: No, Mr. Hamilton; the jury may find that Zenger printed and published those papers, and leave it to the Court to judge whether they are libelous; you know this is very common; it is in the nature of a special verdict, where the jury leave the matter of law to the Court.

HAMILTON: I know, may it please Your Honor, the jury may do so; but I do likewise know they may do otherwise. I know they have the right beyond all dispute to determine both the law and the fact, and where they do not doubt of the law, they ought to do so.

Hamilton, to the jury, went on:

[I]t is a right which all freemen claim, and are entitled to complain when they are hurt; they have a right publicly to remonstrate the abuses of power in the strongest terms, to put their neighbors upon their guard against the craft or open violence of men in authority, and to assert with courage the sense they have of the blessings of liberty, the value they put upon it, and their resolution at all hazards to preserve it as one of the greatest blessings heaven can bestow.

Hamilton reassured all present of his and Zenger's loyalty to King George: "We know His Majesty's gracious intentions to His subjects; he desires no more than that his people in the plantations should be kept up to their duty and allegiance to the Crown of Great Britain, that peace may be preserved amongst them, and justice impartially administered." But could any of this be served "by a governor's setting his people together by the ears, and by the assistance of one part of the people to plague and plunder the other?"

These are excerpts from a long speech. Reading all of it, one can sense the momentum Hamilton was building. He warned the jury of seditious libel prosecutions, of the length to which "such prosecutions may be carried and how deeply the liberties of the people may be affected." Too often were such cases "countenanced by the judges, who held their places at pleasure (a disagreeable tenure to any officer, but a dangerous one in the case of a judge)." He pointed out that one reading aloud from the Bible could be charged with seditious libel. He closed with an appeal to higher justice:

[T]he question before the Court and you gentlemen of the jury is not of small nor private concern, it is not the cause of a poor printer, nor of New York alone, which you are now trying: No! It may in its consequence affect every freeman that lives under a British government on the main of America. It is the best cause. It is the cause of liberty; and I make no doubt but your upright conduct this day will not only entitle you to the love and esteem of your fellow citizens; but every man who prefers freedom to a life of slavery will bless and honor you as men who have baffled the attempt of tyranny; and by an impartial and uncorrupt verdict, have laid a noble foundation for securing to ourselves, our posterity, and our neighbors that to which nature and the laws of our country have given us a right—the liberty—both of exposing and opposing arbitrary power (in these parts of the world, at least) by speaking and writing truth.

The prosecutor, in an indignant reply, argued that the jury need only decide whether Zenger had published the articles (the judge had repeatedly said so); everything Hamilton had said was meant to sow confusion; the law required a verdict of guilty.

By this time the judge's feelings were clearly hurt. He gave his instructions:

> Gentlemen of the jury. The great pains Mr. Hamilton has taken to show how little regard juries are to pay to the opinion of the judges, and his insisting so much upon the conduct of some judges in trials of this kind, is done no doubt with a design that you should take but very little notice of what I might say upon this occasion. I shall therefore only observe to you that as the facts or words in the information are confessed: The only thing that can come in question before you is whether the words as set forth in the information make a libel. And that is a matter of law, no doubt, and which you may leave to the Court.

Hamilton, the consummate professional, was quick to make his peace with the judge: "I humbly beg Your Honor's pardon: I am very much misapprehended, if you suppose what I said was so designed [to cause offense]. Sir, you know; I made an apology for the freedom I found myself under a necessity of using upon this occasion. I said there was nothing personal designed; it arose from the nature of our defense."

The jury retired, deliberated briefly, and returned to the courtroom. Was the defendant guilty or not guilty, asked the clerk, of printing and publishing the libels alleged? "Not guilty," answered the foreman. "Upon which," wrote the chronicler, "there were three huzzas in the hall which was crowded with people." Zenger, the next day, was freed at last from jail.

The Zenger case—the steadfastness of the ordinary man in the dock, his counsel's eloquence, the jury's brave verdict—quickly became celebrated throughout the colonies. Commercial printers, among them Benjamin Franklin, published the trial transcript. The effects on American law were immediate, profound, and lasting. The jury's power to acquit a criminal defendant for reasons of conscience, even against the judge's instructions, was made famous. Excessive bail, which had kept an innocent man in jail for months, was prohibited in federal cases when the Bill of Rights was written half a century later. Hamilton's argument for the right to criticize government foretold the free speech guarantee of the First Amendment. The trial, as Gouverneur Morris, a framer of the Constitution, would say, was "the morning star of liberty" in this country.

Seditious libel stayed on the books, but in the colonies it became virtually a dead letter. Hundreds of people were convicted of this crime in seventeenth-and eighteenth-century England, while in America, throughout the colonial period, there were only about half a dozen prosecutions and two convictions. Grand juries were reluctant to indict and trial juries, whatever the evidence, ordinarily would not convict. Had it been otherwise—had crown-appointed judges issued the verdicts, or juries been compliant—freedom to speak and write and protest in this country could have withered at birth.

Juries gained still more importance as friction over trade laws and taxes grew between the Americans and the crown. The Navigation Acts were designed by Parliament to channel all colonial trade through England, to the colonists' disadvantage. These unpopular laws came to be seen as an insult not just to prosperity but to liberty, and colonial juries balked at enforcing them. Ships impounded by the British under the Navigation Acts were regularly freed by jury verdicts that openly defied the law and the evidence. To bring a smuggler before a jury, complained a Massachusetts governor, "is only trying one illicit trader by his fellows, or at least by his well-wishers." One Boston smuggler who benefited from jury defiance was John Hancock, whose flamboyant signature appears like an exclamation mark at the bottom of the Declaration of Independence.

Great Britain answered the upstart colonial juries by reducing their authority. Courts of vice-admiralty were established to handle maritime cases; in these no juries could be empaneled. The result was more outrage among the colonists.

The Enlightenment, the Age of Reason, the emerging concept of individual rights, the struggle to be rid of English domination after a century and a half of colonial life, and the belief that common men (common men of property, at least) were better equipped than any professional to decide matters of justice, combined to give the jury more power and prestige than it ever had enjoyed before. Free elections and trial by jury, wrote John Adams, were the people's only security "against being ridden like horses, and fleeced like sheep, and worked like cattle, and fed and clothed like hogs and hounds." By the time of the American Revolution the abridgment of jury trials had become a prime grievance, listed among George III's other sins in the 1776 Declaration of Independence. After the war, and after the short-lived Articles of Confederation, the 1787 convention at Philadelphia wrote a jury guarantee for criminal cases into the Constitution (Article III). The 1791 Bill of Rights repeated the guarantee ("In all criminal prosecutions, the accused shall enjoy the right to a speedy and public trial, by an impartial jury. . . .") (Sixth Amendment) and added one for federal civil cases (Seventh Amendment).

The jury, then, entered our national life as an institutional hero. As the Supreme Court would say in the twentieth century, the right to a jury trial was "granted to criminal defendants in order to prevent oppression by the Government." But there was more to it than that. Colonial Americans believed that twelve qualified citizens could do better justice, civil or criminal, than could one official wearing the black robe of a judge. In the early colonies the judges were not lawyers—there was no strong reason to defer to their judgment—and juries, before a clear separation of powers evolved, often did governmental work beyond deciding cases: they set tax rates, regulated prisons, oversaw road-building, and performed other functions later classified as legislative or administrative. The preference for jury decisions continued after the legal profession came into existence. "A clear head and an honest heart," one New Hampshire judge told a jury, are worth "more than all the law of the lawyers." This ethic, coupled with an early shortage of lawyers and the felt need to resist oppression, produced the doctrine of jury nullification—the belief that juries had the right to determine the law as well as the facts, against the judge's instructions if necessary. This was seen not as revolutionary but as basic to justice. John Adams called it "an absurdity to suppose that the law would oblige [jurors] to find a verdict according to the direction of the court, against their own opinion, judgment, and conscience."

What the jury had done in the Zenger case became accepted doctrine. For about a century, jurors were routinely told of their right to nullify, especially in criminal cases. The judge would instruct them on what the law provided, but would often add that if they disagreed they could determine the law by their own lights. Typical was an instruction given by Chief Justice John Jay, who, presiding at a trial in 1794, told the jurors they had the right "to determine the law as well as the fact in controversy."

The heyday of jury nullification lasted into the late 1800s. Juries were told commonly in criminal cases, and at times in civil cases, that they could determine the law according to their own consciences rather than accept the judge's version of it. Linked as it was to the American Revolution and the Bill of Rights, this tradition was seen as central to liberty; it was as widely accepted then as the opposite idea is now.

The opposing view—that law-defining must be the sole province of the judge—developed as the post–Civil War nation became industrialized, the urban working population swelled, the pace of life quickened, and commerce grew more complex. Greater certainty and clarity in the law were demanded. Lawyers, once scarce, were now widely available. Some have argued that there was a deliberate effort, sponsored by commercial interests, to shift power from juries to judges. What is certain is that the reductionist view of the jury as "fact-finder" gained currency. In this view, the jury was limited to deciding what had happened and then applying to its findings the law laid down by the judge. This diminished role for jurors appeared more and more frequently in instructions from the bench. As often happens in the law's evolution, cross-currents were at work. In one courtroom, jurors might be told they had the right to nullify, while in the next county another panel was hearing, from a different judge, that no such right existed. But the antinullification view became dominant and finally, in 1894, it won the Supreme Court's blessing.

The case arose thousands of miles from the nearest domestic shoreline when the second mate of an American freighter vanished at sea in the South Pacific. The disappearance was a mystery until a seaman boasted that he and his friend had killed and gotten rid of the mate. The body would never be found, but there was enough evidence to indict. Sparf and Hansen, two sailors aboard the freighter, were charged with murder and brought back to the United States for trial. The jury heard the evidence and the judge's instructions, deliberated, and came back to the courtroom with a question. Could the defendants be convicted of the lesser crime of manslaughter? No, said the judge; if the defendants were guilty of anything, it would have to be murder: "[I]f a felonious homicide has been committed, the facts of the case do not reduce it below murder." The jury had "the physical power," the judge said, to return a manslaughter verdict, "but as one of the tribunals of the country, a jury is expected to be governed by law, and the law it should receive from the court."

The jury then found Sparf and Hansen guilty of murder on the high seas, a capital offense. The defendants appealed to the Supreme Court, arguing that the judge's instructions abridged the jury's right to nullify—to determine the law for itself if necessary to avoid an unjust result.

A divided Court upheld the convictions. "A verdict of guilty of an offence less than the one charged," wrote the majority, "would have been in flagrant disregard of all the proof, and in violation by the jury of their obligation to render a true verdict." The jury was bound to accept the trial judge's statement of the law. "In this separation of the functions of the court and jury is found the chief value, as well as safety, of the jury system." Two dissenters argued in vain that jurors "in a criminal case, have the right, as well as the power, to decide, according to their own judgment and consciences, all questions, whether of law or of fact" in deciding guilt or innocence.

The opponents of jury power had won. Jury nullification in its pure form—the jury's right to determine questions of law—was put to rest after a distinguished career.

Even while announcing the end of law-finding by juries, the *Sparf and Hansen* Court was careful to note that when a criminal jury acquits— no matter how compelling the evidence of guilt—its decision is final and irreversible. The government can never appeal a jury verdict of not guilty. While the jury no longer can define the law, it has the right to acquit regardless of the law—to say no when the government has gone too far, when a guilty verdict for whatever reason would do violence to fairness, common sense, and conscience.

This ability of the jury to acquit—to extend unarticulated mercy— has saved us from our official selves many times. One of the finest chapters came with the Fugitive Slave Law, passed by Congress in 1850 to force Northerners to return escaped slaves to their Southern masters. This draconian law authorized slaveowners and their agents to "pursue and reclaim" fugitives; required federal officials to help; excluded the fugitive's own testimony from a court proceeding to establish his identity; declared the writ of habeas corpus unavailable; and subjected anyone who harbored or rescued a fugitive to a fine and imprisonment. The law was the main concession to the South in the Compromise of 1850; its authors were trying to hold together a Union being riven by the slavery issue.

The Fugitive Slave Law worked smoothly in the border states, but met with resistance in New England. Neighbors black and white were often outraged when a person—perhaps one they had known for years—was taken from their midst to be returned to slavery. In several cases angry crowds plucked the fugitive from the lawmen's hands and started him on a fast trip to Canada, where he could live free. When the rescuers were put on trial, juries often refused to convict them.

Richard Henry Dana, Jr., who as a younger man had written the seafaring classic *Two Years Before the Mast,* described one such case in 1851. A fugitive slave from Virginia named Shadrach Minkins, also known as Frederick Jenkins, had been seized in the Boston restaurant where he worked and taken to a federal courtroom for a hearing to return him to slavery. His counsel, one of whom was Dana, obtained a three-day delay and left the building. Then, from his office across the street, Dana saw Minkins, who appeared "stupefied by the sudden rescue," being rushed out of the courthouse by a crowd that had snatched him from the marshals. Off they ran toward Cambridge, "like a black squall," wrote Dana, "the crowd driving along with them and cheering as they went." Several days later, Minkins, having been helped along by well-wishers, arrived safely in Montreal. Eight of his rescuers—four black men and four white—were indicted and placed on trial in Boston. Although the Fugitive Slave Law had been cosponsored by the ambitious Senator Daniel Webster of Massachusetts, the prosecutions were highly unpopular. In the first three cases enough jurors held out for acquittal to prevent a verdict from being reached. Discouraged, the government dropped the remaining cases. No one was ever convicted of helping Minkins escape. And Minkins, miraculously spared, stayed in Montreal, where he opened a restaurant, married an Irish woman, and started a family. Despite the cold winters and the difficulties of making a living, he vowed never to return to the United States, even to the North, as long as slavery endured. He told one visitor that he had asked his friends to shoot him if he were ever crazy enough to head for the border. He died in Montreal in 1875.

Under the Fugitive Slave Law, a high proportion of thousands of escaped slaves were returned by judges sitting without juries. But when rescuers were prosecuted, jury trials were available, and many jurors answered the call of conscience.

Conscience, ignited by economic necessity, prevailed again in the

Pennsylvania coal fields in the 1930s. Thousands of miners, thrown out of work by the Depression, had no way to provide for their families. Many of them turned to what quickly became known as "bootleg coal." Working at first only at night and then openly by day, they dug coal where it could be found near the surface on their employers' properties, sold it at bargain prices, and fed their families with the proceeds. This brought a subsistence living at best, but the volume of bootleg coal rose to forty million dollars' worth by 1934. "We gotta live, don't we?" one miner told an interviewer, and pointed out that the coal companies had acquired much of their land by stealing it from the Indians. "Was that a nice thing to do? Well, we're the new Indians, taking what coal we can back from the companies." The mining companies fought back by blowing up illegal holes and causing the arrest of scores of bootleggers. But the effort was in vain; the juries in coal country still believed in the laws forbidding larceny, but would not convict these men and drive their wives and children into still deeper poverty. One company official seemed resigned to the acquittals. "Those fellows," he said in an unguarded moment, "take such gosh-awful chances that in a way they're entitled to that coal."

The most famous examples of jury mercy in recent history came during the Vietnam War, seen by many at the time as "terribly wrong," to use the phrase that came to Secretary of Defense Robert McNamara three decades later. There were countless public protests. In trials of protesters for trespassing, or burning draft records, or obstructing public officials, some juries acquitted in the teeth of the evidence and the instructions; others, feeling obliged to convict, did so.

The so-called Oakland Seven had led a stop-the-draft demonstration outside the Oakland Armed Forces Induction Center in 1967. The demonstrators not only voiced their sentiments, but physically disrupted the conduct of business at the center. The seven were charged with conspiring to commit trespass, creating a public nuisance, and resisting arrest. At the trial there was no question that they did these things. The defense argued, instead, that the war was illegal, the defendants' intentions noble, and the police brutal in dealing with them. All seven were acquitted. Post-trial interviews showed that the jurors had seen a political motive in the prosecution. "I tried to examine the prosecution's argument," said one juror, "but I thought it meant, in other words, that people should be puppets, go along. If that were true, our democratic procedures wouldn't be worth much. I'm not a puppet, I'm a free thinker." Another juror, a colonel in the military, said: "I was very caught up in the details of the case, but I also understood in a brief flash, if they could do that to these boys they could do it to anyone; they can stop all dissent."

At the opposite end of the country, in 1973, twenty-eight religiously motivated antiwar activists were tried in federal court in New Jersey for having destroyed records at a local Selective Service office. The evidence showed that the FBI knew of the activists' plans and planted among them an informant who gave them the tools and knowledge to carry out their act of protest. The trial judge allowed the defendants to testify about their purposes and political beliefs, and received evidence about the Pentagon Papers and the nature of the Vietnam War. He told the jury, at first, that they had no power to acquit against the evidence, but by the end of the trial changed his mind. His earlier advice had been wrong, said the judge, and he told the jury:

[I]f you find that the overreaching participation by Government agents or informers in the activities as you have heard them was so fundamentally unfair to be offensive to the basic standards of decency, and shocking to the universal sense of justice, then you must acquit any defendant to whom this defense applies.

A verdict of not guilty followed for all twenty-eight defendants.

The similar case of Dr. Benjamin Spock and his fellow protesters came out differently. The jurors sympathized with the defendants but found their conviction unavoidable under the judge's instructions. "I knew they were guilty when we were charged by the judge," said one afterward. "I did not know *prior* to that time—I was in full agreement with the defendants until we were charged by the judge. That was the kiss of death!"

These episodes—spanning more than a century and involving the slavery issue, the Depression, and the Vietnam War—show how jury discretion helps us, again and again, to do justice in times of national crisis. The jury rises to these summits. And it rises not from sea level but from a long range of hills where discretion is at work every day. The causes are not always exalted. Sometimes mercy is extended simply because the defendant's conduct, although illegal, is tolerated. Dr. Jack Kevorkian's repeated acquittals on assisted-suicide charges—where the patient, not the doctor, pressed the fatal button—are a likely example. (Dr. Kevorkian's luck ran out when he pressed the button himself.) During Prohibition, bootleggers were hard to convict in areas where the prevailing sentiment was wet. The 1929–30 acquittal rate in federal liquor law prosecutions was 13 percent for cases tried in Kansas, Oklahoma, and Nebraska, 48 percent in New England, and 60 percent in New York. There is no reason to believe that the indictments were any less accurate in the East. A 1973 crackdown on prostitution in San Francisco, with the police using attractive female officers dressed in "clinging" outfits as decoys authorized to arrest men who proposed illicit sex to them, failed when juries refused to convict. Poaching, in some rural areas, has been treated with good-natured laxity. "To the best of my recollection," noted one judge in the 1960s, "there has never been a game law violation verdict of guilty in this county." As the conservation ethic rises, poaching convictions come more easily.

If the jury feels that a conviction will lead to a grossly excessive and cruel punishment, a mercy acquittal may follow, as often happened when simple larceny was a capital offense in England. There are signs of this in some recent inner-city drug cases; drug dealing is not tolerated by juries, but as word spreads about long mandatory prison sentences for nonviolent first-time offenders, jurors will react.

If the police or prosecutors have acted unfairly, an acquittal may result, providing a curb on future official conduct. In a sense there are two distinct questions in any criminal case: is the defendant guilty? And if he is, does the government deserve to win a conviction? The second, at times, may trump the first. Recent examples are the prosecutions of Marion Barry, the District of Columbia's mayor (acquitted of most charges, although caught on a videotape with cocaine, where a girlfriend had set him up for the government), and Oliver North (acquitted of all but minor charges by jurors who probably believed he was a scapegoat for higher officials).

There is an ugly side to the jury's right to acquit. Until not long ago, white men who killed blacks—or civil rights workers—in the South were often freed regardless of the evidence. If a jury decides to acquit out of race prejudice, or any other form of hatred or ignorance, no one can stop it, and no one can reverse the injustice. We must live with the memory of the Emmett Till case and others like it. There have been not only race-based acquittals of guilty whites but convictions of innocent blacks, as the Scottsboro case and Harper Lee's novel *To Kill a Mockingbird* remind us. We can only vow to do better—and nowadays we *are* doing better, as shown by the 1998 trial of Sam Bowers in Hattiesburg, Mississippi. Bowers, as an imperial wizard of the Ku Klux Klan, had ordered a 1966 firebombing that killed Vernon Dahmer, Sr., a black man who was helping other blacks register to vote. Four earlier trials—including two murder trials in the 1960s—had ended with Bowers walking away after all-white juries deadlocked. No jury in Mississippi, said Bowers, would ever convict a white man of killing a black. But this time there was a jury of the New South—six blacks, five whites, and an Asian American. Former Klan members testified that Bowers had been the only Klan official empowered to order a person's death, and that in Dahmer's case he had done so. The jury unanimously found Bowers guilty of murder; the judge sentenced him, at long last, to life in prison; and Bowers was led away by a racially mixed detail of police officers.

Vernon Dahmer, Jr., spoke of his father: "He was working to make sure this day would come." Voter registration, for which the murdered man had died, meant not just electoral power but the right to serve on juries. "This"—the racially diverse jury—"represents America," said Dahmer Junior. "This represents our community. The system has now worked for us."

Jury mercy has ranged from the noble to the humdrum to the disgraceful. But in the main it has served us well. By defeating unjust prosecutions, by protecting the weak against overzealous officialdom, by fending off oppressive uses of the law, jurors have strengthened not just liberty but the rule of law itself—and they still do.

It does not happen every day. In nearly all trials the law as given by the judge, when applied to the evidence, produces a verdict the jurors feel to be just; there is no conflict between law and conscience. When a conflict does arise, it usually is resolved not by open rebellion but by subtle reasoning. Most jurors are respectful; they seek not to defy the law but to make it work.

An example from my court illustrates this. Charlie Renton, as I will call him, was a federal prisoner in California. Renton had spent years in jail for recurring episodes of unarmed bank robbery and drug dealing, all to finance his enthusiastic pursuit of liquor, drugs, and women. Now in middle age, he seemed old beyond his years, burned out, institutionalized, and affable. But Renton was seething over an injustice. Before his latest trip to prison he had entrusted a drinking buddy and fellow drug dealer with $2,500, to hold for him until he got out. The friend, predictably, had spent the money. Renton now wanted it back; his release date was only a year or so away. When polite means failed, Renton mailed a letter from prison, telling the erstwhile friend what he would do to him (death or at least irreversible damage to his private parts) if the money was not repaid. There was no response, so Renton mailed a second threatening letter, and then a third. The letters were filled with vivid profanities. The erstwhile friend's mother turned them over to the police.

A federal prosecution followed, and it was severe beyond any apparent need. Renton obviously had no ability to carry out his threats; he was locked up. His transgressions could have been dealt with quickly and simply through the prison's internal disciplinary system. Instead he was charged with six federal felonies (two per letter): three counts of threatening violence to collect an extension of credit (in violation of a statute aimed chiefly at mob extortion), and three of sending threats through the mail. If convicted, he would face a long additional prison sentence.

Renton was brought to trial in Seattle, where the letters had been received. The drug-dealer former friend, who still owed the $2,500, testified. His mother testified. Renton, in prison garb, took the stand, admitted the key facts against him, called himself "an old fool," and said he had been blowing off steam in a situation where he was helpless to do anything.

Under the law it made no difference whether the defendant meant to, or even could, carry out threats he had made. The defendant was clearly guilty. Yet the jurors, after prolonged deliberation, announced themselves deadlocked. I asked them to try again; they did, and came back still deadlocked. I declared a mistrial.

Soon afterward, the case was settled. Renton was allowed to plead to a single count of sending a threat through the mail, and received a modest additional sentence.

After the case was finished, the engineer-businessman who had been the jury foreman accepted an invitation to come to my chambers and talk about it. He was eager to tell what happened. All twelve jurors, he said, felt that the case was too trivial to be in court—that it had been grievously overcharged and was an imposition on their time and the judge's. Eleven of them, however, decided that under the law and the evidence there was no choice but to convict on all six counts. Only the foreman disagreed. At first he had trouble formulating why. It was a matter of self-respect: "I had to live with myself—the one in the mirror." Then he thought of all the vile language he had heard for years while working on construction projects, and on the street in his downtown neighborhood. Nearly all of it was hot air—mere expressions of emotion. What Renton had written to his debtor, the foreman decided, was "no more than whiskey talk or a figure of speech—not to be taken literally." It was, in other words, not a threat at all but merely an outburst, "in language common to both their vocabularies." In this way the foreman reconciled his sense of justice with the jury instructions. And he stood his ground. It was uncomfortable, but "my honor to myself was more important than what the eleven thought of me."

The jury deadlocked by a vote of eleven to one. But the result, in the end, was fairer than it would have been without the foreman's dissent.

What we glimpsed with the Charlie Renton jury has been shown vividly in recent experiments where jury deliberations—customarily private, but observed in these cases with the consent of the parties, the judge, and the jurors—have been videotaped. *Frontline* and *CBS Reports* have broadcast such programs. In them we see jurors striving not to defy or overcome the law but to apply it sensibly. Even those most out of sympathy with the judge's instructions seek to accommodate them.

Jury mercy is not to be feared. It is one part of the discretion jurors must use in deciding an endless variety of questions: whether a car driver acted negligently, or a physician failed to meet the professional standard of care, or a killer acted with premeditation, or a party's failure to do something called for by a contract was serious enough to be a breach, or competitors met to conspire in restraint of trade or only to talk socially, or stock purchasers were defrauded, and so on. Jurors make judgments, and they do so by using not just the law laid out for them by the judge, but their own sense of justice as well. In this way they keep the law legitimately attuned to community values.

What, then, should jurors in a criminal case be told about their right to acquit for the sake of conscience, regardless of the evidence? The best answer, in my view, is to say nothing. When the occasion calls for it, I will let in evidence of the defendant's motive and belief even if those would fall short of a legal defense. I don't use the imperious phrase "whether you agree with it or not" in jury instructions, but I do tell the jurors what the law provides and that they must find the facts from the evidence and then apply the law to reach their verdict. This provides a structure, a reasoned basis, for the deliberations. Jurors take this definition of their role seriously—I have never had a verdict that seemed to flout or ignore the instructions—but they also know that their sense of justice has a rightful place in court.

THE RULES OF THE GAME

Jurors, like the rest of us, are vulnerable to the fear, prejudice, and confusion that have hanged innocent men and women through the ages. They will rise to difficult occasions, but they need help. They need, above all, impartial judges and fair rules of procedure. If trials are chaotic, if hearsay and harangues and free-floating opinions take over, if no limits define what is relevant, if witnesses cannot be made to face cross-examination, injustice will follow. Nothing in American history shows this better than our seminal trial disaster, the Salem witch prosecutions of 1692. At a high cost in ruined lives, these came at just the right moment to help create, in the century that followed, the rules that protect us from each other—whether we are in the jury box, or in the defendant's chair, or at counsel's table, or in the street going about our business, but open, as everyone is even on the sunniest day, to being subjected to a criminal charge or civil lawsuit.

The witch trials have been described as a case history of mass hysteria, religious extremism, repressed sexuality finding a sadistic outlet, or last-gasp counterattack by a declining Puritan elite. Something can be said for all these views, but the trials' most enduring legacy is a simple and practical one. The judges of Salem and the clergymen who egged them on have been denounced ever since for their bigotry and narrow-minded cruelty. What is usually overlooked is that the trials were by jury; that the accused witches could have been acquitted; and that the jurors, succumbing to official pressure and the prevailing wave of fear, returned guilty verdicts they regretted for the rest of their lives. But skepticism was not entirely lacking in the Puritan soul. The jurors unquestionably wanted to do the right thing, and with anything resembling fair rules of the game the outcome for at least some of the wretches who died on the gallows would have been different.

Massachusetts Bay Colony had been founded, seventy years earlier, as an experiment in the perfectibility of man. The Puritans aimed to create a kingdom of virtue, a "Garden of Christ" in the wilderness. Like all the other American colonies but one, Massachusetts imposed an official religion—in this case, a stark and gloomy creed whose believers lived in mortal fear of damnation. Satan was a tempting presence everywhere; to keep him off, all "vain enjoyment" was forbidden.

The colony's criminal code, although milder than the draconian laws then current in England, relied broadly on the death penalty and was studded with biblical references. One provision made witchcraft a capital offense: "If any man or woman be a WITCH, that is, hath or consulteth with a familiar spirit, they shall be put to death [Exod. 22.18; Levit. 20.27; Deut. 18.10.11]."

At the time, there was nothing unusual in outlawing witchcraft on pain of death. Superstition was engrained in the Western world and modern science was in its infancy. While Isaac Newton was explaining in his *Principia Mathematica* the physics of motion, and Antonie van Leeuwenhoek in Holland was using his microscope to discover a new world of microbes, the great mass of people still feared witchcraft. Over the centuries, thousands of witches had been executed in Europe, chiefly by fire at the stake.

By the time the unusually cold winter of 1691–92 arrived, Massachusetts was in trouble. The colonists recently had fought a brutal and costly war against the Indians, suffered orders by Charles II that undercut their independence, and felt a decline in their own sense of community. Their House of Deputies had found it necessary to adopt a resolution denouncing social friction as "a subversion of the gospel order." A visitor to Boston in 1688 observed that the people were "savagely fractious" in dealing with one another.

Looming over the small colony, to the west, was a dark unbounded wilderness, feared as the source of Indian raids and savage godlessness.

To the east lay the sea and inhospitable England. A sense of isolation grew; if salvation was to come, it must be earned at home. But the dream of an ideal kingdom was yielding to human frailty, and the colony's very existence seemed imperiled. Other settlements along the Atlantic coast had failed and vanished; if God's favor were lost, Massachusetts would follow them into oblivion. Satan, it was clear to many, must be the author of these miseries. Who else would want the Garden of Christ to wither?

As the colony's troubles deepened, clergymen gave sermons prophesying doom and blaming the occult forces of darkness. Increase Mather, the foremost divine of Massachusetts, published in 1684 a collection of tales describing New England witchcraft and sorcery. His son Cotton Mather, an even more zealous preacher, wrote a book about "several very astonishing witchcrafts and possessions." Witchcraft, wrote Cotton Mather, "is the furthest effort of our original sin." The stories he told—of fits, possessions, unnatural ailments and deaths, flights down chimney flues and up onto rafters—were set in Massachusetts. Mather believed them to be true; so did most of his readers.

The ingredients for persecution of an exotic minority were in place: social discord, fear of imminent destruction, the belief that an agent of evil was secretly at work everywhere. The Puritan soul demanded release from these tensions. And the society lacked one element that might have calmed, or at least moderated, the tempest to come: there were no lawyers in Massachusetts. The profession had gotten off to a shaky start in the colony when the first lawyer to arrive, who debarked at Plymouth in about 1624, was soon afterward jailed for scandalous behavior and expelled. By 1641, "pleading for hire" was prohibited by law. Hoping to govern an ideal state, the Puritan leaders saw no need for professional advocates. Distrust of lawyers, in fact, permeated the seventeenth-century colonies. Virginia excluded them from its courts, as did Connecticut. The 1669 Constitution for the Carolinas called it "a base and vile thing to plead for money or reward." The Quakers of Pennsylvania sought brotherhood and harmony—goals believed to be subverted by lawyers. Even had there been lawyers in Massachusetts, they would have been unable to help under the English rule, then still prevalent, that barred them from felony cases.

So the witches of Salem, soon to be charged, would have to face trial without counsel, and without judges trained in the law.

In Salem Village, a small settlement a few miles outside the town of Salem, lived Samuel Parris, a joyless clergyman, with his family and retinue. There was one exotic person in Reverend Parris's household: a female slave named Tituba, brought from Barbados where Parris had lived as the son of a British merchant. In the winter of 1691–92, several adolescent girls of Salem Village became fond of passing what free time they had in Tituba's kitchen. Tituba may have dabbled in the occult arts, and she surely had tales to tell of the warm and distant Caribbean. We cannot know what secrets were shared, but somehow the girls developed frightening symptoms of hysteria. They would scream, fall to the floor, jerk their bodies in convulsions, bark like dogs, cry out in pain from pinches and blows inflicted by invisible tormentors, and recoil in fear of apparitions only they could see. Parris, alarmed and mystified, brought in the village physician. The doctor's resources were thin, and when none of his nostrums worked he announced a diagnosis that exonerated himself: Satan was responsible; the girls were bewitched.

The symptoms spread quickly to other girls in the neighborhood. The same devil who threatened the survival of Massachusetts seemed now to be corrupting its young. Parris enlisted other ministers to help him dig out the truth. Who had afflicted these children? Under interrogation, the girls at first were baffled. Then, yielding to their elders' demands for a confession, they identified three tormentors: Tituba herself; Sarah Good, a pipe-smoking, acerbic crone who often begged from her neighbors; and Sarah Osborne, vulnerable because she had let a man move into her house several months before they married.

Thomas Putnam, father of twelve-year-old Ann Putnam, one of the afflicted girls, joined with three other farmers in swearing out complaints before magistrates in Salem. On February 29, 1692, the magistrates issued warrants and Sarah Good, Sarah Osborne, and Tituba were arrested and jailed on charges of witchcraft.

A hearing began the next day in Salem Village to determine whether the accused women should be held for trial. John Hathorne, a thoroughly devout magistrate, presided. Hathorne would soon become the bane of all witches: from the start he believed every accusation, brushed aside every denial, and assumed the guilt of every suspect. His duty, as he saw it, was to defeat Satan; he would not be put off by wily defenses.

As a cold wind howled outside, the first hearing was held in the wooden, boxlike Salem Village meetinghouse. The chamber, usually devoted to church services, was packed. The afflicted girls sat in the front row. Scribes wrote down what happened, and the records of these preliminary examinations have come down to us in vivid detail. First to be called for questioning was Sarah Good—defiant, disreputable, and, as it happened, pregnant again. Hathorne examined her to produce a confession, assuming from the start that she was a witch.

Q: Sarah Good, what evil spirit have you familiarity with?
A: None.
Q: Have you made no contract with the devil?
A: No.
Q: Why do you hurt these children?
A: I do not hurt them. I scorn it.
Q: Who do you employ then to do it?
A: I employ nobody.
Q: What creature do you employ then?
A: No creature, but I am falsely accused.
Q: Why did you go away muttering from Mr. Parris's house?
A: I did not mutter, but I thanked him for what he gave my child.

Sarah Good was holding firm against a frightening interrogator and a hostile crowd. The magistrate asked the children to look at her and say whether she had hurt them. "Yes," answered the girls, and immediately fell into torment. Now and throughout the trials, this evidence—

the girls' fits of agony in the presence of accused witches—would be the most damning proof. John Hale, a visiting minister, described what he saw: "These children were bitten and pinched by invisible agents; their arms, necks and back turned this way and that way, and were turned back again, so as it was impossible for them to do of themselves, and beyond the power of any epileptic fits, or natural disease to effect. Sometimes they were taken dumb, their mouths stopped, their throats choked, their limbs racked and tormented so as might move a heart of stone. . . ."

Hathorne pursued the luckless woman in the dock:

Q: Sarah Good, do you not see now what you have done? Why do you not tell us the truth, why do you thus torment these poor children?
A: I do not torment them.
Q: Who do you employ then?
A: I employ nobody. I scorn it.

But under the relentless questioning, Sarah Good finally buckled:

Q: Who was it then that tormented the children?
A: It was Osborne.

This pathetic attempt to deflect the attack to a codefendant could only have been self-defeating—for how could Good know that Sarah Osborne afflicted the children unless she was a witch herself?

Next came Sarah Osborne—frightened, ill, leaning on the back of a chair for support, but bravely protesting her innocence in answer to Hathorne:

Q: What evil spirit have you familiarity with?
A: None.
Q: Have you made no contract with the devil?

A: No, I never saw the devil in my life.

Q: Why do you hurt these children?

A: I do not hurt them.

Q: Who do you employ, then, to hurt them?

A: I employ nobody.

Q: What familiarity have you with Sarah Good?

A: None. I have not seen her these two years.

But four of the girls swore that the accused, or her apparition, had pinched and pricked them, and had urged them to write in her book. Sarah Osborne would die in jail a few weeks later, while awaiting trial.

So far the browbeating from the bench had produced no confession. But next came Tituba, and with her the case against Satan blossomed. Tituba began with a denial:

HATHORNE: Tituba, what evil spirit have you familiarity with?

TITUBA: None.

Q: Why do you hurt these children?

A: I do not hurt them.

Q: Who is it then?

A: The devil for ought I know.

This plainly displeased the authorities, and the transcript reveals a terrified slave gradually sensing that her only hope lay in giving them what they wanted—a confession that implicated others.

Q: Did you never see the devil?

A: The devil came to me and bid me serve him.

Q: Who have you seen?

A: Four women sometimes hurt the children.

Q: Who were they?

A: Goody Osborne and Sarah Good, and I do not know who the others were. Sarah Good and Osborne would have me hurt the children but I would not.

There was also "a tall man of Boston"—a warlock.

Q: When did you see them?
A: Last night at Boston.
Q: What did they say to you?
A: They said hurt the children.
Q: And did you hurt them?
A: No, there is four women and one man; they hurt the children and then lay all upon me, and they tell me if I will not hurt the children they will hurt me.
Q: But did you not hurt them?
A: Yes, but I will hurt them no more.
Q: Are you not sorry you did hurt them?
A: Yes.

And Tituba was off on three days of spellbinding testimony. For the onlookers it must have been the drama of a lifetime. Every suspicion about witchcraft was confirmed: there were red cats and red rats that whispered "serve me"; a creature with wings and a woman's face; midnight flights to distant places; a tall man with a yellow bird who tempted women with "pretty things"; a book of Satan to be signed; specters pinching and tormenting the faithful; and magic rituals at witches' sabbaths.

"Who hurts the children now?" asked Hathorne. "I am blind now," answered Tituba. "I cannot see." But her confession convinced the believers that many others, besides the three accused, were embroiled in Satan's conspiracy against Massachusetts.

Tituba, along with the two Sarahs, was held in jail for trial. But unlike them she was safe; her testimony was too valuable to be lost on the gallows.

The afflicted girls, finding themselves the center of attention for the first time in their lives, were faced with demands for more names. A pattern developed: the girls would become possessed by evil spirits;

adult believers would urge them to identify their tormentors; the girls would comply; adults (most notably members of the Putnam family, who had plenty of axes to grind) would swear out complaints before the magistrates; and the accused would be arrested, jailed, and subjected to a preliminary hearing.

Rebecca Nurse, age seventy-one, was a virtuous matriarch with a flock of adoring children and grandchildren, but occasionally she lost her temper. There were old grudges against her, and when several girls named her as a witch, members of the Putnam family testified against her as well. Angered by Rebecca's denials at her preliminary hearing, Thomas Putnam's wife cried out: "Did you not bring the black man with you? Did you not bid me tempt God and die? How oft have you eat and drunk your own demon?" Rebecca, despairing, said, "Oh Lord, help me!" At these words the afflicted girls fell into torment. The magistrates noted that the accused was not weeping. Why not?

A: You do not know my heart.
Q: You would do well if you are guilty to confess and give glory to God.
A: I am as clear as the child unborn.

Rebecca steadfastly denied everything—afflicting the innocent, signing the devil's book, paying apparitional visits, and all the rest of it. "Would you have me belie myself?" She was bound over for trial.

As the spring brought warmth and blossoms to New England, scores of men and women were cried out upon as witches, arrested, and held for trial. They were confined in dark, damp, miserable jails—chained to the wall in the belief that this precaution would keep them from spectrally attacking their victims from prison. Among those jailed was the youngest witch—Dorcas Good, Sarah's daughter, age four and a half.

Elizabeth Proctor, reputable wife of a successful farmer and tavern-keeper, at first escaped being named, but then one of the girls saw her perching on a meetinghouse roofbeam, and another claimed she had pursued her to sign the dreaded book. "Dear child, it is not so," said

Elizabeth. "There is another judgment, dear child." But she was held for trial. Her husband John made the mistake of publicly criticizing the court, and was denounced, subjected to an array of witchcraft charges, and jailed.

As the afflicted girls gained confidence and power, so did the magistrates—especially Hathorne, whose pride of interrogation is visible in the record. Bridget Bishop was charged with afflicting four of the girls and, earlier, having bewitched her first husband to death. She denied everything: "I am no witch."

Q: How is it then, that your appearance doth hurt these?
A: I am innocent.

But the afflicted were "greatly tormented" in Bridget's presence. When she lifted her eyes, the girls' eyes rolled up in their sockets; when she shook her head, the girls' heads twisted from side to side. Didn't this show her guilt?

A: I know nothing of it. I am innocent to a witch. I know not what a witch is.
Q: *How do you know then that you are not a witch?*

This must have passed as a brilliant question. Poor Bridget had no good answer to it.

The biggest catch, the most prominent and surprising witch, was a clergyman, George Burroughs. Ten years earlier, Burroughs, a small and dark man gifted with remarkable strength and agility, had been the resident minister at Salem Village. He had moved to Maine, where he farmed and had a parish and lived with his third wife (he had been twice widowed), her daughter, and his own seven children. In early May, seated at dinner with his family, Burroughs was suddenly confronted by men bearing a summons. They took him out of his house and rode with him on the long trip to Salem Village. There, to his astonishment, he found himself denounced by hostile witnesses who claimed he had repeatedly tortured Ann Putnam, murdered his first two wives and a Mrs. Lawson and her daughter (the decedents' apparitions, in their winding sheets, had said so), and presided as master warlock at witches' sabbaths. No one mentioned that John Putnam, Ann's uncle, still resented Burroughs over an old dispute about a debt. The magistrates found ample evidence to justify keeping him locked up.

By late spring the jails were filled with about a hundred accused witches awaiting trial. Some of these had confessed, and the confessions—uttered out of a confused sense of guilt, or to placate hostile interrogators and save the accused's own skin—buttressed the afflicted girls' evidence.

"Thou shalt not suffer a witch to live," says the Old Testament. Yet confessing to witchcraft proved, at Salem, a sure route to survival. Only one of the fifty-odd suspects who eventually confessed was hanged, and he had repudiated his confession. Confessors were spared to provide evidence against those who would not break loose from Satan's grip.

Sir William Phipps, newly appointed as royal governor of the colony, arrived at Boston Harbor on May 14, 1692. Phipps was a man of good sense but, facing a crisis of law enforcement, he ordained a special court to try the backlog of witchcraft cases. As chief justice he named his deputy governor, William Stoughton, who was both a clergyman and a rising politician. Stoughton, without legal experience, would soon prove to be a judge of iron determination: he wanted guilty verdicts. The court would have six other judges, all members of the governor's advisory council.

The surviving trial records are scantier than those of the preliminary examinations. We know that the first to be tried, on June 2, 1692, was Bridget Bishop, who was vulnerable as a tavernkeeper with a long history of being suspected as a witch. Bridget had a habit of appearing in men's lustful dreams; she was, therefore, a temptress.

A jury composed entirely of church members was sworn. John Cooke, age about eighteen, testified he had seen the defendant's specter one morning at sunrise: "And she looked on me and grinned on me, and presently struck me on the side of the head, which did very much hurt me. And then I saw her go out under the end window at a little crevice about so big as I could thrust my hand into." There was more, attested by other witnesses: Bridget had shown up in the guise of animals, caused children to sicken and die, and given suck to a snake. A jury of women, inspecting her body before the trial, had found a "witch's teat" near her private parts. Bridget never had a chance. The jury found her guilty, and the judges sentenced her to be hanged.

One judge, Nathaniel Saltonstall, resigned in protest; but his gesture was ineffectual, the more so because he promptly took to heavy drinking.

On June 10, 1692, Bridget Bishop was hanged by the sheriff from the limb of an oak tree on a hill near Salem Village.

This first hanging prompted Sir William Phipps to write a letter to the ministers of Boston seeking their advice. There was, in some quarters, doubt over the reliability of spectral evidence. The ministers answered on June 15 in an artful letter probably written by Cotton Mather. The devil, they said, may appear in the shape of an innocent person, so no one should be found guilty on spectral evidence alone. The judges should proceed with "exceeding tenderness" toward the accused. "Nevertheless"—in the next breath—"we cannot but humbly recommend unto the Government the speedy and vigorous prosecution of such as have rendered themselves obnoxious, according to the direction given in the laws of God, and the wholesome statutes of the English nation; for the detection of witchcrafts." This amounted to an endorsement of the special court; the door was open to more guilty verdicts and executions.

As the hearings and trials went on through the summer, an occasional witness would try to demolish the girls' credibility. Daniel Elliott, in defense of Elizabeth Proctor, swore that one of the afflicted had told him that "she did it for sport, they must have some sport." But this was brushed aside, and the girls, as their influence grew, undoubtedly accused men and women not just for sport but out of conviction; power breeds self-belief.

In late June five women were brought to trial, among them Rebecca Nurse. The afflicted girls fell into seizures in court; dozens of witnesses testified against the accused witches; the crowd in the meetinghouse, and the overflow outside, demanded convictions. But Rebecca Nurse was known to be a good woman. She behaved with quiet dignity at the trial, and the jurors knew that many respectable citizens had signed a petition in her behalf. As to her, the jury returned a verdict of not guilty. There was an immediate uproar, a "hideous outcry" by the accusers and their allies. William Stoughton, presiding, made himself heard by asking the jurors if they had considered what Rebecca had said when Deliverance Hobbs and her daughter Abigail were brought in to testify: "What, do you bring her? She is one of us." Stoughton meant that this was incriminating, that "us" referred to the company of witches. The jury went out, deliberated, and came back with a question for the accused, put to her by Thomas Fisk, the foreman: what had she meant by her remark? Rebecca, partly deaf, failed to hear the question and made no answer. The jury retired again and soon returned with a verdict of guilty. The judges sentenced her to death.

In jail, Rebecca Nurse learned that the jury foreman, justifying the verdict, had cited her failure to explain her remark about the Hobbses. She wrote an explanation to "humbly show" the court and jury that she had meant only to say Goodwife Hobbs and her daughter were fellow prisoners. "And I being something hard of hearing, and full of grief, none informing me how the court took up my words, and therefore had not opportunity to declare what I intended, when I said they were of our company."

This explanation was undoubtedly true, but it availed nothing. Rebecca Nurse and four other women, one of whom was the pipe-smoking, irrepressible Sarah Good, were hanged on Gallows Hill on July 19, 1692. The hangings of the time were unscientific. There was no quick breaking of the neck, but death by slow strangulation. Sarah, at the end, was beseeched by a meddling clergyman to confess her witchery. "You're a liar!" she shot back. "I am no more a witch than you are a wizard. If you take my life away, God will give you blood to drink." Years later, as it happened, the clergyman died of a hemorrhage.

On July 23, from Salem prison, John Proctor sent to Increase Mather and four other prominent Boston ministers a heartfelt plea for fair treatment. The judges, juries, and public, Proctor wrote, were "much enraged and incensed against us by the delusion of the devil." He had come to know his fellow prisoners, and they were "all innocent persons." His property had been destroyed or seized, and his son had been tortured to try to force a confession. Proctor asked for a change of judges, since those now seated had "condemned us already before our trials." The five ministers ignored the letter.

On August 5, four men and two women were brought to trial, among them Proctor, his wife Elizabeth, and George Burroughs. Fifty-three neighbors had signed petitions attesting to the Proctors' good conduct and character; their words were blown away by the gale. Burroughs, the accused clergyman brought back from Maine, had now been living in prison with alleged witches for two months, and he knew them to be innocent. He saw that hysteria had overtaken the girls, the judges, and the public. He tried in court to dispel it—not just to clear himself, but to banish a delusion. In a written argument to the jury he said that "there neither are nor ever were witches that having made a compact with the devil can send a devil to torment other people at a distance." But there was evidence that on the eve of trial Burroughs had left toothmarks on the arms of his accusers. He was found guilty, as were the others, and all six were sentenced to death.

Elizabeth Proctor was spared because of pregnancy. The other five were taken by cart to Gallows Hill on August 19. The same minister who had plagued Sarah Good's last moments refused John Proctor's request that he pray with him because, he insisted, Proctor was unrepentant. George Burroughs was allowed to speak last words to the crowd. He spoke so well, from the ladder, that some were in tears. Then he recited, calmly and flawlessly, the Lord's Prayer—a feat, it was widely believed, that no witch could achieve.

The crowd stirred and murmured restlessly; doubt was creeping in. Then Cotton Mather, who had ridden out from Boston for the occasion, spoke from horseback. The devil was able to take on the appearance of an angel, he said; let no one be deceived.

The crowd subsided, and all five witches died bravely.

On September 9, six more people were tried and sentenced to death. Among them was Mary Easty, who with her sister had sent the court a petition from jail asking for fair procedures. Having no lawyer, these women asked the judges "please to be of counsel to us"; to let their local minister and church members testify; to hold the girls' accusations insufficient "without other legal evidence"; and to allow "a fair and equal hearing of what may be said for us as well as against us." For reasons unknown the sister was never brought to trial, but Mary's trial was as one-sided as the others; the petition had no effect on the believers running the court. After the sentencing Mary Easty wrote to the judges again—not for herself, this time, but for the many still awaiting trial:

> I petition to your honors not for my own life for I know I must die and my appointed time is set but . . . that if it be possible no more innocent blood may be shed. . . . I question not what your honors does to the utmost of your power in the discovery and detecting of witchcraft and witches and would not be guilty of innocent blood for the world but by my own innocency I know you are in the wrong way. . . . I would humbly beg of you that your honors would be pleased to examine these afflicted persons strictly and keep them apart some time and likewise to try some of these confessing witches, I being confident there is several of them has belied themselves. . . .

Mary could have saved herself by joining the ranks of the confessors; she explained why she would not do this:

> I know not the least thing of witchcraft. Therefore, I cannot, I dare not, belie my own soul. I beg your honors not to deny this my

humble petition from a poor dying innocent person and I question not but the Lord will give a blessing to your endeavors.

It is hard to see how anyone could fail to be moved by this petition, but if the judges were moved they did not show it. Two weeks later Mary Easty died on Gallows Hill, along with seven others. "What a sad thing," remarked the meddling clergyman who seemed never to miss an execution, "to see eight firebrands of hell hanging there."

Nine more defendants were condemned in September; four of these confessed and were reprieved, and a fifth pleaded pregnancy.

By October 1692, fourteen women and five men had been hanged, one man had been pressed to death under heavy stones for refusing to submit to trial, seven more people had been sentenced to the gallows, about a hundred and fifty were in jail awaiting trial, and about two hundred others had been accused.

There had been repeated requests for procedural changes to eliminate bias and make witch-identification more reliable: John Proctor's plea for a change of judges, for example, and George Burroughs's critique of spectral evidence, and Mary Easty's commonsense proposal that the confessors be examined closely and kept apart. It is striking how closely these arguments by untutored defendants resemble modern legal safeguards. Proctor's request would be called, today, a motion to recuse a biased judge; Burroughs's would be an objection to hearsay and opinion evidence; and Easty's would invoke the rights to confront and cross-examine witnesses. But the judges, led by William Stoughton, were unmoved. None of these ideas, they believed, none of the exculpating testimony offered, could prevail against evidence showing witchcraft. Not a single defendant had been acquitted.

After months in the wilderness, the forces of skepticism and common sense received unexpected help from the afflicted girls themselves. As serial accusers often do, the girls went too far. Their giddy confidence led them to accuse not just the poor and the eccentric, as they had at the start; not just respectable farmers and housewives who happened to have enemies; but now, powerful leaders of the colony as well. The girls cried out on magistrate Jonathan Corwin's mother-in-law; on two sons of Simon Bradstreet, a former governor; on the Reverend John Hale's wife; and on Samuel Willard, the president of Harvard College. Obviously, none of these personages could be a witch, and none was arrested. But if the girls were wrong—as all agreed they were—might they not be wrong in other cases as well?

The clergy, whose support had been crucial to the prosecutors, began to retreat. On October 3, Increase Mather addressed a congregation of ministers at Cambridge. Mather had become worried about the wave of charges and executions, and now implied that the afflicted girls might be unreliable. He uttered one sentence of striking modernity: "It were better that ten suspected witches should escape, than that one innocent person should be condemned." This view, if adopted, would reverse the presumption of guilt that had guided the trials. Mather's sermon was soon published with an introduction signed by fourteen other ministers.

On October 8, Thomas Brattle, a wealthy and respected Boston merchant who was also a mathematician and a member of the Royal Society, wrote and made public a letter criticizing the judges, the evidence, and witch-prosecutions in general:

I would fain know of these Salem gentlemen, but as yet could never know how it comes about, that if these apprehended persons are witches, and by a look of the eye, do cast the afflicted into their fits by poisoning them, how it comes about, I say, that by a look of their eye, they do not cast others into fits, and poison others by their looks. . . .

As to those who had confessed,

there are now about 50 of them in prison; many of which I have again and again seen and heard; and I cannot but tell you, that my faith is strong concerning them, that they are deluded, imposed upon, and under the influence of some evil spirit; and therefore unfit to be evidences either against themselves, or anyone else.

The confessors, Brattle noted, had often contradicted themselves and been caught in lies. Instead of treating the testimony as unbelievable, the judges would "vindicate these confessors, and salve their contradictions, by proclaiming, that the devil takes away their memory, and imposes upon their brain." If so, Brattle reasonably asked, wasn't the devil also influencing the confessors' words at other times?

Sir William Phipps was persuaded. On October 12 he forbade further imprisonments for witchcraft; on October 29 he dissolved the special court.

There remained the many accused still in jail. A new superior court was created by statute, and fifty-two of these cases came before it in January 1693. The icy William Stoughton still presided, but there were new rules: spectral evidence was no longer admissible, and non–church members were eligible for jury service. Forty-nine defendants were acquitted; the other three were condemned but soon reprieved.

Three months later the governor discharged all prisoners remaining, and issued a general pardon. A year after its onset, the witch-hunt was over. But many families had been ruined; in addition to the nineteen executed, four people had died in prison; and, as Thomas Brattle put it, "ages will not wear off that reproach and those stains which these things will leave behind them upon our land."

To their credit, many of those responsible for the Salem witch trials apologized in the years that followed. Samuel Sewall, who had been a judge of the special court, stood in his Boston church pew in 1697 and publicly accepted the "blame and shame" of what had happened. A group of jurors, among them the foreman Thomas Fisk, begged forgiveness in writing: "We ourselves were not capable to understand nor able to withstand the mysterious delusion of the power of darkness and prince of the air whereby we fear we have been instrumental with others, though ignorantly and unwillingly, to bring upon ourselves the guilt of innocent blood." And in 1706 a young woman, still only twenty-six years of age but burdened by a hard life, asked forgiveness in the Salem Village church as Rebecca Nurse's still-bitter kinsmen looked on. She was Ann Putnam, who at age twelve had been an imaginative and quick-witted leader of the afflicted girls. The minister read the words for her: "I desire to be humbled before God. . . . I desire to lie in the dust and earnestly beg forgiveness of all those unto whom I have given just cause of sorrow and offense, whose relations were taken away and accused." Would the congregation forgive this sinner? They would. Ann wept with relief.

In 1711 the Massachusetts general court officially cleared the names of those convicted and ordered compensation paid to the survivors.

But William Stoughton, who had presided at the trials without mercy, and who in 1694 became governor of the colony, never confessed error or asked forgiveness. He had done his duty; his cause had been just; nothing more could be expected. And Cotton Mather, who as an ardent young clergyman had fanned the flames, felt himself unjustly criticized for the role he had played and never got beyond ingenious self-justification.

The Salem trials were a small episode compared to the great European and English witch-burnings, but they left an imperishable memory in this country. Americans, although religious on the whole, saw the harm that fanatical religion can do. The political power of fear was laid bare; as time went on it became clear that not Satan, but earthly pressures had joined with a harsh and unforgiving creed to turn the Puritans against each other.

And the Americans received, as well, a classic lesson in legal procedure. The accused witches whose spirits still haunt the national conscience were convicted in trials without lawyers, or judges trained in the law, or the rights to cross-question accusers and call one's own witnesses, or rules that would keep out hearsay or speculation or other unreliable evidence, or a presumption of innocence, or any of the other protections we now call "due process of law." The absence of these safeguards made a fatal difference. The jurors feared witchcraft, but they were conscientious men who wanted to do justice. Had they been allowed to hear evidence from both sides, had the most flagrantly unreliable testimony been kept out, had the afflicted girls and confessors been kept apart and cross-examined, had there been instructions from the bench requiring proof beyond a reasonable doubt, some of the prisoners surely would have been saved. This is confirmed by the jury's initial effort to acquit Rebecca Nurse, and by what happened later when the rules were changed to exclude spectral evidence. More defendants were tried after that change than had been tried before; the hysteria was waning but the jurors were still God-fearing people who by and large believed in witchcraft; Stoughton still presided; yet forty-nine of the fifty-two accused were acquitted. In the first round of trials the jury failed to do justice, but it failed largely because the trial procedures gave it little chance to succeed.

Few knew it in lawyerless Massachusetts, but the witch trials came at a time when procedural fairness was beginning a great ascent in the mother country. The cause was furthered, unwittingly, by the Stuart kings, who subjected their realm to political and religious trials almost devoid of rules of the game. Sir Walter Ralegh, the poet, adventurer, and courtier, was tried in 1603 on a charge of treasonably plotting to overthrow James I. The main witness against Ralegh was an alleged co-conspirator, Lord Cobham. Cobham, although in the crown's custody, was not produced in court; instead, evidence was given that he had made out-of-court statements implicating Ralegh. There was no way to cross-examine Cobham to test whether the statements were true, or whether he had even made them. Ralegh protested that he "may be massacred by mere hearsay." The argument got nowhere; Ralegh was found guilty, sentenced to death, reprieved, confined for years in the Tower of London, and finally, after adventures and complications not relevant here, beheaded.

Through much of the seventeenth century, the crown pursued one religious or political case after another, menacing English liberty but prompting a countermovement that established rights for the accused. Courts began to view hearsay with suspicion, and by the century's end often excluded it altogether. English judges—pompous though many of them were—deserve credit for originating the rules of evidence. The idea is that juries should not hear testimony that is too shaky, or too far off the point, or unfairly prejudicial; rather than let such material in, the judge simply keeps it out and the jury decides the case based on evidence that is germane and tested by cross-examination. The rules of evidence today apply in civil as well as criminal trials, whether by a judge or by a jury. Most famous is the hearsay rule: Smith cannot be heard to say that Jones told him he saw the defendant steal a horse; Jones has to show up himself, tell his story, and face cross-examination. The hearsay rule is pitted with exceptions that are an arcane delight to some lawyers and a bafflement to others, but its premise— litigants should be able to confront and question the witnesses against them—is sound.

Even more basic is the rule of relevance: evidence will be received only if it tends to prove or disprove a fact that could make a difference in the outcome of the case. This sounds like, and is, a commonsense proposition that keeps trials from becoming interminable. But there is more to it than that. The rule of relevance—as applied in English and American courts—is not just a prosaic method of getting on with the business at hand, but a guarantor of privacy, dignity, and autonomy against the state.

We try cases on specific issues formulated by the pleadings. The complaint in a civil case might say, boiled down: "Your train engineer was negligent—his bad driving of a locomotive wrecked my truck." The railroad's answer says: "Oh, no he wasn't. *You* were negligent when you tried to cross the tracks." The case is limited to those issues. The indictment in a criminal case might tell the defendant: "You robbed the Midland Bank." The defendant, by pleading not guilty, says: "No, I didn't. Prove it." The case is limited to the charge and denial. No one's general character is placed on trial. The law implicitly recognizes Montaigne's observation that "[t]here is no man so good that if he placed all his actions and thoughts under the scrutiny of the laws, he would not deserve hanging ten times in his life."

In many societies it has not been so. The practice elsewhere, all too often, has been to try the "whole person"—to bring in evidence of past convictions, past misbehavior, work record, domestic life, and so on, in the course of deciding guilt or innocence, or who is liable to whom. Litigation in the former Soviet Union was a prime example of this; no legal barriers stood between the omnipotent state and the weak individual. In Anglo-American trials past misdeeds can be considered at a sentencing hearing after a guilty verdict, or perhaps shown to impeach a witness's credibility, but ordinarily cannot be introduced to prove guilt or liability. This narrow concept of relevance means that specific proof is required; bias cannot take its place. As the poet James Fenton has written:

> Oh let us not be condemned for what we are.
> It is enough to account for what we do.
> Save us from the judge who says: You are your father's son,
> One of your father's crimes—your crime is you.

Along with the rules of evidence came other procedural rights. By 1696 defense counsel were allowed to those charged with high treason, and by the mid-eighteenth century any criminal defendant who could afford a lawyer could have one. The arrival of counsel hastened a sea change in criminal procedure. For centuries the accused had been limited to giving his unsworn answer, in open court, to the sworn testimony against him. He was expected to speak; his silence was usually fatal; he had no power to subpoena unwilling witnesses; and any willing witnesses he might find could not testify under oath. Defense counsel won for their clients the right to present sworn testimony by the accused and other witnesses. The presumption of innocence also dawned gradually in the eighteenth century, as did the privilege against self-incrimination.

As the American colonies absorbed these changes, they experienced as well a rise in the standing of lawyers. Commerce and population increased rapidly in the eighteenth century, and there was a mounting need for legal services: to draft wills, write contracts, resolve disputes. Prohibitions against lawyers were dropped. Trained in England, or locally by the apprentice method, lawyers became respected advisers, document-drafters, and advocates. By 1750 a capable professional bar was at work in every major community. And in every colony, some lawyers became community leaders. Thomas Jefferson, John Adams, Alexander Hamilton, James Wilson, John Jay, and George Wythe were all lawyers. Twenty-five of the fifty-six signers of the Declaration of Independence in 1776 were lawyers; so were thirty-one of the fifty-five delegates to the Constitutional Convention of 1787.

Our Constitution was written at the luckiest of times. The European Enlightenment coalesced with the presence here of men versed in history, the classics, and practical politics. Their memories extended beyond the Revolutionary War and the grievances that had led to it. They remembered the rise of trial by jury, the struggles for liberty and justice under the Stuart kings, and the liberating political theories of Locke and Montesquieu. They knew the havoc that could be visited on a people without fair trial guarantees—as in Massachusetts a century earlier.

They wrote a Constitution based on mistrust of concentrated power. The three branches of the federal government—legislative, executive, and judicial—were limited; none could ever seize the royal prerogative the founders had come to abhor. Yet to many the Constitution was not enough without a Bill of Rights. This was promised in order to gain ratification, and was delivered in the first ten amendments, drafted by James Madison and adopted in 1791. The Bill of Rights spoke largely to litigation, and to the history of trials in England and the colonies. It guaranteed to criminal defendants the rights to be informed of the charge, to be tried by an impartial jury, to confront adverse witnesses, to call witnesses for the defense, to have counsel, to refrain from self-incrimination, and to be free of double jeopardy. It afforded security against unreasonable searches and seizures—the fruits of which, under later Supreme Court decisions, are inadmissible as evidence. It assured trial by jury in federal civil cases. And it provided the overarching command of the Fifth Amendment: no person shall be "deprived of life, liberty, or property, without due process of law."

By the end of the eighteenth century the main features of the American litigation system were in place. Trial by jury, revered as a prime institution of democracy, was afforded in state and federal courts. The rules of evidence (most important, the hearsay and relevance rules) were observed, at least in the better-run trials. In the next century, after the Civil War, the Fourteenth Amendment made the basic guarantees of the Bill of Rights applicable to the states. Every state, in addition, had its own bill of rights—and some of these were even stronger, in certain respects, than the federal version. With these hard-won safeguards against injustice, could we ever again inflict upon ourselves anything like the Salem witch trials? Alas, we could and we did.

There were genuine causes for alarm behind the Great Red Scare of the late 1940s and 1950s. The Soviet Union, our recent wartime ally, rang down its iron curtain on Eastern Europe. The Cold War set in for a winter that would last for decades. In 1949 the Russians exploded an atomic bomb and our nuclear monopoly was over; in the same year the Chinese Communists, after a long civil war, gained control over the most populous country on earth; Klaus Fuchs, a young British atomic scientist, was exposed as a spy for the Russians; and in 1950 the Communist forces of North Korea invaded South Korea, provoking an American military response through the United Nations. Americans were gripped by fear of a nuclear war, and with it fear of subversion. How could so much go wrong, so fast, without betrayal from within?

There were a few Communists in post–World War II America, just as there had been a few practicing witches in seventeenth-century New England. There were also spies, as there always are, but the hearings that followed centered not on espionage but on ideology and party affiliation. Let us put aside the question of whether radical dissidents should have been identified and penalized or simply left alone; we are concerned with *how* they were identified—and, in particular, with the crucial difference that rules of fair play can make.

The House Committee on Un-American Activities (HUAC), revived by Congress in 1947 after a wartime dormancy, led the way. HUAC held highly publicized hearings designed to show that Communists had infiltrated everywhere during the thirties and forties. The committee began with the motion picture industry, subpoenaing frightened witnesses who saved their own careers by naming others as Hollywood Communists. Ten writers and directors who refused to answer questions were imprisoned for contempt. The film studios fell into line by adopting a blacklist of those who would not be hired because their loyalty was suspect. Encouraged, the committee went on to accuse others: defense contractors, schoolteachers, college professors, labor union organizers, and many others including, most alarmingly, employees of the government itself. A pattern developed: HUAC's cooperating witnesses, many of whom were ex-Communists seeking absolution, would name others—sometimes hundreds of others—as former party members or sympathizers. The latter were often identified only because they had taken stands on issues that coincided, so it was claimed, with Communist Party positions. To be named was to be stigmatized. If an accused person invoked the Fifth Amendment, guilt was assumed—contrary to a fundamental rule of constitutional law.

HUAC was soon emulated by the Senate Internal Security Subcommittee, formed in 1950, and by an assortment of state legislative committees. In the deepening climate of fear, these bodies aimed to root out domestic Communists—to "expose" them, in the term of the day. The accused were afforded no right to cross-examination. Hearsay and opinion were welcomed. Counsel for an accused was generally confined to whispered consultation with the client. The charge itself was ordinarily vague—not that the person had committed a specific act, but that he or she was, or had been, a Communist or fellow traveler.

Accusation became tantamount to guilt; merely to be named meant, for thousands of citizens, the end of a career or the ruin of a reputation.

For government employees, the committees' work was augmented by administrative boards charged with removing from public service anyone whose loyalty to the United States was found to be uncertain. A federal board was established by President Truman in 1947; many states had counterparts. The federal efforts brought about the discharge or resignation of about 2,200 government workers, none of whom was clearly proved to have been a Communist.

We paid a heavy price for the Great Red Scare. Jobs were lost, careers ruined, passports denied, security clearances revoked, thousands of reputations destroyed. A pall of fear and distrust descended on American public discourse. Even mainstream liberal views came to be seen, by many, as signs of Communist sympathy. The State Department's Far Eastern Division lost its foremost experts, and became, in Averell Harriman's words, "a disaster area filled with human wreckage." To avoid being investigated, to escape being mentioned at all, were prized objectives. For the many who were intimidated, the result was silence.

The similarities between the Red Scare and the Salem trials of 1692 go far beyond any casual use of the term "witch-hunt." In each instance the society felt itself threatened by an adversary whose secret agents could be anywhere—across the street, at the workplace, even in the church. The adversary was seen as infinitely clever and ruthless. Suspects were charged with an arcane status offense—*being* a witch, or *being* a Communist sympathizer—rather than with specific acts of misconduct. The incriminating testimony came largely from reformed sinners who had trafficked with Satan, or with Communism, and who not only were granted mercy but gained credibility the more they admitted past guilt and mendacity. A plausible denial was taken as proof of wily deceit; there was no way to establish innocence. And in the end, the serial accusers were done in by their own excesses. Senator Joseph McCarthy, who cowed official Washington and much of the nation for four years in the 1950s, was discredited when he accused the

United States Army of being in the grip of Communists; like the afflicted girls of Salem, he had gone too far.

Like a sickness, the Red Scare occupied our thoughts while the fever was on us, and is easy to forget once the symptoms have gone away. But we owe it to ourselves to remember. It was a time of public fear— but even in such a time the rules of fair procedure could have been honored. In the committee and board hearings of the 1950s, the rights to cross-examine witnesses, to have full benefit of counsel, to be informed of a specific charge, to be protected from hearsay, and to be presumed innocent, were missing. Their absence, as in the Salem trials two and a half centuries earlier, made a terrible difference.

Reminders of what free-for-all trials are like are occasionally supplied by Congress. However brilliant it may be at legislating, Congress is inept as a trial court, not only because its members have partisan agendas but because it tends to operate without sensible rules. A struggle over the rules—primarily, over whether to hear evidence beyond independent counsel Kenneth Starr's voluminous written report—was the centerpiece of President Clinton's impeachment trial. The 1991 Senate Judiciary Committee hearings on Anita Hill's sexual harassment allegations against Supreme Court nominee Clarence Thomas offered, as law professor Stephan Landsman has written, "[p]erhaps the clearest example of what an adversarial inquiry looks like when no evidentiary rules apply." The issue was simple and the truth could have been determined in a routine trial in any county courthouse. But the contending senators, ignoring what they ever knew about evidence, threw hearsay, unattributed letters, innuendo, gossip, and wild attacks on character into the boiling pot. The result was obfuscation of the issue and a profound embarrassment for Professor Hill, Judge Thomas, and the nation.

Now that the Red Scare and the Cold War are both over, could we again relapse into procedural lawlessness? To recognize that we could is the first step toward preventing that from happening. "Liberty lies in the hearts of men and women," said Judge Learned Hand. "When it dies there, no constitution, no law, no court can save it." But laws and courts can shelter the flame when it flickers in a wind of fear or hatred. The rules of the game—the rules of evidence and the protections afforded to criminal defendants—are not technicalities; they are bylaws of freedom.

Six Deadly Sins

The American justice system, as we have seen, is a great gift from the past, from men and women who stood up to arbitrary power and created the rule of law, often at ruinous cost to themselves. But unlike an old master's painting that can be hung on the wall and admired while the art market rises, the system will hold its value only if it meets new needs and adapts to new conditions. As a social institution, it must evolve to endure. So we face the question our forebears would ask if they were here: are we making good use of what they left to us?

To answer we will have to leave history's high ground, where the views are panoramic and the light as clear as we are likely to get, and descend into the smoke and clamor of battles being waged below, in today's trial courts and courts of appeal.

The visibility will drop, but we will have ample help from critics. The courts, whose grist is conflict and whose work is conspicuous, are always fair game, and should be, in the national pastime of criticizing government. Justice is no mystery—everyone has a sense of it, even from childhood—and second-guessing, irate dissents, and resentment of judicial power will be with us forever.

But these are not the best of times, and complaints about the system are rampant. Words such as "collapse," "crisis," "failure," and "dysfunctional" are in the air. "The truth is there is no justice in America for the people," writes the renowned trial lawyer Gerry Spence, although if that were so his ranch and Learjet would long since have been repossessed and he would be in another line of work. The late Judge Harold Rothwax, of New York City, said that in criminal trials "our courts have substituted formalism for fairness, and, in the process, they are burying the truth." I don't think so, but we need to ask: which complaints are valid? Which reflect only dyspepsia or ax-grinding? Is there a crisis in the courts and, if so, what is it?

We will look first at the Six Deadly Sins of American litigation: overcontentiousness, expense, delay, fecklessness, hypertechnicality, and overload. Like their medieval counterparts, they are hard to escape altogether; how damaging they are, at any given time and place, is a matter of degree. These are sins of process and access—failures in how we do things, and for whom, and at what costs to budgets and sanity. We will see, I believe, that they are faults of the adversary system as presently operated, and not of the jury, although the jury is often blamed for them.

The O. J. Simpson criminal trial, the most-watched in history, showed what can happen when overcontentiousness and false theatrics take over the courtroom. It was not typical of our system, and its deep impression on popular memory is a cause for regret. But like other ruined cases it dramatizes failings that occur, on a smaller scale, in many trials that never make the news.

Simpson was charged with two simple and simultaneous crimes: the knife murders of his ex-wife, Nicole, and her friend Ronald Goldman. The first steps at trial set the tone for the ordeal to come. The potential jurors were required to fill out a seventy-five-page questionnaire probing such matters as whether they owned "hunting or penknives," or had ever written a letter to the editor, or belonged to a political party, or had asked a celebrity for an autograph, or contributed to charities, or attached any personal importance to religion. Their psyches, their ethnic and educational and occupational and religious backgrounds, were pored over by highly paid consultants. They were put through weeks of oral questioning by lawyers armed with peremptory challenges. Each side maneuvered to stack the jury with those deemed, by pseudoscientific guesswork, to be favorably inclined to its cause. Jury selection took two and a half months; by the time the jurors and alternates were finally sworn in, the case should have been over and a verdict returned. Then came nine more months of evidence, argument, and recesses. The jurors, sequestered for the duration to keep them away from news reports, spent day after day in isolation while the judge and lawyers thrashed out legal rulings. Hundreds of bench conferences were held—while the jurors waited. Numerous days off were ordered—while the jurors waited. The examination of witnesses went on at enormous length, often on defense theories drawn from thin air, with no footing in the evidence. Expert witnesses dueled amid clouds of rhetoric. Counsel engaged in sniping, bickering, courthouse-steps sideshows, and after-hours news conferences. Logorrheic closing arguments, with no time limits, inflicted a further misery.

At the end of this marathon, the jurors deliberated for four hours and returned a verdict of not guilty. The verdict was controversial, but it was the process, more than the outcome, that shocked the world. We suffered an international embarrassment, and millions of Americans were left with an abiding fear of ever being called for jury duty.

The Simpson case was not unusually complex. There was scientific evidence, to be sure, but there often is, and there were only a few salient facts: a history of domestic violence; a motive; blood samples, hair samples, shoe prints on the ground; the absence of an alibi; a detective shown to be racially biased and untruthful; and questionable police work in handling some of the physical evidence. A later civil case over the same homicides, brought by survivors of the two victims, took weeks, not months, to try. The civil jury, applying a lighter burden of proof, deliberated for a week, unanimously found Simpson liable, and awarded $8.5 million in compensatory damages (plus, in a follow-up verdict, $25 million in punitive damages). Why, then, did the criminal case become a fiasco? The media, despite their frantic and overblown coverage, were not to blame. A well-run trial can be televised without damage, even with edification. The Simpson trial disintegrated because the judge, although fair-minded and intelligent, remained a passive umpire while the lawyers ran wild. Americans have long been afraid of heavy-handed judges who fail to be neutral, but neutrality and somnolence are not the same thing. The great lesson of *People v.*

Simpson is that the fencepost school of judging—the judge seen as a silent protrusion in the landscape—no longer works, if it ever did.

Overcontentiousness blights many cases, and the problem is far from new. Addressing the annual American Bar Association convention, a renowned legal scholar said: "The idea that procedure must of necessity be wholly contentious disfigures our judicial administration at every point." It obscures the search for truth. "It turns witnesses, and especially expert witnesses, into partisans pure and simple." It permits witnesses to be bullied and jurors alienated. "The effect of an exaggerated contentious procedure is not only to irritate parties, witnesses and jurors in particular cases, but to give the whole community a false notion of the purpose and end of law."

The message could have been delivered yesterday, but the speaker was Roscoe Pound, later a famous dean of the Harvard Law School, and the year was 1906. Pound, despite his trenchant critique, expressed confidence that things would get better. He looked to "a near future when our courts will be swift and certain agents of justice, whose decisions will be acquiesced in and respected by all." We still have a chance to justify Pound's optimism.

"Justice for all," intoned by schoolchildren in the Pledge of Allegiance, is hopeful but not fully descriptive because it overlooks the distorting effects of money. We do have justice, far more than most societies have had, but our system is blighted by expense and inequality.

Three-fourths of the legal needs of Americans having low or moderate incomes go unmet for lack of expert help, according to reliable surveys. This does not mean that all these unfortunates should be in court—the overwhelming majority of their problems can be solved informally—but it does mean that the law affords them less real protection than it gives the affluent. Many professionals devote part or even all of their working lives to solving this problem, but it remains acute. The Legal Services Corporation, established during the Nixon administration as "a permanent part of our system of justice" to provide federal funding and oversight to local legal aid organizations, is valuable but underfunded. The right to have court-appointed counsel in civil cases is recognized far less in the United States than in Western Europe. Our government, with federal and state resources combined, spends about $1.70 per capita on civil legal aid; England and Wales, in contrast, in 1994–95 spent $30 per capita. Pro bono (free) work by lawyers is praiseworthy and sometimes heroic, but fills only a small part of the need. Litigants who come to court without lawyers can be helped along by sympathetic judges, but still have an uphill battle. "Take it from me," says Chief Justice Daniel Wathen of the Maine Supreme Judicial Court, "justice comes hard if you are poor and have to go it alone in court."

In criminal cases, although we provide free counsel to needy defendants we still give unfair advantages to the rich over the poor. The defense purchased for millions of dollars by an accused celebrity bears no resemblance to that given an itinerant murder defendant in a low-budget state, represented by court-appointed counsel and with no expert witnesses, whose trial of a few days' duration may end in a death sentence. Some public defenders are as able as the highest-paid lawyers in private practice, but there are too few of them. In some states, poor defendants get only token representation by underpaid lawyers appointed from the private bar. "Money," the legal scholar John Langbein notes bitterly, "is the defining element of our modern American criminal justice system."

Four-fifths of Americans believe that going to court in civil disputes costs too much; on the whole, even recognizing that to protect rights and proceed with care necessarily involves expense, they are right. Our system prices itself out of the reach of many who need access to it. A primary reason is that pretrial activities—commonly carried on with little or no judicial oversight—have become the main battleground on a scale undreamed of in earlier times. A trial judge may feel gratified that his calendar is under control, with all cases settled or tried on schedule. The lawyers in his court may feel content. What these professionals fail to see is that the parties—the silent participants whose rights and fortunes are at stake—are being bankrupted in the pretrial stages.

In a typical civil action for damages, the plaintiff files a complaint, the defendant delivers a written answer, and the judge sets the case for trial at some future time. That time may be months off, or a year, or two years, or more. In the meantime the lawyers are free to conduct discovery: subpoenaing documents that may become evidence; questioning witnesses and opposing parties under oath (these sessions are called "depositions"—to depose a person, in American lawsuits, is not to topple him from power but simply to ask him questions); and sending written interrogatories for the opponent to answer.

In earlier times there was no discovery. The suit was brought and on the day of trial the parties and their lawyers and witnesses showed up and had it out. This led to surprises, many of them entertaining. But "trial by ambush," thrilling though it was to trial lawyers, fell into disrepute. To put an end to it—to require each side to make its evidence known in advance, avoid surprises, reduce tactical tricks, and promote fair decisions on the merits—discovery was brought into the system about sixty years ago.

To a great extent the results have been salutary. It is now much harder to conceal evidence; a valid case that might not succeed under the old method can be proved by good pretrial work; settlements can be based on adequate knowledge of the facts. The problem is that discovery, meant to be a simple process, can grow into a monster. A single deposition in a hotly contested case may go on for days or weeks. Prolonged and bitter battles may be fought over production of documents, with each side contending the other is hiding the ball. Hundreds of interrogatories may be exchanged, leading to clashes over whether they need to be answered.

The process can be so costly that often more has been spent, by the time the parties sit down to talk settlement, than is at stake in the case. Knowing how poor the cost-risk ratio is—and having heard, perhaps, of Charles Dickens's *Jarndyce v. Jarndyce*—many would-be litigants simply give up their rights.

The advantage that wealthy civil litigants have over poor ones can be nullified by able counsel working pro bono or for a contingent fee (a percentage of the amount recovered, if any); but too often it is not nullified.

Unequal justice worsens as the gap between rich and poor widens. In 1999 the wealthiest 2.7 million Americans—the top 1 percent—had as much after-tax income to spend as the aggregate of the bottom 100 million. The ratio has worsened since 1977, when the top 1 percent had as much as the bottom 49 million.

The justice system cannot change income patterns or abolish poverty, but it can make itself fairer, simpler, and more accessible.

The law's delay, mentioned by Hamlet four hundred years ago in a list of reasons for suicide, has not gotten any better. Anyone who doubts this should talk to the surviving clients in what my law firm called, with growing familiarity as the years went by, the Spokane Gas Case.

It sounded, at first, like a David-against-Goliath contest that would be difficult but short. On the telephone that day in 1975, when I was still in private practice, was one of the Northwest's finest lawyers, Robert McNichols of Spokane. McNichols wanted help in representing twelve local gasoline dealers who claimed they were being squeezed out of business by their supplier, Texaco. His clients—a mix of old-fashioned service-station men who would rather fix engines than pump gas, and forward-looking retailers trying to change with the market—for a long time had not realized the cause of their troubles. They saw other Texaco-brand stations posting retail gasoline prices below what they themselves paid at wholesale. They could not match those prices without selling every gallon at a loss. When they tried to maintain even a slight profit margin they lost customers, even old friends, who thought they were price-gouging. Their businesses were being ruined. When they asked Texaco's field representatives what was going on, they were told only to try harder—to offer more service and smiles and cleanliness. They tried harder, to no avail; in this business price was king.

Finally the truth came out. Texaco was secretly charging a large chain operator, who owned Texaco-brand stations throughout the

Spokane area, three cents per gallon less than it charged the smaller retailers. Not only that, Texaco—as we learned only later, during discovery—was giving a six-cent-per-gallon break to minor-brand retailers who sold the same gasoline under the apt name of Gull. These price differentials, unless we could get rid of them in court, soon would drive out the small station owners.

There was one hope for relief. The Robinson-Patman Act is a federal law meant to level the playing field for small businesses going up against large chains. It bars price discrimination in sales to competing retailers (unless justified by a lower cost of sale to the favored retailer or by the need to meet another supplier's offer). There is a triple-damages remedy for violations. But there are enough technical difficulties to dismay all but the hardiest claimants; few damage awards have ever been won under the Robinson-Patman Act.

We decided to file suit. A contingent-fee agreement made the case economically possible for the plaintiffs. Two younger lawyers—Robert Whaley, of McNichols's firm, and John Ebel, of mine—took over the case and promptly ran into a stone wall. Texaco, represented chiefly by New York lawyers, waged all-out war, as it was entitled to do: every possible argument was raised, delay sought, discovery effort frustrated. We were accustomed to this and the problem was not Texaco but the courts. There was a backlog of cases; months, then years, went by with no trial.

Some clients can be intimidated by a crushing pretrial process; ours weren't. At last the case went to trial before a federal court jury in Spokane. Whaley and Ebel tried it with skill and dispatch against high-quality opposition and, after four weeks, won a handsome verdict for the plaintiffs.

The trial judge, however, decided he had made a mistake in the jury instructions. The jury had been allowed to award damages equal to the illegal price differential multiplied by the volume of the plaintiffs' gasoline purchases. Although that sounds like common sense, and in the past had been an approved way of calculating damages, the judge found that the law had changed: instead of winning damages equal to the price overcharge, the claimants would have to prove the sales and profits they lost because of it, a much harder task. Setting aside the jury's verdict, the court entered judgment for Texaco.

Our clients appealed. An appeal takes time—too much time, ordinarily, because appellate courts function slowly and write more than they need to. The trial record must be typed up, lawyers' briefs written and filed, oral arguments scheduled and heard, and judges' views developed and expressed in print. After a long interval, the United States Court of Appeals for the Ninth Circuit reversed the judgment: the trial judge indeed had wrongly instructed the jury on how to compute damages, but the case should not have been dismissed. A new trial, with corrected jury instructions, would have to be held.

More time went by. In 1985, before a new federal district judge and a different jury, the case went to its second trial. Again the plaintiffs, represented by Whaley and Ebel, proved their claims. On the jury's verdict, for a lower amount this time, judgment was entered in their favor.

Texaco, predictably, appealed. The plaintiffs by now were getting a sense of geologic time. At last, the Court of Appeals decision came down: the verdict was in accordance with law; the judgment was affirmed. The case, we thought, finally had come to a happy ending.

It hadn't. Texaco petitioned the Supreme Court for review, and the Court granted the petition. This was an ominous sign: the high court takes only a tiny fraction of the cases tendered to it; why would it take this one if it agreed with the Court of Appeals decision?

"Equal Justice Under Law," reads the famous inscription on the Supreme Court building's façade. More time went by. Briefs were labored over, printed, and filed. Finally, on a December day, Robert Whaley stood before the Court to defend his clients' verdict. Years of work by both sides were compressed into a few minutes of argument, with questions from the justices. Afterward—while the decision was awaited—Texaco offered to settle the case for $400,000, a figure that lawyers would call "nuisance value." The offer was rejected.

In 1990, six months after the arguments, the Supreme Court filed

its decision. By a unanimous vote, the nine justices affirmed the judgment. Texaco had violated the Robinson-Patman Act; the price discrimination was not legally justified; the plaintiffs could collect their
award. The judgment by this time came to more than $5 million. The
case, at last, was over.

Was the right outcome reached in the Spokane Gas Case? I believe
so—and, more to the point, two juries, one federal appeals court, and
the Supreme Court said so. Was justice done? Alas, the answer must be
no. From the day Robert McNichols first called me to the day the
plaintiffs collected their judgment, fifteen years went by. One plaintiff
had died; others were in declining health; nearly all were out of the service-station business. Time, abetted by courts that seemed never to
have heard that "justice delayed is justice denied," had taken away the
best fruits of victory.

Criminal cases come first on the docket, and civil cases must follow,
often at a great distance. Few cases take fifteen years, but many take
three or five or seven years or more when they don't have to. The result
of glacial slowness is injustice. Some delay is caused by overwork, by
a glut of court business; but with all respect to my colleagues, some of
it isn't.

The sin of fecklessness might also be called entropy, with the courtroom seen as a closed system in which every exertion only adds to the
growing chaos. One example will suffice—an aimless trial for the ages.

In White Plains, New York, the former nursing director of a hospital
sued the hospital and four of its doctors for libel after a no-confidence
vote against her was mentioned in an employee newsletter. Her reputation, she claimed, had been unfairly harmed. The case was not complex. In 1994 it came to a trial by jury. The jurors were given no
estimate of how long the trial would take. They had every reason to
assume it would be short, but soon found themselves sinking in a
quagmire. The lawyers were excruciatingly repetitious and dilatory. To
complete the testimony of two witnesses took twenty-four trial days.
The jurors met with the judge and begged him to move things along.

Nothing changed. Twice more, the jurors asked that the pace be speeded up. There was no improvement. In early December, four months into the trial, plaintiff's counsel still had not rested his case, and the jurors rebelled. If the trial were not finished by the end of the year, they told the judge, they wanted to be discharged; the long, unexpected, and still open-ended absence from their jobs was ruining their private lives. The judge, at a loss, declared a mistrial; the case would have to be redone.

Interviewed later, one juror likened his service to "being sucked down a black hole." Another felt guilt: "My conscience is eating away at me. I started something I didn't finish." The plaintiff's lawyer complained that his client "has been dangling for years" with no resolution of her case. The hospital's lawyer claimed to be "as stunned as anyone at the slowness of this trial." Everyone lamented the waste of time and money. Other litigants, awaiting their turn, suffered from the court's paralysis.

The jurors had sacrificed a part of their lives for nothing—except that the story of this aborted trial, like that of the Simpson case, can spur improvements that must be made.

Our system is accused of hypertechnicality—of being obsessed with procedure at the expense of truth and common sense. The criticism applies to every kind of trial and appeal, but is heard most often about criminal prosecutions. "She got off on a technicality" is a phrase more familiar than "presumed innocent."

Three recent cases will provide a fair sampling of how the "technicality" complaint repeatedly comes up:

In 1999, the Washington State Supreme Court considered the case of a woman who answered a knock on her door and found two city police officers who said they wanted to come in and search her home. The officers were armed and wore black raid-jackets with the word "police" emblazoned in yellow letters across the front and back. Two other officers stood behind the house to "secure the premises."

The police had received a tip that the house contained a marijuana growing operation, but they had no search warrant and no grounds to ask a judge for one. They decided to try a "knock and talk"—a way of getting the householder to consent to a search. If consent is voluntarily given, a warrantless search is legal. In asking the woman to consent, the officers did not tell her that she had the right to refuse. Out of fear, she testified later, she signed a consent form.

The officers searched and found sixty-eight marijuana plants, plus other evidence, in an upstairs room. The woman was convicted of manufacturing marijuana.

The state's highest court, on her appeal, observed that most people, confronted by armed police on their doorstep, are easily cowed into consenting to a search. The Washington state constitution provides that "[n]o person shall be disturbed in his private affairs, or his home invaded, without authority of law." This, said the court, "clearly recognizes an individual's right to privacy with *no* express limitations." It is broader than the federal prohibition of "unreasonable searches and seizures"—and it means that when police attempt a "knock and talk" search at a person's home they must advise her of her right to refuse to consent. Without that advice, most people would be unable to make an informed decision. Because the woman's consent was involuntary under this standard, the conviction was reversed. The illegally obtained evidence could not be used and the defendant would go free.

In a 1998 bank robbery case, a federal district judge had to decide whether to suppress the defendant's confession, which would mean it could not be placed in evidence at the trial. The judge had no doubt that the defendant was guilty of two robberies, in one of which he had pointed a .357 magnum pistol at the teller. But the famous *Miranda* rule requires not only that the police inform an in-custody suspect of his right to remain silent, but also that if he asks for a lawyer during the interview, they cease questioning him until the lawyer is present. In this case the defendant, at the police station, had waived his right to remain silent and had begun to talk, but then had asked to see a lawyer. The police discouraged the idea, saying things would go better for him if he cooperated and that a request for a lawyer would be viewed as a sign of noncooperation. They kept on with the questioning. The defendant admitted the robberies and signed a written confession. Then he called a lawyer—who would have advised him, if consulted earlier, to remain silent. The judge ruled that the confession was involuntary under the *Miranda* standard; the trial would have to go forward without this important piece of evidence.

In a 1995 Illinois federal case, the defendant was charged with fraudulently selling leased cars as if he owned them. The evidence came in, closing arguments were given, and the jury retired to deliberate. Instead of twelve deliberating jurors, however, there were fourteen; the judge, rather than excuse two alternates at the end, let them act as additional jurors. No one objected to this procedure. The jury found the defendant guilty by a 14–0 vote. A federal appeals court in Chicago found a violation of the court rule stating that alternate jurors "shall be discharged after the jury retires to consider its verdict." The verdict, said the court, was reached by "a jury composed of more than the number permitted by the rule." The deliberations of twelve had been joined by two unauthorized others. The conviction was reversed and a new trial ordered.

Were these three decisions hypertechnical? The marijuana grow, after all, had been found in the house; the bank robber really had confessed; and the defrauding car seller had been found guilty by twelve-plus jurors. Or were the decisions wise applications of laws meant to preserve the individual's freedom, privacy, and autonomy against the powerful state?

There are no final or indisputable answers, but here are mine:

The Washington Supreme Court's "knock and talk" decision draws a bright line that will protect privacy and give the police clear guidance. Under federal law the officers' failure to advise the woman who answered the door that she could refuse to consent to a search would be a factor to consider, but not in itself decisive. A federal judge might or might not find the consent to have been voluntary. But this was a case under state law, in state court. By requiring that the advice always be given in Washington, the court honored a state constitutional guarantee of privacy that is stronger than its federal counterpart.

The bank-robbery case, where the confession was suppressed, shows how the *Miranda* rule works to improve police treatment of suspects. Its premise is that the poor and ignorant usually don't know what many of the affluent and well-informed do know: that an arrested person may remain silent, his silence cannot be used against him, and he is entitled to call a lawyer. I think the trial judge was right. I must admit, in all fairness, that I was the trial judge. The jury, by the way, found the defendant guilty of both robberies without having heard anything about his confession.

The third case strikes me as a true example of hypertechnicality. Granted that the judge should have excused the two alternates, what harm was done by his allowing them to deliberate with the other twelve when no one objected? All fourteen jurors voted for a guilty verdict. The useful doctrine of "harmless error" should have been invoked to affirm the conviction.

Even the most avid Bill of Rights supporter must admit that, with hundreds of thousands of criminal cases processed per year, hypertechnicality creeps in at times. Some are so offended by it that they would tear down the fences that protect the accused. I believe they are mistaken. But hypertechnicality, especially in criminal cases, appears often enough to make this list.

Overloaded courts bring to mind a scene in Charlie Chaplin's silent film *Modern Times*. Chaplin, an assembly line worker with a wrench in each hand, must tighten bolts in an endless series brought to him at manic speed by a conveyor belt. He tries frantically to keep up. When he has to scratch his nose, he falls behind and almost gets sucked into the machinery. When the lunch whistle blows he can't stop twitching his wrenches and applies them to a woman visitor's jacket buttons, to her great annoyance. Back on the line, he flails hopelessly against the onrushing bolts.

Something like this is experienced by American judges in courts swamped by burgeoning caseloads. They struggle to maintain quality and keep up, but barely avoid being sucked into the machinery. Improved court management can alleviate the problem, but in big cities and in districts heavily plagued by crime, good management isn't enough.

Saint Paul said in one of his letters to the Corinthians: "[I]t is altogether a defect in you that you have lawsuits one with another."

Napoléon, the sponsor of a groundbreaking legal code, said that lawsuits were "an absolute leprosy, a social cancer."

Ambrose Bierce, in *The Devil's Dictionary,* defined a lawsuit as "a machine which you go into as a pig and come out of as a sausage."

And the famous Judge Learned Hand, who spent his life writing appellate court opinions, said: "As a litigant, I should dread a lawsuit beyond almost anything else short of sickness and death."

Could they all have been wrong? According to the American public, yes. Civil litigation enjoys a phenomenal popularity.

Traditional types of cases—breach of contract, divorce, vehicle accidents, and so on—have proliferated, but we have also seen a growth of new rights. A century ago hardship and deprivation were viewed largely as private misfortunes. Now, in a kinder society, we have come to expect accommodation, fair treatment, compensation—justice, in a word, in all of life's passages. Poverty, injury, unfair treatment on the job, ill health, loss of savings in a failed bank, a pauper's grave—these no longer are seen merely as the workings of fate. Few would want to go back, but the expectation of what has been called "total justice" brings increased business to the courts, and we now have many kinds of lawsuits that never existed before: negligence cases where the plaintiffs themselves also were careless (in earlier times the defense of contributory negligence wiped out those claims); cases about employment rights, child abuse, social security benefits, professional malpractice, product liability, consumer protection; cases about race discrimination, sex discrimination, endangered species, toxic waste disposal; and so on through a list so varied that all the world seems to make its way through the courtroom.

Whether American society heaps too many expectations on the law is an important question but makes no difference to overloaded courts; they must cope with whatever comes through the door.

On the criminal side we have new crimes: securities fraud, racketeering, tax evasion, money laundering, and a host of others. When our republic was founded there were three crimes defined by federal statutes; now there are more than three thousand. Many cases are complex and require long trials, but the chief cause of overloading the criminal courts has been the war against drugs. Drug-related prosecutions in my state, Washington, now account for more than half of all arrests. Chief Justice Richard Guy of the state supreme court warned the legislature in 1999 that unless more resources are provided, "[o]ur courts will become criminal courts almost exclusively. Petty drug-enforcement cases are overwhelming us." Federal dockets nationwide also are heavy with drug prosecutions. Thanks largely to the drug war, and to an obsession with imprisonment in preference to other penalties, our jail and prison population doubled in the 1990s, reached nearly two million in 2000, is the world's largest, and costs taxpayers $40 billion a year to maintain. Our per capita imprisonment rate is six times that of England and seventeen times that of Japan. The 458,000 Americans in prison for drug offenses in 2000 were ten times the number in 1980 and 100,000 more than *all* prisoners in the European Union, whose population is 100 million greater than ours. In the federal system, emulated by some states, long prison sentences are mandated by statutes that mechanically equate drug quantity with length of sentence—ten years for 1,000 marijuana plants, for example, but only five years for 999 plants, regardless of mitigation or surrounding circumstances. (This kind of rigidity leads to hair-splitting worthy of medieval theologians, such as that over what constitutes a "plant." When I last looked into this controversy, three definitions were current in the federal courts: a cutting that has developed roots; a cutting with "root balls" and a "reasonable root system," regardless of whether it could survive transplanting; and a cutting with strong enough roots to be transplanted. A sentence may be doubled, or halved, depending on the outcome of such quibbles.)

Despite the war on drugs, the plague continues. The need to strengthen education and addiction treatment, and to devise more imaginative and flexible criminal sanctions, is obvious.

The great bulk of litigation is pursued in state, not federal, courts. State courts received 91 million new cases in 1998. Between 1984 and 1998, their civil filings rose 34 percent, criminal filings 50 percent, felony filings 82 percent, juvenile filings 73 percent, and domestic relations filings 75 percent—while the country's population went up by only 15 percent. In the same period, criminal cases filed in the federal courts increased by 62 percent and felony cases by 92 percent. In the federal courts of appeal, the number of cases filed per judge increased fivefold in recent years. And it is not just a matter of more cases filed. In both state and federal systems, there is a rise not only in volume but in complexity. More complicated, difficult, and multiparty cases are filed than ever; to decide them takes time.

It is not that Americans are "sue-happy," as many jurors think at the start of their service. Frivolous cases make good stories, but are few in number and are promptly dismissed, for the most part, by the judges. Overload is caused not by frivolity but by the sheer volume of genuine litigation.

Federal and state legislators have failed, in many parts of the country, to provide the resources needed to handle proliferating caseloads. In my state, usually considered an enlightened place, the presiding state trial court judge in Seattle says that lack of funds, coupled with the priority that must be given to criminal and juvenile cases, "will surely result in the diminution, if not the total eclipse, of the public courts as arbiters of civil disputes." The federal districts that border on Mexico are so swamped with illegal immigration and drug cases that they have virtually no time for anything else. Nationwide, except in some rural areas and a few lucky cities, we are short of judges, administrators, and courtrooms. The results are logjams, delay, frustration.

The providing of justice is a service affected by supply and demand. Today in the United States there is a tremendous demand for justice coupled with a firm belief that the courts are where one goes to find it. The most basic problem we face is that demand is outstripping supply; people are seeking more justice, quantitatively, than the system can provide through its traditional methods. The solutions will require both ingenuity and appropriations.

Each of these six faults, adapted for time and context, resembles one of the original Seven Deadly Sins. (Overcontentiousness = anger; expense = avarice; delay = pride [in the form of a stubborn refusal to change outmoded ways]; fecklessness = sloth; hypertechnicality = envy [hypertechnical judges envy, and try vainly to emulate, the deity's unique quality of perfection]; and overload = gluttony. I am glad to report that the seventh one, lust, has no equivalent in court.) These vices reinforce one another; as Chaucer wrote of the originals, in the fourteenth century, they "all run on one leash, but in different ways."

The list may sound formidable but should cause no despair. Countless cases are still decided fairly, swiftly, and economically, and the problems, where they exist, can be solved. Some of them can be solved quite easily, as I hope to show.

At this point, it is important to note that none of the Six Deadly Sins is committed by the jury. They are flaws in today's version of the adversary system, not in the jury's performance. Every one of them can be laid to poor work by judges or lawyers or legislators; none to the work of jurors.

This distinction between the adversary system itself and the jury as part of it tends to be overlooked even by thoughtful critics. Two recent books are illustrative. Law professor William Pizzi, a former prosecutor, gives a telling critique of adversarial excess in American criminal cases and offers helpful comparisons to procedures used in several European countries. Then—on the basis of a few recent "stunning acquittals" and hung juries—he recommends that "we rethink the role of citizens in our criminal justice system" and "move away from juries composed solely of citizens in favor of mixed panels of judges and citizens."

Similarly, lawyer-anthropologist Roberta Katz, while conceding that "[b]y and large, over the past two centuries, the American civil justice system has worked well," argues that now it is "clearly headed for breakdown" and has become "an ugly mix of lottery, gladiatorial combat, and farce." She gives chilling examples of overcontentiousness, expense, and delay. Then, citing a few high punitive damage awards and the alleged difficulty some juries have had with complex cases, she moves from a cogent critique of the adversary system to a suggestion that the jury be dropped in favor of specialized courts composed of experts in whatever field is involved in the dispute.

These proposals by worthy critics tar the jury with a brush that should be saved for legal professionals and politicians. Our trial system's failings—at least the ones discussed so far—are not the jury's fault. But that leaves a big question: as we enter the new century, as we make repairs, should we take the jury with us or leave it to history?

Is the Jury Up to the Job?

Jury critics can draw on a long tradition of skepticism.

The noted misanthrope Mark Twain wrote that "[t]he jury system puts a ban upon intelligence and honesty, and a premium upon ignorance, stupidity, and perjury."

Erwin Griswold, a Harvard Law dean who served as solicitor general of the United States under President Lyndon Johnson, asked: "Why should anyone think that twelve persons brought in from the street, selected in various ways for their lack of general ability, should have any special capacity for deciding controversies between persons?"

Jerome Frank, a law professor who became a New Deal official and then a federal appellate judge, argued that "usually, the jury are neither able to, nor do they attempt to, apply the instructions of the court." Frank—a fountain of ideas, a brilliant man, and a delightful talker— was the twentieth century's most influential jury critic. In two books still widely read, he savaged American trials. Juries, Frank maintained, were ignorant and lawless; they did whatever they felt like doing regardless of the law and the facts. But those who quote Frank today seldom realize that he launched a similar attack against judges. Judges, he argued, do not decide by applying rules of law either; the judge starts with "a conclusion and afterwards tries to find premises which will substantiate it." The rules are just rationalizations: "The judge really decides by feeling and not by judgment." It is not clear what kind of litigation system Judge Frank would have substituted for the one he thought too grounded in human foibles.

There also have been, from the beginning, passionate admirers. The philosopher David Hume called the trial jury "an institution admirable in itself, and the best calculated for the preservation of liberty and the administration of justice, that was ever devised by the wit of man." Tocqueville wrote that "the practical intelligence and political good sense of the Americans are mainly attributable to the long use which they have made of the jury in civil causes." Chief Justice Earl Warren believed that jurors "have maintained a standard of fairness and excellence throughout the history of our country."

The polemics are entertaining, but we must get beyond them. "What have you done for us lately?" is asked of all democratic institutions, and we need to look at whether the jury succeeds today, in the real world. No matter what the federal and state constitutions say, the jury will survive only if it works.

The challenge is sharper than ever because, for the first time in history, the jury has become democratic in the broadest sense. For most of its long life it was composed of male citizens, most if not all of them white, who owned property or otherwise were deemed reliable. In eighteenth-century England, writes a student of the period, "probably 75 percent of the population was rigorously excluded from common juries. They were virtually only seen in court as defendants." "Special juries"—made up of persons of an even higher class than usual, or of experts in a commercial or professional field—were sometimes used to the exclusion of ordinary citizens. The promise of the Civil War amendments to the Constitution—that racial minorities would have full rights of citizenship, including the right to serve on juries—went unkept for a century. Women also were ineligible for jury duty, in most states, until about 1940. The "key man" system—under which the court clerk or marshal would limit jury summonses to those considered reliable—persisted in the federal courts until 1968, when Congress, in the Jury Selection and Service Act, required for the first time that jurors be "selected at random from a fair cross-section of the community." A 1975 Supreme Court decision adopted that standard as a constitutional requirement for state court juries.

Except for a few categories—those who cannot speak English, or are too mentally or physically infirm to serve, or whose civil rights have not been restored following a felony conviction—jurors are now chosen at random from the entire adult citizenry. We have had only about one generation's experience with using so broad a base. What we do has finally caught up with our democratic principles, and the results are still coming in.

To measure jury performance is no easy task. If we put aside the rhetoric of grass-roots enthusiasts who believe that the people can do no wrong, and of cynics who think all laymen are fools (and who probably believe that Shakespeare could not have written the plays because he never went to college), we are left with a slippery question: How can we know whether juries are doing justice?

The answer has to be subjective. While social science can measure rates of conviction and acquittal, the percentage of civil claimants who win, the average size of damages awards, and the like, it cannot measure the *quality* of any verdict, or of verdicts generally. Quality— whether justice is done—remains inescapably a matter of opinion.

The opinions most avidly sought by researchers are those of judges. Trial judges do not claim to be oracles (most of them don't, anyway), but they have more experience with juries than anyone else; they see one trial after another, from beginning to end, and they hear the same evidence the jury hears.

The most famous scholarly work on jury competence was an attempt to quantify trial judges' opinions on a large scale. In *The American Jury,* published in 1966, Harry Kalven and Hans Zeisel of the University of Chicago examined more than three thousand criminal trials by comparing the jury's verdict to what the judge thought about the case. They found the judge agreeing with the jury 78 percent of the time. The Chicago project later examined six thousand civil cases; again, the rate of judge-jury agreement was nearly 80 percent. The areas of judge-jury disagreement were not fundamental but reflected the jury's subtle bringing-in of social values such as mercy— "an impressive way," the authors concluded, "of building discretion, equity and flexibility into a legal system." As for jury comprehension, Kalven and Zeisel found that "contrary to an often voiced suspicion, the jury does by and large understand the facts and get the case straight."

A generation later, surveys continue to show overwhelming judicial approval of the work of juries. In 2000, the *Dallas Morning News* and Southern Methodist University sent questionnaires to all state trial judges in Texas and all federal trial judges in the United States, and got responses from two-thirds of them. The results showed that more than 90 percent believe that juries are conscientious, understand the legal issues, and reach just and fair verdicts. Six in ten said they would rather have their own civil case decided by a jury than by a judge or arbitrator, and eight in ten said they would opt for a jury trial if charged with a crime.

Judge-jury agreement rates on the verdict hover at about 80 percent. If we assume that the judge has a sensible idea of how the case should come out, these agreement and approval rates give heartening news about jury reliability. And judges, by and large, do not assume that their disagreement with the verdict necessarily means the jury was wrong; usually there is room for reasonable minds to differ. A generation ago, in a climate more favorable to trial by jury, the Supreme Court noted that when judges disagree with verdicts "it is usually because [juries] are serving some of the very purposes for which they were created and for which they are now employed."

Like a healthy patient who hasn't seen a doctor for years, but suddenly checks into the hospital with a mysterious illness, the trial jury is currently subjected to batteries of tests and studies, some of which yield valuable data. But because the readings that social science can give us are limited, we must use anecdotal evidence. In the debate over jury performance, there is no way to avoid testimonials.

I offer my own experience not because it is exceptional but because I am sure it is typical. In the hundreds of trials I have seen as a practicing lawyer and judge, the jury nearly always has returned what I believed to be a just and fair verdict. This holds true in cases involving scientific or technical evidence, and in those with racial overtones. I will avoid citing cases I tried as a lawyer, where an advocate's interest in the outcome persists, and mention, as examples, three I have seen as a neutral judge.

In *United States v. Nickell,* a woman in her forties was charged under a federal anti-product-tampering statute with having killed her husband by placing cyanide in pain-relief capsules that he took. Then, several days later, she allegedly put a bottle containing cyanide-laced capsules on a store shelf; a young woman, unacquainted with the defendant, bought the bottle, took one of the capsules, and died. The government's proof at trial was almost entirely circumstantial: Stella Nickell was tied to the homicides by a web of scientific evidence. She took the stand and emotionally denied everything. The jury had to weigh her testimony—and the equally tearful testimony of her accusatory adult daughter, called as a witness for the prosecution— along with that of chemists, fingerprint analysts, and other experts. There had been a flood of media coverage in the months leading up to trial, and to avoid contaminating the jury panel it was necessary to question each potential juror separately, out of the others' presence. Even with that constraint, and with no time limit placed on counsels' questioning, the empanelment was done in two days. The evidence and arguments were completed in less than three weeks. The jury, after five days of deliberation, reached a verdict of guilty that I thought correctly recognized the force of the scientific evidence.

In *Alalamiah Electronic v. Microsoft Corporation,* a Kuwaiti computer software company claimed that Microsoft had taken advantage of the Gulf War's dislocations to breach a contract and induce two key engineers to switch employers and work for the American software giant in Seattle. Microsoft counterclaimed for alleged piracy of its technology. The trial testimony and exhibits were partly in Arabic (translated, fortunately, into English) and included expert testimony from both sides in the disputed areas of computer technology. The jury reached a thoughtful verdict—partly for Alalamiah but mostly for

Microsoft. A few weeks later the case was settled on the basis of the verdict. After the settlement was reached, I wrote to the jurors inviting them to visit my chambers and talk about the jury system. All came except one who called to say he could not leave work. My conversation with these citizens (who had bonded into a cheerful group, as jurors often do) confirmed what was already apparent: they took their work seriously, and they understood the evidence and the law.

In *United States v. Brown,* ten African-American defendants were charged with conspiracy to distribute cocaine in both powder and "crack" forms, and two of them were charged with a variety of related crimes. The jury was composed of eleven whites and one young African-American man. A second black on the panel had been challenged off by the defense. The evidence concerned events up and down the West Coast, from California to Alaska, over a five-year period; more than a hundred witnesses testified, hundreds of exhibits were received, and all counts were vigorously contested by the ten defense lawyers. The evidence and arguments took twenty-four days. The jurors, called upon to reach thirty-one verdicts (ten defendants with multiple counts as to some), took ten days to decide. The questions they sent out during their deliberations were thoughtful and to the point. In the end, the jury convicted five defendants of conspiracy, acquitted four, could not reach a verdict as to one (the government decided not to retry him), and returned an appropriate variety of verdicts on the other counts. The outcome as to each defendant showed a thoughtful assessment of whether guilt had been proved beyond a reasonable doubt. There was never the slightest sign of racial bias in any direction; the unanimous decision was based on the evidence.

The good work of these three juries typifies what I have seen. And in the rare instances where I have thought the jury went astray, no celestial sign reveals that I was right and the jury was wrong.

My jury trials have taken place in the Far West, from the Canadian border to the Mexican, but the same observation of jury quality is made by judges throughout the United States. Here is a nonscientific sampling—the comments of five renowned federal district judges, diverse in background and region, but all having a wealth of trial experience:

Judge Jack Weinstein, Brooklyn, New York: "Our jurors—who are of many diverse ethnic groups and origins—are excellent."

Judge Ann Claire Williams, Chicago, Illinois: "Jurors are devoted to their task, and they do well even in complex cases. Their level of competence is directly related to the lawyers' work; if the lawyers make it understandable, the jurors get it. They are fair and they follow the law. We have cases with racial overtones, but I've never seen a verdict that I thought was affected by racial or any other form of discrimination."

Judge Lyle Strom, Omaha, Nebraska: "Out of hundreds of jury trials, I can count on fewer than the fingers of one hand the verdicts that I thought made no sense. The rest were all reasonable. In complex cases as well as simple ones, twelve jurors do a remarkably good job of coming up with the right answer."

Judge John T. Curtin, Buffalo, New York: "[H]istory and tradition are not the only—or even the primary—reasons that I value our jury system. Most importantly, I believe that our current system does justice and appears to do justice."

Judge William Wayne Justice, Austin, Texas: "Juries in our country are meant to be virtual microcosms of our democratic political community, composed of persons of variant races, ethnicities, cultures, wealth, and gender. In the overwhelming number of instances, the verdicts of these juries are fair. It is true, nevertheless, that individual juries, from time to time, do not operate properly; but in this respect, they merely mirror an imperfect society."

Not all trial judges agree, of course, but I believe the great majority do.

The jurors themselves, even those who begin as doubters, overwhelmingly confirm the jury's vitality. One study found that 75 percent of them leave the courthouse feeling better about justice than when they arrived. A well-run court can produce near-unanimity on this score. In Columbus, Ohio, for example, when eleven hundred jurors were surveyed following service in municipal court in the year 2000, 91 percent said they came away with a more favorable impression of trial by jury than when they started, and 99 percent said they would encourage others to serve.

Here is a sampling of jurors' reports:

Robert Aronson, a law professor, served on a state court criminal jury. "A young African-American man," he wrote,

> was charged with assaulting two white off-duty police officers who were in the process of subduing a second African-American man, who was intoxicated and belligerent. The extensive jury voir dire had failed to determine that two of the jurors lived in the neighborhood where the incident occurred and viewed the young African-American males in the area as "hooligans." Nor did the defense counsel find out that another juror had substantial ties to and identified with the police officers. From my vantage on the panel, it didn't seem possible that the system would work. And yet this jury, a group of people divided by differing experiences, biases and prejudices, was somehow able to work through their contradictory beliefs. In the end, they acted unanimously to acquit through that rare, near-miraculous process of jury deliberation.

Mindy Cameron, the *Seattle Times* editorial page editor, served on two juries in municipal court. The evidence, the burden of proof, and reasonable doubt were clearly understood, she wrote. "It was all quite unremarkable, actually, except for this: No cynicism. Two weeks of jury duty with dozens of other people anxious to get back to their busy lives and I never once heard a cynical remark."

In Phoenix, Arizona, a state court criminal jury's deliberations were videotaped, with the consent of all concerned, by *CBS Reports*. The young Hispanic defendant was charged with armed robbery of an African-American convenience store clerk. As in other recently filmed trials, the viewer sees the deliberations begin shapelessly, gradually take form through an open give-and-take, and finally coalesce in a unanimous verdict (in this instance, guilty). "I'm not exactly real keen, you know, on the American government," said an unnamed woman juror afterward. "I think it can stand a lot of improvement. This made me feel better because of the people in that room. They were just straight-up people, very honest, they wanted to do a good job. It made me feel better about being an American citizen and having the American justice system."

James Gobert, a law professor, was skeptical when summoned for jury service in Tennessee. After serving in several cases, he was a believer:

> It was an eye-opening experience. On the juries on which I served were men and women from all walks of life. They were of different races, different religions and different ethnic backgrounds. Their educational attainments ranged from nuclear physicists with multiple doctorates to high school drop-outs. . . . Somehow or other, all the generational, cultural and class differences managed to be bridged. In the end it was what united us rather than what divided us that was important. What united us was our common pursuit of the right verdict in the case on which we had been brought together. Moreover, this odd collection of individuals was somehow able to function effectively as a group. All of our members contributed to the deliberations and all played a meaningful role in the decision-making process. What most impressed me was the seriousness of purpose with which my fellow jurors approached their task. Contrary to anecdotal stories (probably disseminated by frustrated lawyers who had just lost a case), none of the jurors was in a hurry to go home; all were prepared to put in as much time as it would take to reach the right verdict.

Gobert observed "both a leveling effect (in the sense that gender, class, education and income were irrelevant to one's role as a juror) and an elevating effect (in the sense that persons who were not used to wrestling with knotty problems managed to rise to the intellectual challenge)."

There are, of course, contrary reports. A male juror who served in the mass murder trial of Juan Corona, a farm labor contractor charged with killing twenty-five itinerant men and burying their bodies in shallow graves, said afterward: "Being a juror was a terrible thing. I'm not smart and I'm not educated, and I don't know if it's right to put a person like me in that position of being a judge. It was awful. I had to think like I've never thought before." Yet the Corona jury, capably led by a foreman who had never finished high school, sifted for eight days through a mass of evidence, overcame disagreements and discord, and reached a unanimous verdict of guilty on all counts.

Stephen Adler of *The Wall Street Journal,* in a valuable book on the jury system, describes several cases in which the jury, as he sees it, did poorly. In one, a complex, multiweek price discrimination battle between two tobacco companies, the jury foreman said afterward: "I enjoyed it, had a good time, and would do it again. But as for my opinion of the justice system, I don't believe you can leave law and justice to people who don't know laws and business management." In another, the jury had to decide how much to award a woman who had contracted AIDS through a transfusion of contaminated blood negligently provided by a blood bank. "It was ridiculous," said one juror afterward, "to determine damages without any guidelines. We did muddle through it, but we had no clue." But such reports are a minority, and they arise, more often than not, from mismanagement rather than from dim-wittedness or bias in the jury box. Garbled evidence, aimless days in court, and opaque instructions on the law can bring a bad verdict. When that happens the jury is not the culprit but one of the victims. As Adler points out, "it's often the trial judge who deserves the biggest share of the blame for the disappointing work of juries."

What are the sources, then, of the current sharp attacks on jury competence and integrity? They are based not on analysis of the estimated 150,000 jury trials held each year—neither side in the debate could review all of those—but on a few hung juries and high-profile verdicts thought to be wrong. In civil cases, the critics point to huge damage awards, alleged antibusiness sentiment, and inability to understand complex issues and evidence; in criminal cases, to unjustified acquittals, hung juries, and unfair application of the death penalty.

The indictment, I believe, is false. The jury is not perfect. It has its moments of idiocy, as when Louisville jurors recently chose between murder and manslaughter by tossing a coin—a procedure they thought justified because they agreed unanimously on it to avoid a hung jury. (The coin-flip, naturally, made front-page news across the country; a new trial was ordered.) But the failures are few and usually are due to our giving jurors poor information or saddling them with intractable questions to decide—questions to which no satisfactory answers are likely to be found.

Our tort system—the laws that determine when and to what extent a company or person must compensate another for injuries caused by negligent or malicious behavior or by a defective product—is a mixture of moral standards, efforts at societal control, the desire for vengeance, and the need to compensate innocent victims. Many tort cases involve an individual suing a major corporation, and are seen as battles in the endless struggle of the powerless against the privileged. The tort system is controversial, and although its rules are made by legislators and not by jurors, the jury takes much of the heat.

A recurring question that the tort system imposes on juries is how much to award in punitive damages—damages meant not to compensate the victim but to punish the wrongdoer and set an example for others. A favorite current example is that of an eighty-one-year-old woman who was awarded $2.7 million in punitive damages, on top of $160,000 in compensatory damages, after a McDonald's fast-food outlet sold her a container of scalding-hot coffee which spilled onto her lap, causing injuries, while she was driving a car. Another is an Alabama jury's award of $581 million to punish two corporations for deceiving consumers who bought satellite dishes, even though the claimants had lost only $1,200. Still another is a Florida jury's record award of $145 billion in punitive damages for sick and dying smokers ("For a period of

50 years," said the foreman afterward, "these tobacco companies denied the dangers of their product . . . [the award] would put the companies on notice—not just the tobacco companies, all companies—concerning fraud or misrepresentation of the American public.")

Such verdicts inspire attacks on "runaway juries" by proponents of tort reform, a movement aimed at limiting the remedies available to injured persons.

Whatever the merits of tort reform may be, the often-heard arguments that tort litigation has seen explosive growth, and that juries are open-handed, are not supported by court records. Tort case filings leveled off two decades ago and recently have declined. Of the tort cases that go to a jury verdict, plaintiffs win slightly less than half, and the average award remained constant in the 1990s. The median amount of plaintiffs' verdicts is $51,000, and only about 4 percent of awards include punitive damages.

There is no evidence that juries generally are antibusiness. To the contrary, research and experience both show that jurors support the lawful goals of American business, expect claimants to accept personal responsibility, and are concerned about frivolous or excessive litigation. The "skyrocketing verdicts" and "out of control" tort system, described by such critics as Vice President Dan Quayle's Council on Competitiveness, are imaginary. Jurors do expect employers and manufacturers to deal fairly with employees and consumers, but they reject false claims as firmly as they reject false defenses. As law professor Richard Lempert concluded in a 1999 article: "If there is any single finding that stands out in the 32 years of modern social science research on juries, beginning with *The American Jury*, it is that case facts are the most important determinant of jury verdicts. Ordinarily, their influence dwarfs everything else."

Out-of-the-ballpark damage awards are rare and nearly always are reduced by the trial judge or on appeal. (The punitive component of the McDonald's verdict—although supported by evidence that McDonald's knew it served its coffee dangerously hot, had received more than seven hundred burn complaints in the year before the accident, and had refused to lower the temperature to the level used by other fast-food restaurants—was reduced by the trial judge to $480,000.) Yet it must be recognized that some juries, after hearing evidence of alleged corporate disregard of public health or safety, see themselves as the voice of the powerless and send an overblown and unrealistic "message." The Alabama jurors in the satellite dish case could not have believed that $581 million would ever be collected, and it won't be; the parties settled for an undisclosed sum. Such verdicts may help jurors blow off steam, but they reduce confidence in the system.

The basic problem with punitive damages is that jurors are asked, with little guidance, to discipline a free-enterprise market by imposing open-ended fines on wrongdoers. They hear evidence of the defendant's profits and its related blameworthy conduct. They are instructed that "the purposes of punitive damages are to punish a defendant and to deter [it] and others from committing similar acts in the future," or words to that effect. Even the most thoughtful jurors face a hard task in deciding what it will take to get the attention of this defendant "and others."

That juries in the main are conservative in this area is shown by a recent judge-jury comparison. A study by the U.S. Department of Justice, which reviewed more than ten thousand injury cases tried in 1996 in the nation's seventy-five largest counties, found that judges were three times as likely as juries to impose punitive damages, and that the median award by judges in bench trials was nearly three times that of juries. The punitive damage system may be flawed—"a terrible way to govern ourselves," says law professor Peter Schuck—or it may be the valuable deterrent described by its supporters, but its problems cannot fairly be blamed on the jury.

Jury critics also claim that a randomly picked group of twelve cannot be expected to understand complex legal issues or scientific or technical evidence. This line of attack, more than any other, calls into question the jury's future.

To date, especially in well-run trials, the record is encouraging. When jury instructions are given in impenetrable jargon, or specialized knowledge is imparted confusingly or not at all, the jury of course may fail to understand. So may the judge, the spectators, and the lawyers. A challenge to all modern trial systems—including those that use no juries—is raised by the information revolution and especially by cases that require some grasp of a technical field. But there is almost invariably a fund of intelligence and wisdom in these gatherings of twelve. As law professor Valerie Hans reminds us, the "evaluation of the central issues in most trials depends on basic human judgment, not on highly technical issues understood by only a few experts." The judge must serve as "gatekeeper" to exclude groundless or unscientific expert testimony, and must make sure that the jurors hear adequate explanations. When that is done, they understand the case. As one trial lawyer said, "I would generally rather have a juror who tinkers with their car on the weekends decide my mechanical patent case than a judge who has a Ph.D. in philosophy and no mechanical aptitude."

In the 1980s a few courts carved out a "complexity exception" to the right to trial by jury in civil cases. The federal appeals court in Philadelphia, for example, decided that the right is extinguished if legal and factual difficulties are so great that a jury could fail to understand. The judge, in this view, would decide in advance whether a jury (of unknown composition) would be able to understand the case. At about the same time the federal appeals court in San Francisco reached the opposite conclusion: there is no complexity exception, and "[j]urors, if properly instructed and treated with deserved respect, bring collective intelligence, wisdom, and dedication to their tasks," qualities that are "rarely equaled in other areas of public service." The Supreme Court has not dealt directly with this question. If and when it does, it may recognize that the solution is not to displace the jury but to give it better information, guidance, and working conditions. "Jurors," as three leaders of Arizona's trial reform program recently wrote, "are in fact capable of resolving highly complex cases."

—

In criminal cases, high-profile failures to convict defendants considered obviously guilty have raised a storm of criticism. In the Menendez brothers' first trial, the jurors failed to reach a verdict although the defendants admitted killing their parents. In the Rodney King state court trial, an all-white jury acquitted white police officers of every charge—even the minor one of using excessive force—despite a videotape that showed them mercilessly beating an unarmed black man on the ground. The prosecutors failed to call the victim, Mr. King, as a witness. Lorena Bobbitt was acquitted of mutilating her husband with a knife. Oliver North was found guilty of only minor charges.

Such cases, although they attract feverish attention, are far too small a sampling to suggest jury incompetence. And in each instance there was a mitigating explanation—or, at least, a satisfying sequel. The jurors' disagreement in the Menendez case was over a murder versus a manslaughter conviction, not over whether the defendants should be acquitted. A retrial resulted in murder convictions. The first Rodney King verdict—which I believe was, indeed, a miscarriage of justice—was followed by a federal trial in which two officers were convicted and sent to prison for violating King's civil rights; the victim also received a handsome financial settlement. Lorena Bobbitt presented a battered-wife, mental-irresponsibility argument of considerable appeal. Oliver North's jury reasonably believed that the defendant was a mere cat's-paw for higher officials who escaped prosecution—"a scapegoat," as one juror put it after the trial, "blamed unfairly for following the instructions of his superiors."

When the judge and lawyers do their jobs well the jury performs well, even in trials with saturation media coverage. A fine example was the 1994 prosecution of eleven Branch Davidians over the killing of four federal agents during an assault on a cult compound at Waco, Texas. All were acquitted of murder and conspiracy; seven were convicted of manslaughter or illegal weapons possession; four were acquitted altogether. A just verdict was reached in a difficult and highly emotional case. Another was the 1995 trial and sentence to life imprisonment of Susan Smith, the South Carolina woman who drowned her two young children to be with her lover. The calm and efficient proceeding did credit to all concerned. Yet another was the 1997 trial of Timothy McVeigh over the Oklahoma City Courthouse bombing; the case was well tried, and the revelation in 2001 that the FBI had made an incomplete disclosure of documents to defense counsel is no reflection on the work done by the jurors.

There is no evidence that unjust acquittals are a general or widespread problem. In my experience, juries convict if guilt is proved beyond a reasonable doubt, and otherwise not. That is exactly what they are supposed to do.

The death penalty burdens the jury with the ultimate intractable question: Who deserves to be spared, and who must die? We ask the jury, in most states, because we do not trust anyone else to decide. Yet on this issue we cannot fully trust the jury either. Jurors' answers are imperfect, as are the answers of all other mortals. As Judge John Noonan has written: "For those without belief in human immortality, there is an awfulness about the utter extinction of a human person. For those who are religious, the deliberate human taking of life appears to be the usurpation of a power that belongs to God." And since we don't understand how God metes out life and death, we can hardly expect fallible humans to decide to everyone's satisfaction.

This is not the place to debate capital punishment or the Supreme Court's upholding it as constitutional, but we do need to look at how it affects our trial system and the jury's reputation. The United States is the only Western democracy that still uses the death penalty. Whether one is for or against the penalty in principle, there is no doubt that its application is racially imbalanced, prone to mistakes because of inadequate trial representation of poor defendants, and enormously expensive in time and money. The system, writes federal appeals Judge Betty Fletcher, has it backwards. The intense effort and resources are concentrated at the wrong end. We have inadequate representation at the trial level, which erodes the capacity of judges and juries to acquit the innocent and to save from death those who deserve less severe punishment; we have prolonged review processes that more often than not deflect attention from the real issues of fair trial and possible innocence to arcane examinations of technical bars.

The utter finality of death, and our need to think we are inflicting it fairly, leads to a unique and agonizingly technical brand of appellate review that may go on for a decade or more. Two-thirds of the death sentences are reversed, usually for a new trial or penalty hearing. Yet no matter how long or laboriously we pore over the transcripts of capital cases, we never will find the certitude we seek. The late Justice Harry Blackmun, for many years a supporter of capital punishment, decided near the end of his career that "the decision whether a human being should live or die is so inherently subjective—rife with all of life's understandings, experiences, prejudices and passions—that it inevitably defies the rationality and consistency required by the Constitution." Therefore, he no longer would "tinker with the machinery of death."

The American Bar Association called in 1997 for a moratorium on the death penalty until the nation takes steps to make its application fairer. In early 2000, Governor George Ryan of Illinois, citing a "shameful record of convicting innocent people and putting them on death row," halted all executions in that state. Nationwide, eighty-seven death row inmates have been released as innocent since 1976, and the number is growing with the use of DNA evidence. But the wrongly convicted are only a tiny fraction of the 3,600 now on death row. The law usually gets the right person, and Justice Blackmun's "machinery of death" breaks down most commonly in determining not who is guilty but who among the guilty must die. For that defect, there is no sure remedy. Death penalty trials continue in three-fourths of the states and in the federal system; as long as they do, jurors will be asked to shoulder a burden that no one could carry well.

The national hung jury rate in criminal cases is about 2.5 percent in the federal courts and 5 percent in the state courts. It is even lower in civil cases. A jury's failure to agree does not necessarily mean the case will be retried—it may be dropped or settled—and the occasional hung jury, in my view, is a small price to pay for what we gain with unanimous criminal verdicts. But recent heavily publicized hung juries have led to demands that less-than-unanimous verdicts be accepted. In a few cases a single juror simply refuses to deliberate and sits in a corner until the other eleven give up and a mistrial is declared. (An old story speaks of twelve members of a hung jury leaving the courthouse, with one of them saying: "Those were the eleven most stubborn people I've met in my life!") In a recent Seattle murder trial, a juror announced at the start of deliberations that she did not trust police or prosecutors or judges and would not vote to convict anyone of anything. Eight days of pleading by the other jurors failed to budge her, and a mistrial was declared. She ran from the courtroom without speaking to anyone. (A retrial several months later resulted in a first-degree murder conviction.)

Resentment of legal authority in any form—harbored, for example, by zealots who believe their private militia is a sovereign state and that all other governments are fraudulent—leads to occasional hung juries. But the most disturbing cause of verdicts blocked by juror disagreement is racial animosity. Race, our oldest and deepest domestic problem, finds voice in the jury room—not usually, but at times. In 1998 I presided at the trial of an African American man charged with the crime of "felon in possession"—meaning that, having been convicted of a felony (more than one, as it happened), and having been released from prison, he was then found in possession of a loaded pistol. There was one black juror; all the others were white. The jury could not agree and, after giving every chance for a verdict to be reached, I declared a mistrial. Later I learned from the clerk, who had received an unexpected telephone call from the jury foreman, that the black juror simply had refused to deliberate; it was a racial thing, she said, and that was that. She may have guessed that heavy penalties would apply to this federal offense, and if so she was right; when the defendant was convicted in a retrial, the law, in light of his serious past record, mandated a ten-year sentence.

The disparate impact of criminal law enforcement leaps out from the statistics: blacks make up only 13 percent of the country's population but about 50 percent of its jail and prison population. Congress has ordered prison sentences for crack cocaine dealers one hundred times more severe than those imposed on powder cocaine dealers; almost 90 percent of crack cocaine defendants, but only about 20 percent of powder cocaine defendants, are African Americans. Blacks who kill whites are eleven times more likely to receive the death penalty than whites who kill blacks, and of the five hundred prisoners executed between 1977 and 1998 nearly 82 percent had been convicted of murdering a white person, even though blacks and whites were homicide victims in almost equal numbers. In juvenile courts, among young people who have not been sent to a juvenile prison before, blacks are more than six times as likely as whites to be sentenced to prison.

Conscious racism is now rare in American legal proceedings, but a stubborn residue of discrimination remains. It is entwined with poverty and is traceable far more to the work of police, prosecutors, and judges than to jury verdicts. Those living in poor and blighted city neighborhoods are likelier than residents of more affluent areas to be stopped for driving an old car with broken taillights or missing license plates, or detained for questioning on the sidewalk, or arrested for having succumbed to the drug trade's promise of quick and easy wealth. "Walking or driving while black" may be the only offense perceived by the onlookers.

A prosecutor deciding whether to charge a suspect with the most serious possible crime or some lesser offense is required by law to be race-neutral, but unconscious stereotyping may enter in; the statistics do not tell us how much of the death penalty disparity is caused by prosecutors' charging decisions rather than by anything that happens at trial. To a sentencing judge, a criminal defendant or juvenile offender who has a strong support network, an intact family, and a job or an offer of one presents a more appealing case for probation than one who is on the streets with no visible prospects. Such factors will influence the judge regardless of race or color, but blacks, because of income disparities, commonly have a harder time than whites in showing the court a set of living conditions that would encourage probation or a short sentence.

It is not surprising that two blacks in three believe the criminal justice system is stacked against them. What is surprising is how well mixed-race juries continue to perform.

The case most often cited for racial bias in the jury room is *People v. Simpson,* where the black defendant was acquitted by a predominantly black jury in the face of circumstantial evidence that millions of television viewers thought was conclusive. This may well have been, at least in part, a protest verdict, but there were also questions about the merits. The trial was botched by the professionals; the proof was circumstantial; and the state's main witness, a police detective, lied on the stand and finally admitted he was biased enough to falsify evidence against a black defendant. The jury, it must be remembered, was not asked whether it believed Simpson committed the murders; it was asked whether the state had proved his guilt beyond a reasonable doubt.

Other multiracial juries, time after time, reach sensible unanimous verdicts in criminal cases. An Atlanta jury of eight blacks and four whites convicted Wayne Williams, an African American, in the notorious "missing and murdered children" cases. Another Atlanta jury of eight blacks and four whites convicted Emmanuel Hammond, also an African American, of murdering a white woman. A Chicago jury of six blacks and six whites convicted Mel Reynolds, a black congressman, on charges related to his having sex with an underage former campaign worker. A New York jury of eight whites and four blacks acquitted the police officers who shot Amadou Diallo, an unarmed black man, in the mistaken belief that he was reaching for a gun (a verdict that illustrates how hard it is to convict officers if the jury believes they acted out of panic or confusion rather than deliberate brutality). A few weeks later a Connecticut jury of eleven whites and one black convicted a white policeman of manslaughter for shooting an unarmed black suspect in the back.

As these cases illustrate, multiracial juries usually are able to agree. A typical experience is that of a Los Angeles rabbi who reported for jury duty with great reluctance and only when told he could be arrested if he failed to appear. To his surprise, he found jury service "one of the most fascinating and fulfilling adventures" he had had in years. In five days of deliberations in a criminal case, he "learned that if you take a dozen strangers (a cross-section of our city—several Latinos, some Anglos, a nisei, an African American, and one Westside rabbi) who share only their citizenship, the English language, and a common civic duty, amazing things can happen." No medals were awarded for jury duty, the once-skeptical rabbi noted, but the "feelings that experience can engender are reward enough. More than enough."

Today there are high acquittal rates in some inner cities where jurors and defendants are predominantly black or Hispanic. The feelings of minorities that the system is stacked against them clearly are at work. So is a spreading realization that prison terms for drug-dealing, especially in the federal system, are harsh beyond the expectations of nearly all jurors. Acquittals on these bases are another episode in the long history of jury discretion. They are not a reason to despair of our communal devotion to justice; in fact, given the uneven impact of criminal law enforcement, what is remarkable is the high degree of jury harmony. In some societies, riven by ethnic or religious divisions, hatred swamps the ethic of equal justice, and juries are not usable. We are not at that point. If we ever reach it, we will lose much more than trial by jury.

The usual alternative to a jury trial is a trial to the judge—a bench trial, as it is called. We have plenty of those, where no party has demanded a jury or the case by its nature, for historical reasons, carries no right to one (in admiralty or divorce or injunction claims, for example). Bench trials can be entirely satisfactory and I would be the last to say that judges generally are incompetent. But jury critics tend to assume, without demonstrating, that judges are better able than juries to decide cases. There is nothing to warrant that assumption. Judges do have law degrees, and tend to be more articulate than jurors commonly are in explaining their decisions. (Juries, of course, don't have to explain, and their occasional attempts to do so are sometimes felicitous, sometimes not.) But the ability to articulate should not be confused with the ability to do justice. "The power to argue strongly," the Canadian writer Robertson Davies observed, "and what I may call the puzzle-solving and examination-passing cast of mind, is often the possession of people of arid and limited perception and uneducated heart." Some of the most elaborately rationalized judicial opinions in history have been profoundly unjust; most of the great jury verdicts have not been explained at all.

The United States, *The Washington Post* found in a 1996 study, "is becoming a nation of suspicious strangers, and this mistrust of each other is a major reason Americans have lost confidence in the federal government and virtually every other major national institution." Yet it must not be assumed that poll-engendered observations mean that trial by jury has failed or must fail. There is a crucial difference between what a citizen says in casually answering a pollster and what he or she experiences while serving in court. What Tocqueville said a hundred and sixty-five years ago about jury service being a great educator is still true. In well-tried cases, nearly all jurors find themselves caught up in the quest for justice.

Are twelve heads better than one? Yes, and not just because twelve jurors collectively are more perceptive than the judge. The jury brings fresh energy and a current of common sense, of elemental fairness, into the stream of justice; it brings not just group intelligence and dialogue but community values. The balances between liberty and criminal law enforcement, between business enterprise and responsibility to consumers, between an injured person's right to damages and the defendant's probable ability to pay, are struck by the community's conscience. The result in a given case may be debatable, but is greatly legitimized if it comes from a jury.

There are juries elsewhere in the world, chiefly in former outposts of the British Empire, but the American jury is by far the most vital and influential. More than 90 percent of the world's criminal jury trials, and nearly all of its civil jury trials, take place in this country. Democracy can exist without juries, as we see in the governments of Japan, Western Europe, and other parts of the world. Yet I cannot help thinking that for us the jury is the canary in the mine shaft; if it goes, if our people lose their inherited right to do justice in court, other democratic institutions will lose breath too. We don't need to let that happen.

Better Trials

Trials are only a part of our system, but they are the apex, the model, the part that is open to the public, reported in the media, dramatized in TV shows and movies, recounted in popular books, and even broadcast live. They are the part that everyone knows about. Even in cases that end in settlement or plea bargain (the great majority), the prospect of trial helps shape the outcome. Trials are central to both the perception and the reality of justice, yet far too often we have let them become muddled, slow, expensive, and divorced from the search for truth. We must do better, and the question is how.

Some law professors, and even a few judges, argue that we should make a fresh start by dropping the adversary trial method, with its heavy civilized-fight legacy, and adopting a continental European system. The Europeans—the French, Germans, Italians, Dutch, and others on the Continent—follow the legal tradition of ancient Rome, which is a millennium older than England's common law and far more widespread in today's world. We would be foolish not to pay attention to it.

A continental system—to begin a necessarily oversimplified summary—relies on logic and codification and overwhelming central power, implemented through judges who are not former trial lawyers but civil servants trained for a lifetime career on the bench. It has less interparty strife than we do, no jury as we know it, and no powerful trial lawyers. The process is seen not as a partisan conflict but as an official inquiry into the truth; for that reason it is called "inquisitorial," although in modern democracies it bears little resemblance to the religious inquisitions of the past. Gone is the institutionalized torture that prevailed for five hundred years, from roughly 1300 to 1800, when continental criminal defendants, unlike those in England and its colonies, were routinely tortured under judicial supervision to extract confessions. The European model eliminates theatrics, witness-coaching, partisan experts, and lawyers' inflated egos clamoring for attention. The judges take over at the start, run the inquiry, and decide the case. "The sporting spirit," Sybille Bedford has written, "the notion of the law as a game of skill with handicaps to give each side a chance, is entirely absent on the Continent."

In European criminal trials there are no rules that keep out some kinds of evidence while allowing other kinds. Hearsay, for example, can be received if the judges think it should be. Witnesses are encouraged to talk in their own words rather than being tightly hemmed in by questions; a witness telling what he or she saw may go on for half an hour or more without interruption. Spontaneity may allow a prejudicial remark to slip out now and then, but is considered worth the risk. The lawyers play a secondary role; the judges do nearly all the questioning; interruptions are rare. Lawyer coaching of witnesses before or during trial is prohibited. The whole process is less rigid than ours, less rule-bound, less dependent on lawyering skills.

In civil litigation as well, European practice is judge-centered. In Germany, to take a leading example, the evidence in a civil case is gathered by a judge, not by the lawyers. The lawyers may suggest the names of witnesses to be questioned, but may not interview or coach them. The trial is not a single event but a series of hearings; one step at a time, the judge adds to the case dossier. The judge brings out the testimony; the lawyers may ask follow-up questions, but are not the main interrogators. Each witness testifies once, rather than being subjected to interviews followed by a deposition followed in turn by trial testimony. Settlement is discussed as the case goes along; the judge may help by giving tentative views of the likely outcome. When the evidence is complete, the lawyers argue orally or in writing. In argument—as distinguished from fact-gathering—the lawyers function as advocates. The judge then gives a written decision with fact findings and legal reasoning.

Professor John Langbein, an admirer of German civil litigation, argues that only "inertia and vested interests justify the waste and distortion of adversary fact-gathering. The success of German civil procedure stands as an enduring reproach to those who say that we must continue to suffer adversary tricksters in the proof of fact."

We can and should learn from our fellow democracies in Europe—far more than American judges and lawyers have done. The main lesson is that an active judge—a good one—can be a blessing. In our system the power to run trials and decide outcomes is divided among judge, jury, and counsel. In the late colonial era the king's judges, seen as arbitrary and oppressive, left an abiding fear of the bench and helped inspire our constitutional guarantees of trial by jury. The jury's heyday lasted for about a century after the Revolution. Then came a further shift of power, this time to the lawyers; we came to accept that lawyers run trials, while the judge is inert and the jurors are passive listeners treated more like sheep than decision-making citizens.

Any improvements—even minor ones—will require breathing more life into the long-dormant trial judge. But in my view we should never adopt a continental-type system in the United States, even if we could.

European criminal prosecutions, however efficient they may be in some countries (not all), are based on a dimmer view than ours of constitutional rights. The Fifth Amendment, for example—the part of it that guarantees a defendant's right not to incriminate himself—is a great Anglo-American phenomenon. In most parts of Europe, unlike the United States, an accused person's silence may be considered against him. Also missing are the protections we have against hearsay and against inferences of guilt based on the defendant's past record. An acquittal in a European trial court is not final as it is in the United States; the government can appeal and continue to pursue the accused. The separateness of the defendant and the government—the individual's dignity and autonomy against the state—is not preserved as it is in American courts. Our staunch protection of individual rights is buttressed by the adversary system.

The Europeans lack trial by jury. In some countries lay judges sit with professionals in criminal cases, join in the deliberations, and vote on the verdict. But the professional judges dominate; these mixed panels are not juries. A continental system has no comparable institution that empowers citizens to do justice, bonds the courts to the community, and legitimizes difficult trial outcomes.

And a system that relies so heavily on judges invites not just sloth and incompetence but corruption. Everything depends on how good or bad the judges are—a variable on which we should never stake everything. We need to remember, along with the polished systems of today's Holland and Germany and Sweden, those of corruption-plagued Latin America (which are continental in origin) and of the twentieth-century European fascist regimes. Judge-ruled court systems can fall prey to bribery or tyranny; strong, deeply rooted roles for citizens and lawyers in the trial courts are safeguards against judicial decay.

The European systems, in comparison to ours, have larger judicial bureaucracies and fewer lawyers. Most of them are burdened, as we are, by too much expense and delay in civil litigation. And however skilled and conscientious European judges may be, they are government employees; a system so judge-dependent can never attain the vitality of one that makes full use of private counsel's energy and initiative.

Consider, for example, a civil case tried several years ago against former dictator Ferdinand Marcos of the Philippines and his wife, Imelda. In 1981, hit men burst into a labor union hall in Seattle and gunned down two young Filipinos, Silme Domingo and Gene Viernes. Both victims were activists in an International Longshoremen's and Warehousemen's Union (ILWU) local that represented fish cannery workers in Alaska. The killers fled. Grief and outrage spread through the city, especially in the neighborhoods where thousands of Asians live. The families of Domingo and Viernes were devastated.

Following a police investigation, three local Filipino gang members were charged, tried, convicted of the murders, and sentenced to life imprisonment. That could have been the end of it. Many assumed that a dispute over union-hall dispatch practices—over who got the cannery jobs—had motivated the killings. One faction of hot-headed Filipinos, according to this theory, had assassinated another.

But the theory was false. Domingo's sister, Cindy, was determined that justice be done. Viernes was survived by a sister, a girlfriend, and two young children. The families knew that Domingo and Viernes had been outspoken opponents of the Marcos regime. Just a month before their deaths, they had won passage of a national ILWU resolution calling for a task force to monitor government-sponsored brutality against labor unions in the Philippines. The survivors believed Marcos was behind the murders. But how could they prove it?

They hired a lawyer, Michael Withey, who agreed to work for a contingent fee—no charge unless damages were recovered. Withey filed a civil suit in federal court against Ferdinand and Imelda Marcos. To begin the case was in itself an act of bravery; for months afterward the surviving family members, fearing reprisals, wore bulletproof vests.

Withey expected, and met, massive legal resistance. The Marcoses, ably defended by American counsel, were at first dismissed from the case as "heads of state"—a category immune from suit. Following an appeal and the Marcoses' ouster in the uprising that brought Corazon Aquino to power, they were reinstated as defendants. But to dig up evidence implicating them was enormously difficult. Withey took two years away from his practice to work on this case alone, but still needed, and got, help from others in his firm. Documents had to be found and witnesses examined at locations thousands of miles apart, to put together circumstantial evidence, piece by piece. A potential key witness was murdered in Seattle. Depositions, required by court order, were taken of Ferdinand and Imelda Marcos in their refuge in Hawaii, and of Marcos's allies residing on the Pacific Coast. U.S. government documents were obtained, under the Freedom of Information Act, from federal agencies that tracked the Philippine government's "intelligence" activities in this country. Experts on Marcos's covert operations were found and consulted.

In 1989, eight years after it was filed, the case for Domingo and Viernes at last came to trial before Judge Barbara Jacobs Rothstein and a federal court jury in Seattle. By this time Marcos had died, but his estate and his widow Imelda remained as defendants. It took Withey and his cocounsel three weeks to present their evidence. They proved that Marcos's intelligence operatives in this country had monitored Domingo and Viernes; that Marcos himself knew of the ILWU resolution the two young men had promoted; that a Marcos ally in San Francisco maintained a secret fund from which $15,000 was paid to another Marcos friend in Seattle whose gun was used in the murders; and that from that amount $5,000 was delivered to the hit team that fired the shots.

They proved that the American government had warned the Marcoses not to conduct antidissident operations in this country. They showed Ferdinand Marcos, in a videotaped deposition taken in Hawaii, admitting that he operated an intelligence network in the United States—and then, when the questions came closer to home, taking the Fifth Amendment (which can be considered in a civil trial, unlike a criminal prosecution).

The jury returned a unanimous verdict that the Marcoses had conspired with others to murder Domingo and Viernes, and awarded the families $15 million—more than their counsel had asked for.

To win the judgment was one thing; to collect it was another, given the confusion over the Marcoses' assets and the new Philippine government's competing claims against them. While on appeal, the case was finally settled for $3 million. But its importance far transcends the compensation won by the families. In a complex and frightening situation, against great odds and across international boundaries, justice was done. The rule of law prevailed over a dictator's power.

The work of private counsel, devoted to their clients' cause, was vital to this achievement. "The outcome," Michael Withey said later, "was inconceivable without the adversary system." It might have been conceivable, but it surely was improbable.

The case of Domingo and Viernes was exceptionally hard, but in run-of-the-mill cases as well we gain energy, depth, and insight from the adversaries' partisan labors. I see this day after day in the courthouse grist of injury claims, breach of contract, felony prosecutions—the gamut. What we need is not to jettison the adversary method or trial by jury, but to help them work under modern conditions and enlist them more firmly in the search for truth. We should aim not for Utopia but for incremental reforms—"the only method of improving matters," Karl Popper wrote, "which has so far been really successful, at any time, and in any place." Popper may have overstated his case, but when it comes to American trials, he was right.

The repair work is under way—not in all courts, but in a growing number. Almost unknown to the public, a surge of trial reform—led by those famously conservative groups, the judges and the organized bar—has begun. Justice is a collaborative effort, but the Arizona Jury Project, headed by Judge Michael Dann of Phoenix, deserves mention for its seminal work. In early 2001 a three-day "jury summit," sponsored by the National Center for State Courts, drew nearly four hundred judges, administrators, and academics to New York City. While there were and are differences of opinion about what should be done, there is a rapidly growing consensus that change is needed. My recommendations are not unique, but are based on what I have seen succeed in the courtroom.

Modern societies hold that direct democracy, as practiced in ancient Athens, with all citizens voting on questions of the day, is no longer practicable—there are too many people, too many issues, too many time-consuming complexities. We elect officials and turn the business of governing over to them; they must do a passable job or face defeat at the next election.

The great exception to this modern delegation of power has been the trial jury. In the jury room our people work directly as governors. But the job can't be done by an empty jury box; to realize the promise of this now fully democratic institution, we need to have citizens appear for duty when called. Some courts, notably in major cities, are plagued by low response rates to jury summonses. In the District of Columbia, a 1998 study found that nearly 20 percent of citizens summoned for jury duty simply ignored the summons, an additional 43 percent did not receive the summons in the first place (due, apparently, to faulty lists), and less than 25 percent of those summoned actually appeared and qualified for jury duty. In some cities less than 20 percent of those called upon actually serve; most of the others beg off or simply ignore the summons. The nonresponders are disproportionately the poor and members of minority groups, so that low turnouts not only make it hard, at times, to empanel twelve, but also lessen the representative quality of the juries that decide cases. The loss of diversity, in turn, lowers the jury's stature and the acceptability of its verdicts.

What causes citizens to ignore or evade jury summonses? Is it lethargy, or fearfulness, or a sense of futility? Research suggests that the answer, for the most part, is none of those. Financial worries, it appears, account for most jury panel absenteeism. Jurors' daily fees are abysmally low in many places—$10 per day in most counties in my state for the last forty years, for example—and many cannot afford to lose time from work when their pay for performing a governmental duty falls far short of their living expenses. When fees are raised to a reasonable level, the increase in turnout is dramatic. El Paso, Texas, recently showed what can be done. Its juror response rate rose from 22 to 46 percent when the daily pay was raised from $6 to $40. In New York City, response rates have been vastly improved by an increase of the daily fee to $40, a guaranteed first postponement by telephone, and a well-publicized appearance before a jury compliance officer for selected shirkers. Noncompliance in New York can bring a fine of up to $250 or other sanctions; one bond trader was sentenced to five hundred hours of community service for sending his auto mechanic to impersonate him on the jury panel. Reasonable compensation, decent working conditions, and enough enforcement to show that ignoring or evading a jury summons is risky will ease the absenteeism problem. And through those who serve, well-run courts will spread the word that jury service is not just a duty but a pleasure.

While making it easier for financially pressed citizens to serve, we should make it harder for the affluent and well-connected to escape. About half the states have ended the long-standing jury service exemptions for doctors, lawyers, teachers, funeral directors, and other professional and business people. The rest should follow suit. Undue hardship must remain a ground for being excused, but should not be equated simply with a busy life elsewhere. Well-educated people who serve on juries are usually glad they did, and the courts need them.

A final lingering obstacle to democratic jury selection is the outmoded notion that every panelist who has heard or read about the case should be excused. In this day of mass communications, that often means disqualifying the most alert and capable and seating only the least aware and least interested. As Mark Twain observed, when "the very cattle in the corrals" know about the case, it is hard to find intelligent jurors, other than hermits, who have never heard of it. Jurors are often asked if they can put aside any pretrial publicity and decide the case on the evidence and the law. Some will say no. In my experience, those who answer yes usually deserve to be taken at their word. We do not automatically disqualify the judge who has seen pretrial news accounts; the jury will be improved if we give its members the same consideration.

From the moment they report for duty, jurors should be treated with the courtesy and respect due to officers of the court. They should not be kept waiting for hours or days on end; with good court administration, they don't have to be. The "one day or one case" limitation now becoming popular puts a reasonable limit on the disruption of their lives. Nor should they be pent up in oppressive surroundings. Despite our nation's prosperity, many courthouses are run-down and over-crowded; judges cannot change that, but can make sure that jurors get a fair allocation of whatever space exists. And every new panel, in every courthouse, should get a prompt and clear orientation on what it's all about—the court, the flow of civil and criminal cases, the jurors' duties, the roles of the judges and lawyers. Most jurors arrive on the first day full of hope or at least curiosity. To inspire them at the start is both easy and wise.

Of all the flaws in our current system, jury empanelment is the most embarrassing. "The way juries are selected in this country," Anthony Lewis has written, "in high-profile cases especially, is outrageously expensive and damaging to respect for law." Why should it take days, weeks, or even months to pick a jury? It shouldn't—but it often does, leaving the public frustrated and the jury demoralized before the first witness takes the stand. The chief cause is uncontrolled jury questioning by lawyers—voir dire, as it is called. In many state courts counsel have virtually open-ended leave to question potential jurors, sometimes for days on end.

The theoretical purpose of voir dire is to ferret out bias or prejudice and thus ensure a fair jury. But other purposes have crept in: to stack the jury with partisans, to implant a favorable picture in the jurors' minds, to "win the case" before the evidence begins. The questions on voir dire often become intrusive, repetitive, even insulting.

Fair juries can be empaneled with little or no voir dire by the adversaries. In this country the federal court tradition has been that the judge does the questioning, with the lawyers listening and taking notes. That method assures brevity but forfeits potentially valuable questioning by counsel.

The best solution is to allow follow-up voir dire by the lawyers, after the judge questions the panelists first, subject to two conditions. The first is that counsel's questions must go to the panelists' qualifications to serve—to their experiences, attitudes, affiliations, and feelings germane to possible bias—and must not be a disguised attempt to win them over at the outset. This is easily enforced by the judge. The second condition is a time limit—fifteen minutes per side, for example, with counsel free to ask for more time if they think they need it. Requests for additional time are rare; often, after the judge finishes the first round of questioning, the lawyers do not even need their full allotted time per side.

By this method, a fair and impartial jury usually can be empaneled in an hour or two, even in a multiparty case.

Challenges to potential jurors are of two kinds: those for cause (kinship or friendship with a party, admitted or demonstrated bias, or some other disqualifying factor), and those for which no reason need be given. The latter are called *peremptory* challenges or "strikes." Peremptories are afforded to each side, by statute or court rule, up to a certain number. (In federal court, the numbers are ten for the defense and six for the prosecution in felony cases, and three per side in misdemeanor and civil cases.) No one quarrels with challenges for cause, but peremptory strikes raise a sharp difference of opinion. The Ninth Circuit Court of Appeals recently called them "an important statutory right that courts have considered vital to an impartial jury trial." But Judge Constance Baker Motley of the federal court in Manhattan, urging in 1996 that peremptories be banned, called them "an unnecessary waste of time and an obvious corruption of the judicial process." There is much to be said for Judge Motley's view. Trial lawyers know that peremptory challenges are commonly used to select not impartial jurors but favorable ones—jurors whose education, work history, race, ethnicity, and so on are thought to augur well for the client's cause. Often this means getting rid of the best-educated or most perceptive jurors. The misuse of peremptory challenges—creating, as it does, the impression that all that matters is who decides, not the merits of the case—contributes heavily to public cynicism about trials.

The irony is that lawyers, although steeped in superstition on the subject, are very poor at guessing who will be a favorable juror and who won't. One case from my early life as a trial lawyer illustrates the point.

I was defending a nighttime jazz musician and daytime Boeing mechanic who will be known here as Leonard Rockworth. Mr. Rockworth was charged with grand larceny—the theft of a large number of expensive tools from his employer. These tools, regrettably, had been found in his basement at home, and some of them had been missing from Boeing for a long time. Rockworth's explanation was that he had only borrowed the tools to use in his home workshop; he always meant to return them, he said, but had never gotten around to it. One panelist, a man in his sixties, was a retired Boeing foreman. He denied any prejudice, but he looked tough and it was clear that his life must have been plagued by tool thieves; surely he would be pro-prosecution. Following the bar's conventional wisdom, I used the first peremptory challenge to excuse him. Later, at the morning recess, the retired foreman walked up to me in the hallway. He was obviously displeased. "Why did you throw me off that jury?" he said. "I worked for that damned Boeing Company for twenty-five years and hated them every day, and I can't wait to get back at them!" (Rockworth was acquitted anyway, which makes the story easier to tell. Furthermore, he never paid his bill, and, four decades later, still owes me the entire fee of $250. But given my obtuseness during jury selection, who can blame him?)

The unreliable hunches of lawyers are now aided, or compounded, by a lucrative business known as jury consultancy, whose practitioners reportedly are paid the astounding total of $200 million to $400 million per year (the amount is hard to determine). Among other services, the consultants help lawyers select jurors for their background, body language, and presumed subconscious activity. Even if these prophecies were accurate—a highly dubious assumption—they would still serve no good purpose; they are not meant to, and don't, help empanel a fair and well-qualified jury. Beyond that, as the legal scholar Jeffrey Abramson has written, the use of these consultants amounts to "a sustained attack on the worth of jury trials. For if scientific jury selection actually works, then facts and evidence play a subordinate role in trials."

Peremptory challenges have become even more vexed since 1986, when the Supreme Court in *Batson v. Kentucky* barred the prosecution from using them to remove minority persons of the same race as the defendant. Some prosecutors had done that for decades to get rid of black jurors where the defendant on trial was African American. Since *Batson* appeared, the principle has spread to race-based peremptories by the defense, to civil cases, and to challenges motivated by a juror's sex. When a challenge that appears to violate the expanded *Batson* rule is made, the judge must find out if there is an innocent, nondiscriminatory reason for it; if there isn't, the judge must set aside the challenge and leave the juror in the box. The result is a new complication, plus occasional mendacity by counsel dreaming up an innocent-sounding reason for a race- or gender-based challenge.

A few points can be made in favor of peremptory challenges. Someone at counsel table may correctly sense a juror's bias that no amount of questioning will bring out, leaving a peremptory as the only remedy. Voir dire questioning may be inhibited by fear of alienating a juror if counsel know that no peremptories will be allowed. And, it is said, peremptories give the parties a say in who will decide the case and thus enhance their comfort level at trial (an argument which overlooks the fact that if a peremptory challenge increases one side's comfort level, it usually reduces the other's).

To a trial judge, it is saddening to see well-qualified and impartial jurors, many of them idealistic and eager to serve, knocked out of the box for no good reason. The challenged jurors, no matter how thoroughly reassured by the judge, often feel rejected.

We should make two changes. First, we should reduce the number of peremptory challenges to three per side. For a party to have as many as twenty peremptories, as some states permit in felony cases, accomplishes nothing except to spread the impression that the system is being manipulated. For any legitimate purpose, three strikes are enough.

Second, since peremptory challenges are not required by the Constitution, we should experiment with abolishing them. With fifty state jurisdictions and ninety-four federal districts, we could adopt local-option rules to try out the change on a small scale. If it is true that any slight contribution peremptories make to the cause of justice is out-weighed by their misuse to eliminate good jurors, the inordinate time they take in many courts, and the implicit message they send that the outcome will depend not on the merits but on who happens to wind up in the jury box, we should not put up with them forever. At the same time, we should make challenges for cause flexible enough to give the judge leeway in assuring a fair jury. Challenges for cause can be stated in writing and ruled on by the judge without telling the jury which side made a challenge and without mentioning rejected challenges except to say, "No others will be granted."

With voir dire reasonably limited as to time and subject matter, the jurors are fresh, interested, and ready to work when counsel rise to give their opening statements. The process may be even better if peremptory challenges are eliminated.

From time immemorial, each jury had twelve members. Some attribute this to Jesus having had twelve apostles, but no one really knows how the number was set; the jury's origins are too befogged in medieval history. What we do know is that twelve worked well. The number was big enough to provide collective wisdom and a strong cross section, yet small enough to permit collegial deliberations leading, usually, to a unanimous verdict. In the early 1970s, the Supreme Court decided that states could use smaller criminal juries—juries of six or eight, for example, instead of the traditional twelve. Some states made this change to save time and money (although little of either was at stake). Many federal districts took a similar approach in civil cases, adopting local rules that cut the size of the civil trial jury from twelve to six. In letting all of this happen, the Supreme Court said that the jury's having twelve members, rather than some other number, was a mere "historical accident" devoid of current significance. It did not explain why this accident had endured for seven centuries.

At about the same time, the Court upheld nonunanimous criminal verdicts of guilty, as long as nine of twelve jurors agreed; the risk of undermining public confidence in trial outcomes was accepted for no compelling reason. This too marked a sudden change; while some states had long permitted supermajority verdicts in civil cases (ten to two or nine to three, for example), unanimity was the traditional requirement for a criminal conviction or acquittal. Finally, as the jury began to weaken in the face of these decisions, the Court drew a line: in a serious criminal case, the state must provide a jury of at least six members, all of whose votes, if there are that few, are necessary for a valid conviction. Having discerned no magic in twelve, the Court has found magic in six.

At the time, only a few predicted that these jury-reducing decisions would damage the institution, but that is exactly what has happened. It is now widely recognized that juries of six are far less representative of a diverse society, and more prone to eccentric verdicts, than juries of twelve. What should have been obvious at the start has been confirmed by studies as scientific as possible given the subjective nature of the task. Twelve jurors represent the community more fully than six, bring more collective wisdom to the courtroom, and are likelier to reach a sound verdict that will enjoy public support. The difference in cost between a full-size jury and a truncated one is minuscule.

There is a dawning recognition that the detour into mini-juries should be ended, at least in felony cases and substantial civil trials. The federal courts have stayed with twelve for felony cases and, after two decades of letting each district determine its own civil jury size, have recently adopted a salutary rule: the judge in a federal civil case may now empanel a jury of twelve, or of six, or of any number in between. There are no alternate jurors. If a juror is excused during the trial for illness or some other reason, the jury is still validly constituted as long as six or more remain. Since no one is an alternate, everyone in the jury box is fully engaged from the start. A growing number of judges, using this rule, empanel civil juries of twelve. The work of these full-size juries is nearly always excellent.

—

"Too often," Justice Sandra Day O'Connor has written, "jurors are allowed to do nothing but listen passively to the testimony, without any idea what the legal issues are in the case, without permission to take notes or participate in any way, finally to be read a virtually incomprehensible set of instructions and sent into the jury room to reach a verdict in a case they may not understand much better than they did before the trial began." Especially in complex litigation, jurors need information at the start. An automobile collision or a simple larceny case may need little explanation, but in patent law, medical malpractice, commercial transactions, antitrust, securities fraud, and a myriad of other fields, the jury needs to be told at the outset what to look for. Jurors should not have to sit through days or weeks of testimony while wondering what difference it all makes. Mini-opening statements by the lawyers before empanelment—as short as five minutes—can help not only to raise jurors' comprehension but to engage their interest. The judge may need to summarize what the main legal elements will be. That puts an extra burden on the judge who, thinking the case may settle and go away, and who has plenty of other work to do, would rather deal with jury instructions only at the end. But it is worth the effort.

Jurors in criminal cases often have been sequestered for the duration of the trial. Confined to hotel rooms, limited to the company of each other and the court bailiffs, separated from their families, and given access only to preclipped newspapers and censored television, they have led a miserable existence in the name of impartiality. The theory is that they must be kept free of any outside influence—whether of bribery, or blundering comments by a friend, or inadvertent exposure to a prejudicial news story. But sequestered jurors tend to become irritable, dispirited, and fractious with each other. Any gain in purity is outweighed by damage not just to the jurors' personal lives, but to their ability to work together. And there is, in this practice, a note of condescension. To sequester jurors is to tell them, in effect, "We do not trust you."

Consider, in contrast, what is done in a bench trial, where the judge performs the jury's function as fact-finder and returns the equivalent of a verdict. We do not expect the judge to move to a hotel, lock himself in every night, be separated from his family, and see newspapers only after they have been clipped by the bailiff. We trust the judge to follow the rules and avoid outside communications about the case. We should do the same with jurors. It is enough to tell them the ground rules emphatically at the start, and remind them from time to time during the trial. They generally respect those rules. A juror who doesn't, and is found out, can ordinarily be excused without disrupting the trial. The risk that a trial may be marred by extrajudicial communication with a juror is small enough that the outmoded practice of sequestration should, with rare exceptions, be ended.

At the same time, judges can exercise their power to order that trial counsel refrain from making out-of-court statements that are likely, through media dissemination, to prejudice any party's right to a fair trial. In Great Britain the press is prohibited by law from publishing details that could influence a jury. In this country the First Amendment bars any such press restriction, but reasonable limits on lawyer speech are permitted. When those limits are enforced—as they were in the Oklahoma City bombing trials—even the lawyers usually are grateful; they have enough work to do in the courtroom without having to wage a second-front battle in the media. When lawyer posturing before the cameras is ruled out, everyone gains.

A simple and easily made change can transform the jury's courtroom experience: run trials without interruptions. The Simpson criminal trial jurors spent many days waiting in the jury room, or in hotel rooms, while the judge and lawyers thrashed out the admissibility of evidence and other legal points. They waited more hours while the judge and counsel held hundreds of "sidebars"—private huddles to argue and decide objections. Although that case is an extreme example, the practice is followed in many courts: one side asks for a conference; the judge grants the request and sends the jury out; the jurors, sitting in enforced idleness for hours or even days, become bored, frustrated, and resentful. Who wouldn't?

None of this is necessary, and the solution is very simple. The jurors are kept in the courtroom, listening to an uninterrupted flow of evidence, during all jury hours. There is no need to send them out of the room, or have them wait, while legal points are decided. Nearly all objections can be stated by counsel in a short word or phrase—"hearsay" or "irrelevant," for example—and ruled on by the judge immediately. Objections are not argued unless argument is asked for by the judge. If a hearing or argument is needed, it can be held at the next recess or after jury hours, or early the next morning, without interrupting the flow of evidence. Sidebars are avoided. Occasionally it is necessary to ask counsel to go to another subject or call another witness until an evidentiary dispute is decided, but that too can readily be done.

The stop-and-start trial—the trial in which jurors wait outside while the judge and lawyers talk in private—is easily replaced by the cogent, focused, smooth-running trial. Even lawyers who start out obstructive end up liking it. As federal judge Edward Rafeedie of Los Angeles, an expert expediter, points out, the "trial then takes on a beautiful rhythm that makes it a joy for the court, counsel, and, most of all, the jury."

A federal rule tells the judge to "exercise reasonable control over the mode and order of interrogating witnesses and presenting evidence so as to (1) make the interrogation and presentation effective for the ascertainment of the truth, (2) avoid needless consumption of time, and (3) protect witnesses from harassment or undue embarrassment." Similar rules, or inherent court powers, exist in every state. Yet, surprisingly, many judges have seen themselves as mere passive umpires who will let the trial run whatever course it may take, and who will speak only when counsel see fit to raise an objection. The result, all too often, is long-windedness, meandering detours into the irrelevant, and deadly repetition. ("They repeated things again and again as if we were idiots," said one of my daughters-in-law after jury service, which she nevertheless enjoyed.) A fair hearing does not mean endlessness. Counsel on both sides often do such a fine job that the judge need only rule on objections raised; but when the need arises to save the jury's time, not to mention its sanity, the court should use its long-standing power to move the proceedings along.

Trial time belongs to the public, and needs to be conserved like any other public asset. In some civil cases, especially those burdened by complexity and interparty hostility, it is well to set a trial time budget in advance. After getting the lawyers' estimates of how much time they will need, the judge sets a budget of so many trial days, the time to be divided equally between the two sides, with each side's questioning time (whether on direct or cross-examination) to be counted toward its quota. The judge or a clerk keeps track of the hours used and can tell the parties, at the end of any day, where they stand. There must be reasonable flexibility—the parties may be granted additional time if need is shown—but in practice the trial nearly always finishes at or within the time prescribed.

Time budgets are now provided for in the federal rules, but have always been within the court's inherent power. They are especially helpful now, with the demand for trial time far outstripping the supply in many jurisdictions. This technique, like any other, must be used with sensitivity. When it is, the results are nearly always favorable. "We had a better trial than we would have had without the time limit" is a typical comment by lawyers and clients.

Modern trials often call for an understanding of evidence about a specialized field. Jurors need help in understanding complex evidence—so do judges—and help is at hand.

Computer-generated summaries, videotapes, and other technological wonders can bring arcane subjects to life. The judge must make sure they are used fairly—which means, for one thing, that computer-generated dramatizations generally should be avoided. While data summaries are helpful, as are photographs and videotapes of actual

places and events, a computerized reenactment of how one side contends an accident happened, or some other event occurred, is usually
too much like a TV commercial to deserve a place in evidence.

If one side has markedly greater resources than the other, and would
gain an unfair advantage in a high-tech spending contest, there are
ways to keep the playing field level—for example, by directing that
resources such as computerized databases be shared.

Expert witnesses are the main sources of enlightenment about scientific or technical subjects. Of all our American trial practices, none is
more baffling to a European visitor than our use of partisan experts.
Typically, where expert testimony is needed—as to medicine, accounting, machinery design, commercial customs, shipboard practices, or
any number of other specialized fields—each side will hire its own witnesses, pay them, and help them get ready to testify. The judge serves
as gatekeeper to keep out the most unreliable testimony. But even after
that screening is done, swearing contests between opposing experts are
notorious. Experts are frankly seen as partisans; a leading trial lawyer
recently referred to them, at an advocacy training program, as "additional counsel" for the side that hires them. Some experts, of course,
have too much integrity to fall into that pattern and will stoutly say
whatever they believe, no matter where the chips fall. But in many
cases the jury is left with sharply conflicting expert views and with the
feeling that neither side's hired guns can be trusted.

The European approach is entirely different: an expert, if needed, is
appointed by the court, and testifies in aid of the court's inquiry. The
parties do not hire expert witnesses.

Consistent with maintaining the adversary system, we should not
extinguish the parties' right to call expert witnesses, who often do valuable work. But we must make better and wiser use of the court's ability
to appoint an expert of its own. The court "may appoint expert witnesses of its own selection," says a federal rule; state rules are similar.
The idea is to raise the judge's or jury's understanding of whatever field
is involved. Court-appointed experts have testified to good effect in
cases involving construction, accounting, computer technology, medi-

cine, and other specialized areas. Sometimes they serve without pay as
a public service; sometimes, when the parties are affluent, they receive
compensation equally from the litigants. They are open to cross-examination by both sides. Care must be taken to assure that the jury sees
the court-appointed expert as a helpful witness, not as the messiah. But
the dismay over partisan experts is greatly reduced, and confidence in
trials enhanced, when judges make careful use of their power to bring
disinterested expertise into the picture.

In the turbulent trials of earlier centuries, jurors asked questions, inter-
rupted testimony, even argued with witnesses. For a long time, however, we have been in the era of the passive juror. Judges, fearing that
some untoward word might slip out or some irrelevancy be uttered—
fearing also, and more profoundly, chaos in the courtroom (order shat-
tered, people shouting, the gavel banging in vain)—have required
jurors to sit silently and listen. A juror seeking to ask a question is told,
ordinarily, to subside; anything that matters will be brought out by the
lawyers. Once active participants, the jurors have been turned into
receptacles. This cramped view has made jury service both less effective
and less enjoyable.

A fair way to invite juror questions has been developed. The judge
explains at the start how it works: a juror with a question writes it on a
note and hands the note to the clerk, who gives it to the judge. The
judge reads the note silently and may put the question himself, or
deliver the note to counsel for their consideration, or, if the question is
out of bounds or superfluous, simply leave it unasked.

Experience has shown that jurors often ask excellent questions. The
lawyers gain knowledge of what needs to be explained or clarified. The
jurors gain increased understanding and a sense of participation. There
is no loss of rationality or decorum.

The traditional view has been that jurors should not take notes because
to do so might distract their attention from the witness, whose every
expression and nuance should be observed. Here again a groundless

distrust of jurors is at work. Nearly all judges take notes, even in bench trials where they must assess witness credibility. Why treat the jurors less favorably than the judge? Note-taking helps some jurors remember; many courts are finally allowing it. In a long trial, jurors may also benefit from memory aids such as labeled photographs of the witnesses who have testified and notebooks containing copies of the key exhibits for both sides.

Jury service is made harder than it needs to be by lawyers' and judges' addiction to legalese. It is laziness that prompts us to say "subsequent to" instead of "after," "execute the instrument" instead of "sign the lease," and "intentionally misstated" instead of "lied." Here is an example of what jurors are commonly subjected to—an instruction given in a Nevada trial for attempted murder:

> It is not essential that the willful intent, premeditation or deliberation, shall exist in the mind of the defendant for any considerable length of time before the actual perpetration of the crime. It is sufficient if there was a fixed design or determination to maliciously kill distinctly framed in the mind of this defendant before the shots were fired.

The only pithy phrase is "before the shots were fired," and even that is in the passive voice. The language comes from appellate court decisions, which, however profound they may be, are a poor source of words for the jury. With some effort, the jury may figure out what this instruction means:

> The state does not have to prove that the defendant planned for a long time to kill the other person. It is enough if he intended to kill him and fired the shots for that purpose.

Many legal concepts come packaged in unfamiliar words. The jury is entitled to have those words translated, and to have the court's instructions given succinctly and in plain English, with a written copy for each juror.

Sinking into the soft mattress of legalese is easier than speaking plainly. A career in law enforcement seems to foster a similar addiction. People never get out of the car; they always "exit the vehicle." "He applied his canine to the vehicle," said a police witness recently in my court. He did not mean that his fellow officer had bitten a tire with his eyetooth, but that he had sent his dog into the car to sniff for drugs.

Giving up legalese will be like giving up smoking: everyone in the vicinity will benefit.

Disagreements and doubts in the jury room often lead to questions sent out to the judge, usually by way of a note. Can you explain more what "beyond a reasonable doubt" means? Is a failure to pay on time always a breach of contract? Did *X* testify that the car ran the red light, or only that he wasn't sure? The bench's traditional answer has been unhelpful. "Remember the evidence and read the instructions again," jurors have been told, "and then decide the case." This has the virtue of effortlessness, but it is far better for the judge, after consulting with counsel, to give a meaningful answer. Jurors are entitled to something better than a rebuff. In a bench trial, we don't expect the judge to be content with a brush-off when she questions counsel during final arguments; jurors' questions should be treated with similar respect.

Occasionally a jury will send out a note saying it is deadlocked and asking what to do next. The judge's traditional answer can be summed up in two words: keep trying. In a criminal case that admonition can be given only once, as a rule, lest the jurors feel coerced to reach a verdict. If the jurors still don't agree, a hung jury and a mistrial may follow. Although hung juries are rare, and may lead to settlements rather than retrials, each one produces anticlimax and frustration. Many hung juries can be avoided by better responses to the messages from the jury room. When a deadlock is reported, the judge can ask the jurors if it would help to hear additional argument by counsel on some phase of the case. In a civil case, she can offer to have the parties present more evidence on whatever point is dividing the jury. She can ask if further instruction on a point of law might help. By responding in these ways, instead of stonewalling, the judge may open the way to a verdict while preserving fairness for both sides.

These are modest reforms, and some will argue that they don't go far enough. I believe that if adopted in full they will give our trials the focus, brevity, and economy they need. They empower the jury and activate the judge as supervisor of the search for truth, while keeping the freshness, rigor, and energy of the adversary method. The Simpson trial and the White Plains libel case, for example, would have been entirely different if handled in this way.

To make these changes is easy. Most of them can be accomplished, with no amendment of the rules, simply by judges using their existing powers to make trials better. (Exceptions are increasing juror pay and reducing or abolishing peremptory challenges, which would require changes in the law.) When these reforms are adopted, trials are strengthened and there is no downside; all concerned—juries and judges, parties and lawyers and the public—come out ahead.

The Church and the Streets

Cases are brought and then tried—so it has been since time out of memory, and so the pattern lives on in our heads. But in reality a fundamental change has taken place. No more than one criminal case in ten is actually tried. Nearly all the rest are disposed of by plea bargains; to keep going, the criminal justice system relies on negotiated guilty pleas.

The picture is similar in civil litigation. A civil trial can be a thing of beauty, and many are, but at least 90 percent of civil cases are settled or dismissed.

So while we reform trials, we must be aware that most cases never see one. We have developed, beneath the surface, a legal culture of settlement; compromise, not trial, is now the dominant method of lawsuit resolution in the United States. To hark back to earlier chapters, we have moved farther from the combative Anglo-Saxon showdowns and closer to the mediation ways of the Gold Coast Ashanti. We square off and circle each other, but usually stop short of a full battle.

This massive shift from trial to settlement has come, without forethought or intent, through the market forces of justice. People need to get their disputes resolved. When trials are expensive, risky, and slow, they turn elsewhere to satisfy that need. In our society they have turned to settlement.

An emphasis on reaching agreement is no cause for regret, and may even merit celebration, but serious flaws remain in this part of our legal life. Ordinarily, the key events leading to a plea or a settlement take place in private—in lawyers' offices, deposition rooms, document depositories—with little participation or even awareness by the trial judge. In dollars spent, time devoted, and importance to the outcome, the work of discovery and negotiation usually is the ball game. Yet most judges, focused on trials and comfortable in the courtroom and chambers, have tended to ignore the larger arena where most of the action takes place. The pretrial process in countless cases, left untended, has fallen victim to overzealous partisanship and the unfair results that come with it.

The courthouse has been like a church and pretrial like the streets outside. In the church, a black-robed figure presides and everyone is on good behavior, saying good morning, kneeling at the right times, singing the hymns together. But most of the time the congregants are out of sight, and when they are in the streets they go at each other with tire irons and baseball bats.

Judges need to walk into those streets, and many are doing so. To make improvements there is harder than to reform trials, because we are dealing not with a single focused event in the judge's presence but with a series of events, usually extending over weeks or months, occurring in the judge's absence. Yet trials, and trial by jury, can be healthy only as the summit of a system that itself is healthy. If civil litigants are financially exhausted before they reach the courthouse steps, if delay puts justice out of reach, if criminal defendants lack any real voice in plea negotiations, if overaggressive or dishonest behavior during pretrial is rewarded, trials become little more than museum exhibits.

In civil litigation the great problem has been discovery—the pretrial process of gathering documents and other tangible evidence, asking and answering written questions, and taking depositions. The expense of uncontrolled discovery—and the bitterness engendered by discovery wars of attrition or concealment—can bury the merits of a case.

Yet all discovery is open to judicial supervision. The judge may set time and subject matter limits, or the court may do so by rule; Arizona, for example, now limits any deposition to four hours unless all parties agree to a longer time or the judge orders one. The judge may decide, in a simple case, that no depositions will be taken; once the documents

THE CHURCH AND THE STREETS

are produced and witness lists exchanged, the case is ready for mediation or trial. The judge may—and nearly always should—set a firm
early trial date, bearing in mind that discovery, in a variant of Parkin-
son's Law, will expand to fill the time available for its completion.
Nothing turns off the expense spigot so firmly as a prompt trial. And
the judge should make clear that he is willing and able to rule quickly
on any discovery dispute. That may be done by an order setting the
ground rules: civil behavior will prevail, there will be no obstructive
tactics or undue repetition, and the lawyers may place a conference
telephone call to the judge to get a ruling on any discovery dispute.
The tedious process of adjourning a deposition, filing a written
motion, briefing it, and then obtaining a written ruling, is avoided.
This method brings great benefits with few telephone calls; the mere
knowledge that the judge is available tends to eliminate the problems.
When a call does come, the judge usually can take it at once or at a trial
recess, and make a ruling immediately. In cases where discovery problems are numerous or complex, a discovery master—who, if the parties
can afford it, may be a private lawyer compensated by them—can be
appointed to provide similar services. By these methods, discovery can
be tamed; when it is, the lawyers are as grateful as everyone else.

The desirability of settlement goes back a long way. Jesus, according to
Saint Matthew, said: "Agree with thine adversary quickly, whiles thou
art with him in the way; lest haply the adversary deliver thee to the
judge, and the judge deliver thee to the officer, and thou be cast into
prison." We have tended to forget the "quickly" part. Because the
courts have treated settlement as a kind of accidental by-product of litigation, one left entirely to the parties, closure often comes later than it
should—after too much money has been spent, time lost, emotions
inflamed. Recognizing this, litigants are turning more and more to
alternative dispute resolution—ADR—which can be done at any stage
of a case. The phenomenal growth of ADR, and especially of mediation, over the past decade marks a sea change in American civil litiga-

tion. Although called an "alternative" method of dispute resolution, mediation is quickly becoming the standard. It does not conflict with trial by jury, but supplements it in a beneficial way.

One of the first to see this trend was Gerard Shellan, a widely admired presiding judge of the King County Superior Court in Seattle. Judge Shellan made himself available for settlement conferences at seven o'clock on most weekday mornings, before trial hours; in twelve years he held about 1,200 such conferences, nearly all of them successful. In 1989, believing that the traditional pattern of discovery and trial had grown too expensive for most people, he resigned from the bench and became a private mediator. Since then, while donating a large part of his fees to charity, Judge Shellan has mediated 1,800 more cases, many of them highly complex, of which 95 percent have settled. "Nowadays," he says, "most civil case lawyers expect mediation, not trial, to be the process." With Shellan's help, mediation training and a free clinic have been established at the University of Washington School of Law.

Litigants flock to mediation for the simplest of reasons: it offers justice through an affordable and satisfying process. A mediator (unlike an arbitrator) does not reach a decision or enter a judgment. Instead, by serving as go-between, adviser, listener, and shuttle diplomat, the mediator helps the parties and their lawyers reach agreement. The case is ended only if and when both sides are willing to accept a compromise.

A mediation lasting half a day may settle a case that would take weeks to try. And the process, if done well, achieves more than simply ending the dispute. It also gives the litigants a version of their day in court. They are given a chance to vent—to make their arguments and express their feelings, usually out of the presence of the other side, to a sympathetic listener. Mediators often find that the main thing a party wanted was a chance to tell his or her story. There is catharsis in this, and in reaching, with the mediator's guidance, an agreed solution. The emotional as well as financial needs of the litigants are served, and the expense, stress, and risks of trial are avoided.

Arbitrations—informal trials before one or more privately selected arbitrators who decide the case—also have surged in popularity, and in 2000 outnumbered court trials for the first time.

Private ADR firms, offering the services of retired judges and other dispute resolution experts, have sprung up in every major city. Among practicing lawyers, serving as mediator or arbitrator has become a new and profitable specialty. Abraham Lincoln foresaw the value of this when he was a leading Illinois trial lawyer. "Persuade your neighbors to compromise whenever you can," he advised his colleagues. "Point out to them how the nominal winner is often a real loser—in fees, expenses, and waste of time. As a peacemaker the lawyer has a superior opportunity of being a good man." Churches, neighborhood clubs, and business associations now offer similar services in disputes ranging from family crises to patent infringement. The greatest benefits, as usual, go to the litigants who are best informed and best represented; major corporations make frequent use of ADR in settling lawsuits among themselves.

The question is not whether ADR will succeed on a grand scale—it will—but whether it will be publicly provided, to the poor as well as the affluent, through the courts. It must be if we truly aspire to justice for all.

A 1998 statute requires that ADR be made available in all federal courts, but Congress was only trying to catch up with a reality already sweeping the country. A leading example of what should be done is provided by the federal district court in San Francisco. That court, led by Magistrate Judge Wayne Brazil and the late Judge Robert Peckham, has developed a comprehensive set of ADR options, chiefly mediation and early neutral evaluation (in which an expert listens to condensed versions of the parties' contentions and gives them a nonbinding opinion of their prospects). Another is the federal court in Kansas City, Missouri, which has hired Kent Snapp, an experienced trial lawyer, as a highly productive full-time mediator. Snapp had retired to a life of ease, but came back to the legal wars because, as he puts it, "I missed the stress and chaos." A study has shown that between May 1994 and December 1996, Kansas City federal mediation saved the litigants $16 million in fees and expenses. Still another example is the Maricopa County superior court at Phoenix, Arizona, which offers a full range of ADR clinics with explanatory brochures and a roster of qualified neutrals.

In the federal court for western Washington we have had, for more than twenty years, a panel of volunteer lawyers who serve as civil case mediators. The program began as a temporary measure to alleviate a backlog, but succeeded so well that it has become a mainstay of this district's federal justice. For the first decade or so the lawyer-mediators served without compensation; thousands of cases were resolved with their help. Over time, the program's popularity, and ever-growing demands on the mediators' working time, led to a rule change permitting the parties to pay the mediator if they agree to do so. Now, more often than not, the mediator is compensated by agreement.

The expense and delay of civil litigation are prompting not just American courts, but those in Europe as well, to develop quick and economical versions of the traditional day in court. The Dutch have devised a popular method called the *kort geding*. It evolved from the procedure used to decide whether a preliminary injunction should be issued at the start, and offers a short hearing, available in any civil case, in which the judge listens briefly to both sides and then tells them what their chances in a full action appear to be. The process is similar to the "early neutral evaluation" method used in parts of this country. The usual result is settlement, and the average *kort geding* case is finished within six weeks from its start. Satisfaction with the process is reported to be high.

Court-connected ADR programs, some using full-time staff ADR specialists, are springing up in state and federal courts nationwide. Many judges themselves offer judicial settlement conferences—a form of mediation—to litigants who need them. These, of course, are done without charge. A judge skilled in helping parties reach agreement nearly always can achieve success.

—

In criminal cases, plea bargaining, the dominant mode of resolving cases, usually is done by the contending lawyers with no help from the court. The prosecutor and defense counsel meet, talk, and decide how the case should come out. The prosecutor's chief weapon is the threat of more serious charges or a heightened sentence if a deal is not struck; the defense lawyer's leverage is the need of the prosecutor and the court for a plea bargain because of overcrowded calendars.

The compromise they reach may have little to do with the facts of the case; for that reason, some critics argue that plea bargaining subverts justice and should be prohibited. I don't think that is a wise or practicable proposal; the parties should have the ability to reach a fair and voluntary compromise of a criminal case. "Voluntary," though, is a key word, and these days it often rings hollow when plea bargaining is distorted by the government's superior bargaining power. Mandatory sentencing laws—for example, those requiring heavy fixed prison terms for drug dealers regardless of their age or mitigating circumstances—effectively shift discretion from the judge to the prosecutor. The prosecutor, not the court, has the power to exempt a defendant from the mandatory prison term, either by reducing the charge or pronouncing that defendant "cooperative." So intense is the pressure that some defendants plead guilty to lesser offenses they did not commit rather than take their chances on a trial. The process is further skewed by the use of cooperating witnesses—accomplices of the defendant, usually, who are promised light sentences, or even nonprosecution, if they testify for the government. These witnesses may be of doubtful reliability but often are indispensable. Since the judge ordinarily can show leniency to a cooperator, the sentencing disparities can become enormous: a half-dozen entrepreneurs, for example, all of whom entered the country in the same cocaine-carrying plane or boat, may be given sentences ranging from probation to decades in prison.

What the plea bargaining process needs most urgently is the repeal of mandatory prison-term statutes that deprive the court of any chance to use common sense or sound judgment in sentencing. That would go far toward restoring balance to the negotiations. With or without that change, the process needs neutral help, and the courts should provide it. Judges traditionally have stood aside; court rules, intended to prevent plea coercion, prohibit the trial judge from taking part in plea bargaining. But there is nothing to prevent another judge of the same court from aiding the negotiations upon request.

The story of one young Mexican woman illustrates what can be done. She was charged with having taken part in a conspiracy to distribute cocaine. Although she had only answered a few telephone calls for her drug-dealing husband, and had no prior record, she faced a mandatory prison sentence of five years. Neither the prosecutor nor anyone else involved thought that would be fair—she had never dealt drugs herself and she had small children to care for at home—but the prosecutor felt unable simply to reduce or drop the charge. Cooperation with law enforcement was her only possible route to escape the five-year sentence; without that, the sentencing judge would have no choice. Her husband and his closest accomplices already had been tried and found guilty, so she would not have to testify against them. But she was afraid to provide a single word of help in the government's effort to locate other cocaine suppliers. Terrified, she was headed for disaster. The trial judge, with both sides consenting, appointed me to assist in plea negotiations. I met with her, the defense lawyer, the prosecutor, and an interpreter. The young woman was at first so frightened she could hardly speak. I put her at ease by talking to her in Spanish— not well or fluently (which would be beyond me), and not about the case, but about her family and hometown. When we got to the subject at hand we used the interpreter, and the U.S. attorney reasonably proposed that she answer three simple questions—whether she had ever seen *X, Y,* or *Z* at her house—in return for which the government would pronounce her cooperative, and the five-year sentence could be avoided. Able by this time to listen to what her lawyer and I were saying, the young woman accepted the offer. Then, at an interview attended by both counsel, she answered the government's three questions. A few days later she pleaded guilty and was sentenced by the assigned judge to probation. She had avoided five years in prison, and her children would still have their mother. It may be argued that the sentencing laws should not compel such maneuvering to reach a just result; but sometimes they do.

Mediation in criminal cases must be done with great care; not just the interest of the defendant and the prosecutor, but those of the victim and the public are at stake. A capable mediator can serve those interests well where one-on-one plea bargaining, with no help from a neutral, might fail.

To extend the court's reach from the "church" into the "streets" will require increased versatility by judges and greater use of proxies—staff attorneys, discovery masters, and mediators. The change will take us one step toward Europe, where judges are more active than ours have been, without sacrificing any valuable part of what we have. We will still have momentous trials, and trials for all who need them. But the justice system will be complete only when it brings economy, fairness, and speed into the vast litigation arena outside the courtroom. Litigants will come to the courthouse of the future expecting not just a well-run trial, if trial proves necessary, but expense control, case management, and expert help in reaching agreement. By providing those services, the courts can keep their central place in dispute resolution.

LITIGATION IN THE TWENTY-FIRST CENTURY

We are still walking the road that began with the hue and cry and took us through trial by ordeal or magic, the invention of trial by reason and evidence, the rise of the jury as a check on arbitrary power, the evolution of rules of fair play, and the jury's democratization in a highly industrialized and diverse society. Where we go from here is largely up to us. We can decide where the road will lead.

If we choose to, we can have a future in which trial by jury is not just preserved but is better than ever; those with low incomes, or none, have access to justice; ADR is offered both in courts and in neighborhood centers; and plea bargaining in criminal cases is free of coercion by either side. In civil cases, we can and probably will redefine a standard "day in court" to mean not a full-fledged trial but a brief appearance before a judge or other neutral who will listen, advise, and help the parties reach agreement. At the same time, we can provide a full and fair trial to those who need one. All this will be affordable and open to us if we want it enough to build carefully on what we have.

Judges can accomplish much of what has to be done, but an adversary system like ours can flourish only if the lawyers also do their jobs well. There is much reason to believe that they will. Lawyers, like any other providers, are subject to market forces; they must respond to the demand for high-quality affordable service. They are doing so, for example, by embracing ADR. Beyond that, the great majority of the nation's 900,000 lawyers are conscientious professionals who care not only about fees but about justice, just as doctors care not only about billings but about health.

I have known many lawyers who were and are justly admired: they honor the rules, deal honestly with opponents, serve their clients faithfully, and donate valuable time to deserving causes. There are far more of them than the public realizes. Nevertheless, the last three decades have seen a marked decline in the bar's good name and morale. A recent chairman of the ABA's Litigation Section, himself a distinguished trial lawyer, called it a "sea change" in reputation: "The whole lot of us are now seen by broad segments of the public—from corporate executives to the poor—as a blot on society; expensive, elitist, overpaid, unethical, mean-spirited Rambos."

Thoughtful lawyers agree that something like this has happened. The Supreme Court changed the profession in the 1970s by ruling that bar associations and state regulators may not prohibit lawyers from advertising or soliciting. Now, in a bottom-line-obsessed society, with heightened competition for clients and weakened ethical constraints, lawyers jostle for business in ways that traditionally were deemed unprofessional. Self-promoters trumpet their prowess in talk shows and press conferences. Advertising and client solicitation are widespread and widely unwelcome. Traditional courtesy among lawyers has faded, while hostility and abuse have increased. Whether the public is helped by any of this is doubtful; what is certain is that the bar has been damaged.

The American Bar Association model rules of professional conduct say that every lawyer "has a responsibility to provide legal services to those unable to pay and personal involvement in the problems of the disadvantaged can be one of the most rewarding experiences in the life of a lawyer." Many state bar codes have similar provisions. Yet pro bono work is performed to any substantial degree only by about one practicing lawyer in four, with the other three usually pleading lack of time. "There is a great need out there—especially with governments cutting back on legal aid to the poor," says Matthew Kenney, a successful Seattle trial lawyer. Kenney devotes half his working hours to pro bono, but his efforts to persuade colleagues to contribute far less than that bring more promises than results.

"You became a judge at just the right time," one of my former partners told me. "Practicing law is not the pleasure it used to be."

Yet even in this new setting, every lawyer can choose to be upright, ethical, and publicly quiet. Paradoxically, the able lawyers who make that choice tend to enjoy more worldly success than those who don't. And the making of that choice by hundreds of thousands is the one sure way to elevate the bar's good name.

Today there is a strong movement among lawyers to rejuvenate the profession's high ideals. I believe that movement can succeed, but the bar—recognizing both its privileged position in society and the unmet needs of the nation's poor and middle-income people—needs to make two improvements in its service to the public. It should reduce its opposition to "unauthorized practice" by nonlawyers who help people with simple legal matters not involving contested court proceedings— with simple wills and agreed-upon divorces, for example. Paralegals can be trained to handle such matters competently, and enlarging the corps of service providers will be vital to any full-scale effort to solve the problem of unequal justice. The profession needs also to close the gap between its ideal of pro bono service and the reality that too few lawyers do anything to fulfill it. A requirement that each lawyer devote so many hours per year to work without charge for those who cannot pay, or provide some equivalent service, should be considered. Students at several law schools recently have adopted mandatory pro bono for themselves as a graduation requirement—a generous decision that marks an encouraging trend.

Success will also depend on the public. Any court system must have a public that will, by and large, abide by the rules of litigation and accept the results. Ours in particular needs jurors who will show up—will report for jury duty instead of ducking it—and will put in the time needed, listen impartially, and decide intelligently. If the American public ever becomes so divided or selfish or ignorant that these requisites go unmet, the justice system will fail (along with everything else). I don't think that will happen.

—

The legislatures, federal and state, are entitled to be sure that funds appropriated for the courts are well spent. The problem has not been any lack of that assurance, but simply a refusal to provide for unmistakable needs. Overload—a true crisis in many courts—cannot be eliminated without resources.

Neither can the chronic difficulty of extending justice to the poor. If every lawyer in the country gave time to pro bono work, and every legislature adequately funded court operations and juror compensation, there would still be a need to open the system to those who cannot pay. To satisfy that need will require appropriations—for public defenders, legal aid providers, and the establishment of neighborhood dispute resolution centers. The cost would be modest; the gain in social well-being would be enormous.

The public, it appears, would support reasonable funding. A recent American Bar Association–sponsored survey turned up a remarkable statistic: when asked to estimate how much of the federal, state, and local budgets is spent on civil and criminal justice, the respondents said, on average, 27 percent. Most expressed a willingness to devote more to these functions. Their impressions were no doubt influenced by the prominent role trials play in the media.

The correct answer is about 3 percent—four-fifths of which goes to police and correctional functions. Nationwide, only six-tenths of 1 percent of public funds goes to the rest, including the courts. The United States courts—some of which are swamped with lawsuits—receive two-tenths of 1 percent of the federal budget. When legislators recognize that taxpayers expect timely justice, and are willing to pay the reasonable cost of getting it, adequate funding may follow.

Because the trial jury is part of a legal culture whose health is linked to its own, this book has looked beyond the courthouse walls. We do need improvements in society at large—especially in access to justice and in eliminating the effects of poverty and race—as well as in the courtroom. But to make our system work in the twenty-first century, we do not need to abandon its main features.

We do not need to weaken the requirement that a criminal case verdict be unanimous. The cost of the unanimity rule is small, and its value in causing jurors to listen carefully to one another, and occasionally in avoiding an unjust conviction, is great. The federal courts require unanimity in civil cases as well. Almost thirty states, for many years, have accepted nonunanimous civil verdicts (of ten to two, for example), and that is reasonable. But in criminal cases we should stand our ground nationwide.

We do not need to stack jury panels to assure greater minority representation. African Americans and Hispanics have tended to be underrepresented on juries. To remedy this, some scholars propose to lessen the randomness of jury selection by deliberately adding minorities to the roster and subtracting an equal number of whites. But the assumption behind this idea—that jurors vote, or should vote, as ethnic or interest-group representatives—is false. We are a nation of Protestants, Catholics, Jews, Muslims, Buddhists, and believers in countless other creeds, plus atheists and agnostics. We came, or our forebears came, from Europe, Asia, Africa, and all parts of the Americas. What we have most deeply in common is our devotion to the rule of law. That shared value, the foundation of justice, is undermined if we pick jury panels according to race or ethnicity or any factor other than citizenship itself. The way to increase minority participation is not to manipulate the roster but to make it as inclusive as possible while eliminating economic barriers to service.

Above all, we do not need to abandon trial by jury. The main current of fairness and intelligence among the populace, the basis of self-government, is still there. Everyone knows that fools are sometimes elected to public office, even against worthy opponents, but few contend that elections should be abolished. Instead, we vow to do better— to pay more attention, increase voter turnout, get qualified candidates to file, maybe even limit the pernicious influence of money in politics.

We aim to make elections better, not to give them up. So it should be with that other great invention of democracy, the trial jury.

As a new century begins, the jury's work is often difficult; we have moved from simple farm boundary disputes to battles over computer software copyrights, from cattle rustling to securities fraud, from basic swearing contests to evidence at the frontiers of technology. Racial and economic divisions continue to plague us. Yet the trial jury is showing that courtroom justice is still safe in the hands of the people. The jury faces fresh challenges in the complexity of its work and the divisive stresses felt by its members, but it will succeed, as it has succeeded in the past, if we give it a fair chance. That means improving its working conditions in court, the information and guidance it receives, and the system of justice that surrounds it.

Remember what happened when William Penn entreated the jurors in his 1670 trial to "give not away your right." "Nor will we ever do it!" came a voice from the jury box. Our answer should be the same.

A bibliography on the vast landscape glimpsed in this book could fill a tome in itself, and these notes list only a sampling of books, articles, and case reports of interest. For those who want to read more about trial by jury, I recommend six works as indispensable:

Alexis de Tocqueville, *Democracy in America,* trans. Francis Bowen, ed. Phillips Bradley (New York: Alfred A. Knopf, 1976 [1840]), contains the classic analysis of the jury as a political institution. Jerome Frank, *Courts on Trial* (Princeton, N.J.: Princeton University Press, 1949), strikes me as wrong in many respects, but is often cited and remains a trenchant critique of the jury. Harry Kalven, Jr., and Hans Zeisel, *The American Jury* (Boston: Little, Brown, 1966), is the first major assessment of jury performance using social science methods. Jeffrey Abramson, *We, the Jury* (New York: Basic Books, paperback ed., 1995), is a first-rate history of the criminal jury and its connection to American liberty. A law review volume, "The American Civil Jury: Illusion and Reality," 48 *De Paul Law Review* No. 2 (1998), thoroughly analyzes the research done on the civil jury's performance in the late twentieth century. *World Jury Systems*, ed. Neil Vidmar (New York: Oxford University Press, 2000), describes the varieties of trial by jury currently found in the world and assesses their strengths and weaknesses.

INTRODUCTION

xiii   The Tocqueville quotation is from *Democracy in America,* p. 285.

xiii–xiv "With about 1.5 million Americans serving . . ." The estimate is from the National Center for State Courts. See Paula L. Hannaford, et al.,

"How Judges View Civil Juries," 48 *De Paul Law Review* 247, 252 n.25 (1998).

The population/congressional representation figures are drawn from *Historical Statistics of the United States*, vol. 2 (Washington, D.C.: United States Bureau of the Census, 1975), p. 1084; J. D. B. DeBow, *Statistical View of the United States* (Washington, D.C.: United States Senate, 1854), p. 82; and Steven A. Holmes, "After Standing Up to Be Counted, Americans Number 281,421,906," *New York Times,* December 29, 2000, A1.

CHAPTER 1: THE ENDANGERED JURY

1   The "very palladium of free government": see *The Federalist No. 83,* 499 (Alexander Hamilton), ed. Clinton Rossiter (New York: New American Library, 1961).

"Were I called upon . . .": *The Papers of Thomas Jefferson, 1789,* vol. 15, ed. Julian P. Boyd and William H. Gaines, Jr. (Princeton, N.J.: Princeton University Press, 1958), 282–83.

"[A] howling anachronism": Franklin Strier, "Justice by Jury Is a Myth," *Los Angeles Times,* July 18, 1994, B7.

2   On the role of money in the initiative process: David S. Broder, *Democracy Derailed* (New York: Harcourt, 2000).

On the history of the right to vote and voter apathy today: Alexander Keyssar, *The Right to Vote: The Contested History of Democracy in the United States* (New York: Basic Books, 2000).

2–3   Chief Justice Burger on the civil jury: Warren E. Burger, "Agenda for Change," 54 *Judicature* 232, 234–35 (1971); "The State of the Federal Judiciary—1971," 57 *American Bar Association Journal* 855, 858 (September 1971); and "The Use of Lay Jurors in Complicated Civil Cases," Remarks to the Conference of State Chief Judges (August 7, 1979).

Michael Lind on the criminal jury: "Jury Dismissed," in *Postmortem: The O. J. Simpson Case,* ed. Jeffrey Abramson (New York: Basic Books, 1996).

Judge Babiarz is quoted in Mark Curriden, "Tipping the Scales," *Dallas Morning News,* May 7, 2000, 1A.

Valerie Hans is quoted in Mark Curriden, "Putting the Squeeze on Juries," 86 *American Bar Association Journal* 52 (August 2000).

Professor Alschuler's comment is from his article, "Explaining the Public Wariness of Juries," 48 *De Paul Law Review* 407, 411 (1998).

Judge Posner's prediction is from his article, "Juries on Trial," 99 *Commentary* 49 (1995).

3–5   On Governor Wilson's demand for less-than-unanimous jury verdicts: Bill Boyarsky, "The O. J. Simpson Murder Trial: Unanimous Verdicts Also on Trial," *Los Angeles Times,* July 19, 1995, A17.

The percentage of federal criminal charges tried to a jury: William Glaberson, "Juries' Role Erodes in Nation's Courtrooms," *New York Times,* March 2, 2001, A1. The same article points out that federal appeals courts are reversing certain types of jury damage awards twice as often as they did a decade ago. See also Kevin M. Clermont and Theodore Eisenberg, "Anti-Plaintiff Bias in the Federal Appellate Courts," 84 *Judicature* 128 (2000).

On the Texas battle over jury verdicts, see *Wal-Mart Stores, Inc. v. Gonzales,* 968 S.W. 2d 934 (Tex. 1999), and earlier cases cited in that decision.

On the withdrawal of whole areas from the jury's reach, see the excellent series by Mark Curriden and Allen Pusey, "Juries on Trial," *Dallas Morning News,* May–Nov. 2000. Professor King's quote is at 24A in the May 7, 2000, edition.

The Supreme Court's patent case is *Markman v. Westview Instruments, Inc.,* 517 U.S. 370, 388 (1996).

In favor of a "complexity exception": *In re Japanese Electronic Products Antitrust Litigation,* 631 F.2d 1069, 1088–89 (3rd Cir. 1980). Against it: *In re United States Financial Securities Litigation,* 609 F.2d 411, 430–31 (9th Cir. 1979).

On the increased use of summary judgments in civil cases, see Charles A. Wright, et al., *Federal Practice and Procedure* (1995 &

Supp. 1999), at §2529; James A. Henderson and Theodore Eisenberg, "The Quiet Revolution in Products Liability: An Empirical Study of Legal Change," 37 *U.C.L.A. Law Review* 479 (1990); Eric Schnapper, "Judges Against Juries: Appellate Review of Federal Civil Jury Verdicts," 1989 *Wisconsin Law Review* 237.

"Why have a jury at all?": William Glaberson, "Juries, Their Powers Under Siege," *New York Times,* March 2, 2001, A1.

5   Low turnouts for jury duty: Robert G. Boatright, "Why Citizens Don't Respond to Jury Summonses and What Courts Can Do About It," 82 *Judicature* 156 (1999).

6   On the trend in England, see Sally Lloyd-Bostock and Cheryl Thomas, "The Continuing Decline of the English Jury," *World Jury Systems,* ch. 2. "[A] different brand of justice altogether": D. J. McBarnet, *Conviction: Law, the State and the Construction of Justice,* quoted in Lloyd-Bostock and Thomas, p. 89.

Ronald Jay Cohen is quoted in Mark Curriden, "Putting the Squeeze on Juries," 86 *American Bar Association Journal* 52 (August 2000).

CHAPTER II: CIVILIZED FIGHTS

7   *Brown v. Board of Education* is reported at 347 U.S. 483 (1954).

8–11   The Hamilton-Burr duel and its historic setting are described in Joseph J. Ellis, *Founding Brothers: The Revolutionary Generation* (New York: Alfred A. Knopf, 2000), and Arnold A. Rogow, *A Fatal Friendship: Alexander Hamilton and Aaron Burr* (New York: Hill and Wang, 1998). I have accepted Professor Ellis's view of what probably happened when the shots were fired. Accounts are also given in biographies of the two men: John C. Miller, *Alexander Hamilton: Portrait in Paradox* (New York: Harper, 1959); Richard Brookhiser, *Alexander Hamilton, American* (New York: The Free Press, 1999); and Milton Lomask, *Aaron Burr: The Years from Princeton to Vice President, 1756–1805* (New York: Farrar, Straus and Giroux, 1979).

The duel's political meaning is analyzed in Joanne B. Freeman, "Dueling as Politics: Reinterpreting the Burr-Hamilton Duel," 53 *William and Mary Quarterly* (April 1996).

Gore Vidal's novel *Burr* (New York: Ballantine Books, paperback ed., 1990) gives a droll contrarian view of Burr's life and misfortunes.

11–16   Cain and Abel: Genesis 4:1–17.

A good short survey of legal anthropology, with a bibliography, is Simon Roberts, *Order and Dispute: An Introduction to Legal Anthropology* (New York: St. Martin's Press, 1979). Among the classics in the field are Bronislaw Malinowski, *Crime and Custom in Savage Society* (London: Kegan Paul, 1926), and E. Adamson Hoebel, *The Law of Primitive Man* (Cambridge, Mass.: Harvard University Press, 1961).

Litigation vignettes from around the world are offered in John H. Wigmore, *A Kaleidoscope of Justice* (Washington, D.C.: Washington Law Book Co., 1941).

A sampling of ancient and modern trial stories and methods, beautifully illustrated, is *Law: A Treasury of Art and Literature,* ed. Sara Robbins (New York: Hugh Lanter Levin Associates, Inc., 1990).

16–17   Sophocles mentions a hot-iron ordeal in ancient Greece. A sentry is denying that he or his companions committed the forbidden act of burying the corpse of a slain enemy:

> *We were all ready to take hot iron in hand*
> *And go through fire and swear by God and heaven*
> *We hadn't done it, nor knew of anyone*
> *That could have thought of doing it, much less done it.*

Sophocles, *Antigone,* in *The Theban Plays,* trans. E. F. Watling (New York: Penguin Books, 1951), p. 133.

The account of the Barotse trial by ordeal is from Margaret Carson Hubbard, *African Gamble* (New York: G. P. Putnam's Sons, 1937), p. 129.

18–20   "Nothing makes us men . . .": Michel de Montaigne, 1 *Montaigne Essays,* trans. John Florio (London: J. M. Dent, 1980), p. 47.

Abrams v. United States is reported at 250 U.S. 616 (1919). Justice Holmes's opinion is illuminated in Anthony Lewis, *Make No Law: The*

Sullivan Case and the First Amendment (New York: Random House, 1991).

20–21   The kinship of trials and theater is described in Milner S. Ball, "The Play's the Thing: An Unscientific Reflection on Courts Under the Rubric of Theater," 28 *Stanford Law Review* 81 (1975).

"Life is painting a picture . . .": "Address to the Fiftieth Anniversary of the Harvard Graduating Class of 1861 (June 28, 1911)," in *The Occasional Speeches of Justice Oliver Wendell Holmes,* ed. Mark D. Howe (Cambridge, Mass.: Belknap Press, 1962), p. 161.

CHAPTER III: FROM REVELATION TO VERDICT

23–28   Life in England a millennium ago can be glimpsed in Christopher Brooke, *From Alfred to Henry III, 871–1272* (New York: Norton, 1969); Robert Howard Hodgkin, *A History of the Anglo-Saxons* (London: Oxford University Press, 1939); and R. I. Page, *Life in Anglo-Saxon England* (New York: G. P. Putnam's Sons, 1970).

A sampling of Ælfric's homilies, translated into modern English, is given in *Anglo-Saxon Prose,* ed. and trans. Michael Swanton (London: J. M. Dent, 1975).

28–31   The old English trial methods are described with wit, and a total lack of nostalgia, in Charles Rembar, *The Law of the Land: The Evolution of Our Legal System* (New York: Simon & Schuster, 1980). See also Alan Harding, *A Social History of English Law* (London: Penguin Books, 1966).

32–36   On the rise of trial by jury, see Theodore Frank Thomas Plucknett, *A Concise History of the Common Law*, 5th ed. (London: Butterworth & Co., 1956); R. C. van Caenegem, *The Birth of the English Common Law,* 2d ed. (Cambridge, England: Cambridge University Press, 1988); Leonard W. Levy, *The Palladium of Justice: Origins of Trial by Jury* (Chicago: Ivan R. Dee, 1999); Rembar, *The Law of the Land;* and Stephan A. Landsman, "A Brief Survey of the Development of the Adversary System," 44 *Ohio State Law Journal* 713 (1983).

The importance of the English local courts, as distinguished from the royal courts, is examined in John P. Dawson, *A History of Lay Judges* (Cambridge, Mass.: Harvard University Press, 1960).

36–37   On the irrational values that survive in modern trials: Moffatt Hancock, "Conflict, Drama and Magic in the Early English Law," 14 *Ohio State Law Journal* 119 (1953).

37–41   *Regina v. Dudley and Stephens* is reported at 14 Q.B.D. 273 (1884). The case, and the history of cannibalism among the shipwrecked, are recounted unforgettably in A. W. Brian Simpson, *Cannibalism and the Common Law: The Story of the Tragic Last Voyage of the* Mignonette *and the Strange Legal Proceedings to Which It Gave Rise* (Chicago: University of Chicago Press, 1984).

A classic article using a made-up case to pose similar dilemmas for the bench is Lon L. Fuller, "The Case of the Speluncean Explorers," 62 *Harvard Law Review* 616 (1948). Postscripts celebrating Professor Fuller's article, a half-century later, are at 112 *Harvard Law Review* 1834 (1999).

Whitman's poem, "I Sit and Look Out," was first published in 1860 as *Leaves of Grass* No. 17 and appeared in its current form in 1871.

CHAPTER IV: THE JURY BREAKS FREE

43–45   William Penn's life story is told in Catherine Owens Peare, *William Penn: A Biography* (Philadelphia: Lippincott, 1957), and Mary Maples Dunn, *William Penn: Politics and Conscience* (Princeton, N.J.: Princeton University Press, 1967). His letters are collected in *The Papers of William Penn,* ed. Mary Maples Dunn and Richard S. Dunn (Philadelphia: University of Pennsylvania Press, 1981).

45–49   On the evolution of criminal jury trials, see Thomas Andrew Green, *Verdict According to Conscience: Perspectives on the English Criminal Trial Jury, 1200–1800* (Chicago: University of Chicago Press, 1985), and John H. Langbein, "The Criminal Trial Before the Lawyers," 45 *University of Chicago Law Review* 263 (1978).

"[I]t requires no manner of skill . . .": William Hawkins, *A Treatise of the Pleas of the Crown,* vol. 2, 6th ed., ed. Thomas Leach (Dublin: Eliz. Lynch, 1788), ch. 39, §2, at 564.

Sir Thomas Smith's description of English criminal trials is in *De Republica Anglorum* (1583).

49   The Green quotation is from *Verdict According to Conscience,* p. 98.

51   *The Diary of Samuel Pepys,* vol. 1, ed. Robert Latham and William
            Matthews (London: HarperCollins, 1995), p. 265.

52–58   The primary source for the Penn-Mead trial is "The Trial of William
            Penn and William Mead, Told by Themselves," 6 *State Trials* 951
            (1742).

58–59   Chief Justice Vaughan's 1671 opinion in *Bushel's Case* is at 124 Eng.
            Rep. 1006. The case is analyzed in Green, *Verdict According to Con-
            science,* pp. 200–64.

            For a comparison of American juries to other "inheritors of Anglo-
            American law," see "The Common Law Jury," 62 *Law and Contempo-
            rary Problems* No. 2, ed. Neil Vidmar (1999), and particularly Nancy
            Jean King, "The American Criminal Jury," and Stephan Landsman,
            "The Civil Jury in America," in that issue.

59   The Pennsylvania guarantee of trial by jury dates from 1682, and is set
            out in *The Earliest Printed Laws of Pennsylvania, 1681–1713,* ed. John
            D. Cushing (Wilmington, Del.: Michael Glazier, 1978), p. 202.

            CHAPTER V: JURIES AND LIBERTY IN THE UNITED STATES

61–62   The standard "whether you agree with it or not" instruction is from the
            Benchbook for U.S. District Court Judges (Federal Judicial Center,
            1995), p. 95.

            The California abortion protesters' trial: Alan W. Scheflin and Jon
            M. Van Dyke, "Merciful Juries: The Resilience of Jury Nullification,"
            48 *Washington and Lee Law Review* 165, 181–82 (1991); Irene Jack-
            son, "DA's Office Decries Jury-Nullification Ad," *San Diego Union-
            Tribune,* January 26, 1990, B1; Michael Granberry, "Abortion Protest
            Juries Told to Ignore Nullification Ad," *Los Angeles Times,* January 27,
            1990, B1.

            The Scheflin and Van Dyke article cited above gives examples of
            pro-nullification leaflets and advertisements aimed at jury panelists.

            The "jury power information kit" is provided by the FIJA, P.O. Box
            59, Helmville, MT 59843-9989.

            The Seattle letter to the editor is from the *Leschi News,* June 1998.

63–68   The primary source for the Zenger trial is James Alexander, *A Brief Narrative of the Case and Trial of John Peter Zenger (1735)* (Cambridge, Mass.: Harvard University Press, 1963). The narrative is reproduced in a short illustrated biography, Livingston Rutherford, *John Peter Zenger* (New York: Chelsea House, 1981). See also John Guinther, *The Jury in America* (New York: Facts on File Publications, 1988).

69–70   Juries and the American Revolution: Albert W. Alschuler and Andrew G. Deiss, "A Brief History of the Criminal Jury in the United States," 61 *University of Chicago Law Review* 867 (1994).

          "[A]gainst being ridden like horses": *Boston Gazette,* Jan. 27, 1766, cited in 1 *Papers of Adams,* vol. 1, ed. Robert J. Taylor (Cambridge, Mass.: Belknap Press, 1977) p. 169.

70–72   The Supreme Court statement is from *Duncan v. Louisiana,* 391 U.S. 145, 155 (1968).

          "A clear head . . .": Richard E. Ellis, *The Jeffersonian Crisis: Courts and Politics in the Young Republic* (New York: Oxford University Press, 1971), p. 115.

          "[A]n absurdity to suppose . . .": *Legal Papers of John Adams,* vol. 1, ed. L. Kinvin Wroth and Hiller B. Zobel (Cambridge, Mass.: Belknap Press, 1965), p. 230.

          John Jay's instruction: *Georgia v. Brailsford,* 3 U.S. (3 Dall.) 1, 4 (1794).

          The heyday and decline of jury nullification: Jeffrey Abramson, *We, the Jury*; Alan Scheflin and Jon Van Dyke, "Jury Nullification: The Contours of a Controversy," 43 *Law and Contemporary Problems* 51 (1980); and Scheflin and Van Dyke, "Merciful Juries."

          A historical summary of the American jury's law-finding function, and of its colonial-era administrative powers, is given in Matthew P. Harrington, "The Law-Finding Function of the American Jury," 1999 *Wisconsin Law Review* 377.

72–73   *Sparf and Hansen v. United States* is reported at 156 U.S. 51 (1895).

73–74   The Fugitive Slave Law cases are discussed by Abramson and numerous other authors. An excellent recent book on the Minkins case is Gary Collison, *Shadrach Minkins: From Fugitive Slave to Citizen* (Cambridge, Mass.: Harvard University Press, 1997). See also Stanley W. Campbell, *The Slave Catchers: Enforcement of the Fugitive Slave Laws, 1850–1860* (Chapel Hill: University of North Carolina Press, 1970).

74–75   The bootleg coal cases: William E. Leuchtenburg, *Franklin D. Roosevelt and the New Deal 1932–1940* (New York: Harper Torchbooks, 1963), p. 25; Louis Adamic, *My America* (New York: Harper, 1938), pp. 316–24.

75–77   The Vietnam protesters' cases: Steven E. Barkan, *Protesters on Trial: Criminal Justice in the Southern Civil Rights and Vietnam Antiwar Movements* (Rutgers, N.J.: Rutgers University Press, 1985); Joseph L. Sax, "Conscience and Anarchy: The Prosecution of War Resisters," 57 *Yale Review* 481 (1968).

77–79   Dr. Kevorkian: Pam Belluck, "Dr. Kevorkian Is a Murderer, Jury Finds," *New York Times,* March 27, 1999, A1.

         Prohibition cases: Kalven and Zeisel, *The American Jury,* pp. 291–93.

         The San Francisco prostitution crackdown: Scheflin and Van Dyke, "Jury Nullification: The Contours of a Controversy."

         Poaching cases: Kalven and Zeisel, *The American Jury,* pp. 287–89.

         Marion Barry: Jonathan I. Z. Agronsky, *Marion Barry: The Politics of Race* (Latham, N.Y.: British American Publishing, 1991).

         Oliver North: Jeffrey Toobin, *Opening Arguments: A Young Lawyer's First Case: United States v. Oliver North* (New York: Viking, 1991). The case on appeal is reported at 910 F.2d 843 (1990).

         The Emmett Till case: Stephen J. Whitfield, *A Death in the Delta: The Story of Emmett Till* (New York: The Free Press, 1988). The Scottsboro case is *Powell v. Alabama,* 287 U.S. 45 (1932).

         The murder conviction of Sam Bowers, and the comments of Vernon Dahmer, Jr., are reported in Rick Bragg, "Jurors Convict Former Wizard in Klan Murder," *New York Times,* August 22, 1998, A1.

81–82   Nullification not to be feared: See Jack B. Weinstein, "The Many Dimensions of Jury Nullification," 81 *Judicature* 168 (1998). Some courts, however, see the jury's ability to acquit on grounds of conscience not as a desirable part of the law but as an invitation to lawlessness. See *People v. Williams*, 21 p.3d 1209 (Cal. 2001).

Conflicting views on what to tell the jury in this regard are stated eloquently in *United States v. Dougherty*, 473 F.2d 1113 (D.C. Cir. 1972).

CHAPTER VI: THE RULES OF THE GAME

84–102   The primary source for the Salem witch trials is *The Salem Witchcraft Papers: Verbatim Transcripts of the Legal Documents of the Salem Witchcraft Outbreak of 1692*, 3 vols., ed. Paul Boyer and Stephen Nissenbaum (New York: Da Capo Press, 1977). Among the many books on the subject are Frances Hill, *A Delusion of Satan: The Full Story of the Salem Witch Trials* (New York: Doubleday, 1995); Peter Charles Hoffer, *The Salem Witchcraft Trials: A Legal History* (Lawrence: University Press of Kansas, 1997); Chadwick Hansen, *Witchcraft at Salem* (New York: George Braziller, 1969); and John Putnam Demos, *Entertaining Satan: Witchcraft and the Culture of Early New England* (New York: Oxford University Press, 1982). An insightful article is "The Witches of Salem Village," in Kai T. Erikson, *Wayward Puritans: A Study in the Sociology of Deviance* (New York: Wiley, 1966). Frances Hill, *The Salem Witch Trials Reader* (New York: Da Capo Press, 2000), reproduces and comments on selected contemporary documents. Arthur Miller's play *The Crucible,* based on the trials, is splendid not only to watch but to read, and is available in a Penguin paperback edition.

102–3   Sir Walter Ralegh's case is reported at *State Trials,* vol. 2 (1603), and is described in Richard O. Lempert and Stephen A. Saltzburg, *A Modern Approach to Evidence: Text, Problems, Transcripts, and Cases,* 2d ed. (St. Paul, Minn.: West Publishing Co., 1982), p. 349. The rise of the rules of evidence is traced in a fine old book, James Bradley Thayer, *Preliminary Treatise on Evidence at the Common Law* (Boston: Little, Brown, 1898). See also J. M. Beattie, *Crime and the Courts in England, 1660–1800* (Princeton, N.J.: Princeton University Press, 1986); Stephan Landsman, "The Rise of the Contentious Spirit: Adversary

Procedure in Eighteenth Century England," 75 *Cornell Law Review* 497 (1990); and John H. Langbein, "Historical Foundations of the Law of Evidence: A View from the Ryder Sources," 96 *Columbia Law Review* 1168 (1996). Mirjan R. Damaska, in *Evidence Law Adrift* (New Haven, Conn.: Yale University Press, 1997), argues that jury trials and party control of fact-gathering are declining and that, as a result, the rules of evidence have lost their moorings.

103–5   "There is no man so good . . .": *Montaigne Essays,* vol. 3, 239.

James Fenton's poem is from *Children in Exile: Poems 1968–1984* (New York: The Noonday Press, 1994), p. 31 (reprinted with permission).

The legal profession's ups and downs are chronicled in Lawrence M. Friedman, *A History of American Law,* 2d ed. (New York: Simon and Schuster, 1985).

105–6   On the constitutional safeguards for criminal defendants, see Richard C. Cortner, *The Supreme Court and the Second Bill of Rights: The Fourteenth Amendment and the Nationalization of Civil Liberties* (Madison: University of Wisconsin Press, 1981); Anthony Lewis, *Gideon's Trumpet* (New York: Random House, 1964); Morton J. Horwitz, *The Warren Court and the Pursuit of Justice* (New York: Hill and Wang, 1998); and Joseph G. Cook, *Constitutional Rights of the Accused* (Rochester, N.Y.: Lawyers Cooperative Publishing Co., 1974). Current articles on one of the accused's protections are collected in R. H. Helmholz, et al., *The Privilege Against Self-Incrimination: Its Origins and Development* (Chicago: University of Chicago Press, 1997). See also Leonard W. Levy, *Origins of the Fifth Amendment: The Right Against Self-Incrimination* (New York: Macmillan, 1986).

106–9   On the anti-Communist hysteria and the resulting injustices, see Richard M. Fried, *Nightmare in Red: The McCarthy Era in Perspective* (New York: Oxford University Press, 1990); Griffin Fariello, *Red Scare: Memories of the American Inquisition* (New York: W. W. Norton & Co., 1995); and Richard H. Rovere, *Senator Joe McCarthy* (New York: Harcourt, Brace, 1959). One woman's ordeal with the federal loyalty program is recounted in Selma R. Williams, *Red-Listed:*

Haunted by the Washington Witch Hunt (Reading, Mass.: Addison-Wesley, 1993).

109–10   On the Senate's debate over whether to hear evidence beyond the Starr report: Allison Mitchell, "The Trial of a President: The Overview; Senate, in Unanimity, Sets Rules for Trial; Witness Issue Put Off," *New York Times,* January 9, 1999, A1.

The Hill-Thomas embarrassment is analyzed in Stephan Landsman, "Who Needs Evidence Rules, Anyway?", 25 *Loyola of Los Angeles Law Review* 635, 635–38 (1992).

"Liberty lies in the hearts of men and women . . ." Quoted in Gerald Gunther, *Learned Hand: The Man and the Judge* (New York: Alfred A. Knopf, 1994), p. 548.

CHAPTER VII: SIX DEADLY SINS

111–12   Gerry Spence's quotation is from his book *With Justice for None: Destroying an American Myth* (New York: Times Books, 1989).

Judge Rothwax's book is *Guilty: The Collapse of Criminal Justice* (New York: Random House, 1996).

112–14   A keen critique of overcontentiousness in American courts is Marvin E. Frankel, *Partisan Justice* (New York: Hill and Wang, paperback ed., 1980).

The story of O. J. Simpson's criminal trial is expertly told in Jeffrey Toobin, *The Run of His Life: The People v. O. J. Simpson* (New York: Touchstone, 1997). The case "could mark a turning point in our legal history, the moment when the need for America to reinvent a fair and workable trial procedure became too obvious to deny." Albert W. Alschuler, "Our Faltering Jury," in *Postmortem: The O. J. Simpson Case,* ed. Jeffrey Abramson (New York: Basic Books, 1996).

On overcontentiousness leading to unjust convictions, see Jim Dwyer, Peter Neufeld, and Barry Scheck, *Actual Innocence: Five Days to Execution and Other Dispatches from the Wrongly Convicted* (New York: Doubleday, 2000).

Roscoe Pound's speech is "The Causes of Popular Dissatisfaction with the Administration of Justice," 29 *Reports of the American Bar Association* 395 (1906), reprinted in 35 F.R.D. 241, 273 (1964). See also Gordon Van Kessel, "Adversary Excesses in the American Criminal Trial," 67 *Notre Dame Law Review* 403 (1992).

"We still have a chance to justify Pound's optimism"—but only if we do much better than the system did in the ruined case described in Jonathan Harr's masterful book *A Civil Action* (New York: Random House, 1995). A defense lawyer's response is Jerome P. Facher, "The View from the Bottomless Pit: Truth, Myth, and Irony in *A Civil Action*," 23 *Seattle University Law Review* 243 (1999).

114–17   On unequal money/unequal justice, see Lois G. Forer, *Money and Justice: Who Owns the Courts?* (New York: Norton, 1984). On the Legal Services Corporation, see Terry Brooks, "The Legal Services Corporation: 2001 and Beyond," 40 *The Judges' Journal* 30 (Winter 2001). That article quotes Justice Wathen and cites the comparative expenditures on legal aid. Recent articles on access to justice are collected in "Conference on the Delivery of Legal Services to Low-Income Persons: Professional and Ethical Issues," 67 *Fordham Law Review* 1713 (1999). See also Talbot D'Alemberte, "Tributaries of Justice: The Search for Full Access," 73 *Florida Bar Journal* 12 (1999).

The United States lags behind other Western democracies in financially supporting legal services for the poor. See Earl Johnson, Jr., "The Right to Counsel in Civil Cases: An International Perspective," 19 *Loyola Law Review* 341 (1985). Justice Johnson, a California state appeals court judge, asked in 1999: "[S]ince the right to counsel in civil cases is now deemed 'a fundamental human right' by most of western civilization, how much more is required before it becomes an essential ingredient of due process in this country?" Quoted in Leonard W. Schroeter, "Attorney Representation: An Essential Right or Not?", *Washington State Bar News,* December 1999.

Professor Langbein's quotation is from his article "Money Talks, Clients Walk," *Newsweek,* April 17, 1995, 32.

On the costs of civil litigation: *Justice for All: Reducing Costs and Delay in Civil Litigation* (Washington, D.C.: The Brookings Institution, 1989); Roberta Katz, *Justice Matters: Rescuing the Legal System for the Twenty-First Century* (Seattle: Discovery Institute, 1997).

On the current legal needs of low- and middle-income Americans: *Report on the Legal Needs of the Low-Income Public,* American Bar Association Publication No. 4290018 (January 1994).

On the growing income disparity: David Cay Johnston, "Gap Between Rich and Poor Found Substantially Wider," *New York Times,* September 5, 1999, A16.

117–20   The Spokane gasoline dealers' case, in its final incarnation in the Supreme Court, is *Texaco Inc. v. Hasbrouck,* 496 U.S. 543 (1990).

120–21   On the White Plains trial, see Raymond Hernandez, "Westchester Trial Illustrates the Burdens of Jury Service," *New York Times,* December 19, 1994, A1; Mark Hansen, "Jurors Demand a Speedy Trial," 81 *American Bar Association Journal* 26 (March 1995).

121–24   On "the obsessive pursuit of law in contemporary American culture," see Paul F. Campos, *Jurismania: The Madness of American Law* (New York: Oxford University Press, 1998).

The "knock and talk" case: *State v. Ferrier,* 136 Wn.2d 103 (1998).

The case of the bank robber: *United States v. Rodley,* No. CR98-41WD (W.D. Wash. 1998), *affirmed* 2000 U.S. App. Lexis 5952 (March 20, 2000).

The case of the deliberating alternates: *United States v. Ottersburg,* 76 F.3d 137 (7th Cir. 1996).

125–27   "[I]t is altogether a defect . . .": 1 Corinthians 6:7.

Napoléon's quotation can be found in *Memorial de Sainte Hélène,* vol. 4, p. 7, quoted in Joseph Parkes, *A History of the Chancery Court* (London: Longman, Rees, Orme, Brown, and Green, 1828), p. 457.

Ambrose Bierce's quotation is from *The Devil's Dictionary* (New York: Oxford University Press, 1999).

"As a litigant . . .": Learned Hand, "The Deficiencies of Trials to Reach the Heart of the Matter (November 17, 1921)," in *Lectures on Legal Topics: 1921–1922* (New York: MacMillan, 1926), p. 105.

Modern society's heightened expectations of justice are described in Lawrence M. Friedman, *Total Justice* (Boston: Beacon Press, paperback ed., 1987). See also Steven Keeva, "Demanding More Justice: Whether Americans Get What They Want From the Legal System Depends on Its Ability to Stretch Limited Resources," 80 *American Bar Association Journal* 46 (August 1994).

Chief Justice Guy's warning is reported in Hunter T. George, "Chief Justice Warns of Court Overload," *Seattle Post-Intelligencer,* January 14, 1999, B1.

On the national obsession with imprisonment: Joseph T. Hallinan, *Going Up the River: Travels in a Prison Nation* (New York: Random House, 2001).

On prison populations and caseloads: Bureau of Justice Statistics, *Correctional Populations in the United States, 1996,* NCJ Publication No. 170013 (Washington, D.C.: United States Department of Justice, Office of Justice Programs, April 1999); *Examining the Work of State Courts, 1998* (National Center for State Courts, 1999); *Judicial Business of the United States Courts* (Washington, D.C.: Administrative Office of the United States Courts, 2000); Jesse Katz, "U.S. Prison Population Hits the Two Million Mark," *International Herald Tribune,* February 16, 2000, 1; *Newsweek,* Special Report, November 13, 2000; and various issues of *The Third Branch* (Washington, D.C.: Administrative Office of the United States Courts).

A grass-roots movement to substitute treatment for imprisonment of nonviolent drug offenders seems to have begun. See Timothy Egan, "Crack's Legacy: A Special Report; In States' Anti-Drug Fight, a Renewal for Treatment," *New York Times,* June 10, 1999, A1.

On failures to provide adequate funding, see Barbara Wolfson, *Justice Denied: Underfunding of the Courts* (Washington, D.C.: Roscoe Pound Foundation, 1994).

The presiding judge's statement: Brian Gain, "Civil Cases in the Courts: Are They Being Squeezed Out?", *King County Bar News,* July 2000.

128–29   They "all run on one leash ...": Geoffrey Chaucer, "The Parson's Tale," line 949, in *Canterbury Tales,* ed. A. C. Cawley (New York:

Everyman's Library, 1992). The original reads: "Alle they renne in o lees, but in diverse maneres."

William Pizzi's book is *Trials Without Truth* (New York: New York University Press, 1999).

Roberta Katz's book is *Justice Matters: Rescuing the Legal System for the Twenty-First Century* (Seattle: Discovery Institute, 1997).

CHAPTER VIII: IS THE JURY UP TO THE JOB?

131–32 Skeptics and believers:

Mark Twain, *Roughing It* (Hartford, Conn.: American Publishing Co., 1872); Erwin Griswold, "1962–63 Harvard Law School Dean's Report," quoted in Kalven and Zeisel, *The American Jury*, p. 5; Jerome Frank, *Law and the Modern Mind* (New York: Brentano's, 1930), pp. 108, 172, and *Courts on Trial* (Princeton, N.J.: Princeton University Press, 1949), p. 123; David Hume, *The History of England*, vol. 1 (1754) (New York: John B. Alden), p. 77. Tocqueville's statement is from *Democracy in America*, p. 285. Chief Justice Warren's comment is from his foreword to Charles W. Joiner, *Civil Justice and the Jury* (Englewood Cliffs, N.J.: Prentice Hall, 1962).

132 Exclusions from jury panels in eighteenth-century England: Douglas Hay, "The Class Composition of the Palladium of Liberty," in *Twelve Good Men and True: The Criminal Trial Jury in England, 1200–1800*, ed. J. S. Cockburn and Thomas A. Green (Princeton, N.J.: Princeton University Press, 1988), p. 354.

The historic use of special juries, chosen for expertise or social class: James Oldham, "The History of the Special (Struck) Jury in the United States and Its Relation to Voir Dire Practices, the Reasonable Cross-Section Requirement, and Peremptory Challenges," 6 *William and Mary Bill of Rights Journal* 623 (1998), and James Oldham, "The Origins of the Special Jury," 50 *University of Chicago Law Review* 137 (1983).

On the evolution of democratic jury panels in the United States: Abramson, *We, the Jury*; Comment, "Developments in the Law: The

Civil Jury," 110 *Harvard Law Review* 1407 (1997). The federal statutes governing jury selection and service are at 28 U.S.C. §§1861–1878. The Supreme Court's 1975 decision is *Taylor v. Louisiana,* 419 U.S. 522 (1975).

133–34 Regarding jury competence and integrity: Abramson, *We, the Jury;* Stephen J. Adler, *The Jury: Trial and Error in the American Courtroom* (New York: Times Books, 1994); Harry Kalven, Jr., and Hans Zeisel, *The American Jury;* John Guinther, *The Jury in America* (New York: Facts on File, 1988); *Verdict: Assessing the Civil Jury System,* ed. Robert E. Litan (Washington, D.C.: The Brookings Institution, 1993); Valerie P. Hans and Andrea J. Appel, "The Jury on Trial," in *A Handbook of Jury Research* (Philadelphia: American Law Institute/American Bar Association, 1999); Stephan Landsman, "The Civil Jury in America: Scenes From an Unappreciated History," 44 *Hastings Law Journal* 579 (1993); Comment, "Developments in the Law: The Civil Jury," 110 *Harvard Law Review* 1409 (1997); Valerie P. Hans and Neil J. Vidmar, *Judging the Jury* (New York: Plenum Press, 1986); and James Gobert, *Justice, Democracy and the Jury* (Brookfield, Vt.: Ashgate Publishing Co., 1997).

The Chicago project's findings on civil juries are reported in Harry Kalven, Jr., "The Dignity of the Civil Jury," 50 *Virginia Law Review* 1055 (1964).

The *Dallas Morning News*/Southern Methodist University Survey is reported in Allen Pusey, "Judges Rule in Favor of Juries," *Dallas Morning News,* May 7, 2000, 15.

On the recent statistics showing judges' agreement with verdicts and approval of juries' work, see Paula L. Hannaford, B. Michael Dann, and G. Thomas Musterman, "How Judges View Civil Juries," and Richard Lempert, "Why Do Juries Get a Bum Rap? Reflections on the Work of Valerie Hans." Both articles appear in 48 *DePaul Law Review* 2 (1998).

The Supreme Court's statement appears in *Duncan v. Louisiana,* 391 U.S. 145, 157 (1968).

135–36 The appeal in *United States v. Nickell* is reported at 883 F.2d 824 (9th Cir. 1989).

Alalamiah Electronic v. Microsoft Corporation, No. C91-789WD (W.D. Wash.), is unreported.

The judgments in *United States v. Brown,* No. CR96-548WD (W.D. Wash.), that were appealed were affirmed at 182 F.3d 928 (9th Cir. 1999), and *United States v. Walton,* 182 F.3d 930 (9th Cir. 1999).

137   Judge Weinstein's comment on jury quality is from his article "Considering Jury 'Nullification': When May and Should a Jury Reject the Law to Do Justice," 30 *American Criminal Law Review* 239 (1993).

Judge Curtin's comment is from his article "A System That Works," 26 *Litigation* 3 (Fall 1999).

The observations of Judges Williams, Strom, and Justice were given in interviews or correspondence with the author.

137–40   Three-fourths come away with a more favorable view: Stephen J. Adler, *The Jury,* p. 240. The survey reports on juror satisfaction in Columbus, Ohio, were provided by Thomas H. Shields, Jury Commissioner, Franklin County Municipal Court. Reports by jurors about their service: Robert H. Aronson, "A Jury of One's Peers," *Prologue* (Seattle Repertory Theatre, October 1995); Mindy Cameron, "Judging the Jury System: Guilty of Serving Justice," *Seattle Times,* November 28, 1993, B6; *CBS Reports,* "Enter the Jury Room" (CBS television broadcast, April 16, 1997); James Gobert, *Justice, Democracy and the Jury* (Brookfield, Vt.: Ashgate Publishing Co., 1997); Victor Villaseñor, *Jury: The People vs. Juan Corona* (New York: Dell, 1977), p. 266; Adler, *The Jury,* pp. 142–43, 175. A Manhattan murder jury's turbulent deliberations are described in D. Graham Burnett, *A Trial by Jury* (New York: Alfred A. Knopf, 2001).

140–41   150,000 jury trials per year: the estimate, reported at Abramson, *We, the Jury,* p. 251, is from researchers at the National Center for State Courts.

The Louisville coin-flip: Associated Press, "Jury Flips Coin in Murder Case," *Seattle Times,* April 26, 2000, A1.

141–43   An informative book on how business defendants fare in jury trials is Valerie P. Hans, *Business on Trial: The Civil Jury and Corporate Responsibility* (New Haven, Conn.: Yale University Press, 2000).

On punitive damages and tort reform: Stephen Daniels and Joanne Martin, *Civil Juries and the Politics of Reform* (Evanston, Ill.: Northwestern University Press, 1995); Symposium, "The Future of Punitive Damages," 1998 *Wisconsin Law Review* 1; Marc Galanter, "An Oil Strike in Hell: Contemporary Legends About the Civil Justice System," 40 *Arizona Law Review* 717 (1998); "A Step Above Anecdote: A Profile of the Civil Jury in the 1990s," 79 *Judicature* 233 (1996); "National Punitive Damages Conferees Find 'No Crisis,'" 4 *Civil Justice Digest* No. 6 (Roscoe Pound Foundation, 1997); Mark Thompson, "Applying the Brakes to Punitives," 83 *American Bar Association Journal* 68 (September 1997); Stephen G. Chappalear, "Jury Trials in the Heartland," 32 *University of Michigan Journal of Law Reform* 241 (1999); Mark Curriden, "Power of 12," 87 *American Bar Association Journal* 36 (August 2001).

The Supreme Court has held that a grossly excessive punitive damage award violates due process of law. *BMW of North America, Inc. v. Gore,* 517 U.S. 559 (1996).

The McDonald's coffee case is reported in Andrea Aerlin, "A Matter of Degree: How a Jury Decided That a Coffee Spill Is Worth $2.9 Million," *Wall Street Journal,* September 1, 1994, A1. Details of the judge's reduction of the award and the settlement of the case are at *Greene v. Boddie-Noell Enterprises,* 966 F. Supp. 416, 418 n.1 (W.D. Va. 1997).

In the wake of the $581 million verdict, the latest in a series of outsized awards in Alabama, the state legislature adopted statutory caps for punitive damages. David Firestone, "Alabama Acts to Limit Huge Awards by Juries," *New York Times,* June 2, 1999, A16. On the settlement of the satellite dish case, see "Many Multi-Million Dollar Verdicts Reviewed," *Legal Intelligencer,* March 2, 2000, 4.

The $145 billion award against tobacco companies is reported in Rick Bragg and Sarah Kershaw, "Juror Says a 'Sense of Mission' Led to Huge Tobacco Damages," *New York Times,* July 16, 2000, A1.

Professor Lempert's article is "Why Do Juries Get a Bum Rap? Reflections on the Work of Valerie Hans," 48 *DePaul Law Review* 453, 462 (1998).

The typical punitive damages instruction wording is from *Manual of Model Civil Jury Instructions for the District Courts of the Ninth Circuit* (1997 ed.), p. 85.

The Justice Department study finding juries more conservative than judges is reported in Jess Bravin, "Surprise: Judges Hand Out Most Punitive Awards," *Wall Street Journal,* June 12, 2000, B1. See also William Graberson, "A Study's Verdict: Jury Awards Are Not Out of Control," *New York Times,* August 5, 2001.

Professor Schuck's comment is quoted in Barry Meier, "Jury's Action Raises Concerns for Tobacco Industry," *New York Times,* July 16, 2000, 17.

144   Understanding complex issues and evidence: *Jury Comprehension in Complex Cases: Report of the Special Committee of the ABA Section of Litigation* (Chicago: American Bar Association, 1990); Robert D. Myers, et al., "Complex Scientific Evidence and the Jury," 83 *Judicature* 3 (1999) ("Jurors are in fact capable of resolving highly complex cases."); Joe S. Cecil, Valerie P. Hans, and Elizabeth C. Wiggins, "Citizen Comprehension of Difficult Issues: Lessons from Civil Jury Trials," 40 *American University Law Review* 727 (1991); Neil J. Vidmar, ed., "Is the Jury Competent?", 52 *Law and Contemporary Problems* 4 (1989); Richard O. Lempert, "Civil Juries and Complex Cases: Taking Stock After 12 Years," in *Verdict: Assessing the Civil Jury System,* ed. Robert E. Litan (Washington, D.C.: Brookings Institution, 1993); Joseph Sanders, "Scientifically Complex Cases, Trial by Jury, and the Erosion of Adversarial Processes," 48 *DePaul Law Review* 355 (1998).

Valerie Hans's reminder is from her book *Business on Trial,* p. 224.

". . . who tinkers with their car . . .": Quoted in "Abolition of Jury Trials in Patent Cases," 34 *IDEA: The Journal of Law and Technology* 77, 86 (1994).

On the complexity exception, see notes at p. 197.

145–46   The cases of the Menendez brothers, Rodney King, Lorena Bobbitt, Oliver North, the Branch Davidians, Susan Smith, Timothy McVeigh, and Terry Nichols have saturated the press and are discussed in books and articles including *Postmortem: The O. J. Simpson Case*; Pizzi, *Trials*

Without Truth ; and Albert Alschuler, "Explaining the Public Wariness of Juries," 48 *DePaul Law Review* 407, 413 (1998). On the Oliver North case, see Jeffrey Toobin, *Opening Arguments*. An analysis of the Rodney King videotape as evidence is Elizabeth F. Loftus and Laura A. Rosenwald, "The Rodney King Videotape: Why the Case Was Not Black and White," 66 *Southern California Law Review* 1637 (1993).

146–47   Judge Noonan's remarks about the death penalty are from *Jeffers v. Lewis,* 38 F.3d 411, 427 (9th Cir. 1994) (dissenting opinion).

Inadequate trial representation: Lise Olsen, "Uncertain Justice," *Seattle Post-Intelligencer*, August 6–7–8, 2001.

The average stay on death row for the sixty-eight inmates executed in 1998 was ten years and ten months. Richard Carelli, "Average Stay on Death Row Down Slightly," Associated Press, December 13, 1999.

Judge Fletcher's quotation is from Betty B. Fletcher, "The Death Penalty in America: Can Justice Be Done?", 70 *New York University Law Review* 811, 826 (1995).

Two-thirds of death sentence cases reversed on appeal: James S. Liebman, Jeffrey Fagan, and Valerie West, *A Broken System: Error Rates in Capital Cases, 1973–1995,* at http://justice.policy.net/jpreport (2000). See also Fox Butterfield, "Death Sentences Being Overturned in 2 of 3 Appeals," *New York Times,* June 12, 2000, A1.

Justice Blackmun's statement is from *Callins v. Collins,* 114 S. Ct. 1127, 1134–35 (1994) (denial of certiorari) (Blackmun, J., dissenting).

The American Bar Association's call for a moratorium on the death penalty is reprinted and discussed in James E. Coleman, Jr., ed., "The ABA's Proposed Moratorium on the Death Penalty," 61 *Law and Contemporary Problems* 1 (1998). On Governor Ryan's halt of executions in Illinois, see Dirk Johnson, "Illinois, Citing Faulty Verdicts, Bars Executions," *New York Times,* February 1, 2000, A1. On the possibility that other states may follow suit, see Mark Hansen, "Death Knell for Death Row?", 86 *American Bar Association Journal* 40 (June 2000).

148–51   The hung jury rates in federal and state criminal cases: Michael J. Saks, "What Do Jury Experiments Tell Us About Jury Decisions?", 6 *Southern California Interdisciplinary Law Journal* 1, 40 (1997); Kenneth S.

Klein and Theodore D. Klastorin, "Do Diverse Juries Aid or Impede Justice?", 1999 *Wisconsin Law Review* 553, 562 n.53. Continuing research is reported in Paula L. Hannaford, Valerie P. Hans, and G. Thomas Munsterman, "How Much Justice Hangs in the Balance?", 83 *Judicature* 59 (1999).

"In a recent Seattle murder trial . . .": Ian Ith, "One Juror Forces Mistrial for Anderson," *Seattle Times,* March 5, 1999, A1.

On race as a factor in criminal justice, see David Cole, *No Equal Justice: Race and Class in the American Criminal Justice System* (New York: The New Press, 1999); Leadership Conference on Civil Rights, *Justice on Trial: Racial Disparities in the American Criminal Justice System* (2000); Rita J. Simon and Craig Dicker, "Race in the Jury Room," in *A Handbook of Jury Research* (Philadelphia: American Law Institute/American Bar Association, 1999); Jeffrey Rosen, "One Angry Woman," *New Yorker,* February 24 and March 3, 1997; and National Center on Institutions and Alternatives, "As Millennium Approaches, One Million African Americans Behind Bars" (January 14, 1999, press release). Racial disparities in juvenile court are described in a 2000 report sponsored by the Justice Department and six foundations. See Fox Butterfield, "Racial Disparities Seen as Pervasive in Juvenile Justice," *New York Times,* April 26, 2000, A1. On the death penalty's disparate racial impact: Amnesty International's report, *Killing with Prejudice: Race and the Death Penalty* (1999). The federal death penalty, as well as those of the states, is implicated. See Marc Lacey and Raymond Bonner, "Reno Troubled by Death Penalty Statistics," *New York Times,* September 13, 2000, A14.

Paul Butler, in "Racially Based Jury Nullification: Black Power in the Criminal Justice System," 105 *Yale Law Journal* 677, 679 (1995), argues that "[t]he decision as to what kind of conduct by African-Americans ought to be punished is better made by African-Americans themselves, based on the costs and benefits to their community, than by the traditional criminal justice process, which is controlled by white lawmakers and white law enforcers." A condensed version of this article appears in the December 1995 edition of *Harper's* magazine.

Doubt on whether the Simpson jury reached a nullification verdict is cast by Nancy S. Marder, "The Interplay of Race and False Claims of Jury Nullification," 32 *University of Michigan Journal of Law Reform* 285 (1999).

On the Wayne Williams convictions, see Art Harris, "Atlanta Jury Convicts Williams of Two Murders," *Washington Post,* February 28, 1982, A1.

On the Emmanuel Hammond conviction, see Gary Pomerantz, "At Love Trial, a Compelling Human Drama," *Atlanta Journal and Constitution,* March 11, 1990, D1.

On the Mel Reynolds convictions: Edward Walsh, "Reynolds Guilty on All Counts," *Washington Post,* August 23, 1995, A1.

On the acquittal of the officers who shot Amadou Diallo: Jeffrey Toobin, "The Unasked Question," *New Yorker,* March 6, 2000, 38.

On the Connecticut jury's conviction of Scott Smith: Associated Press State and Local Wire (March 14, 2000).

The rabbi-juror's experience is reported in Sanford Ragins, "Justice at the Grass Roots," 83 *Judicature* 312 (2000).

Tension in the jury room is especially high in cases involving harsh mandatory sentences. C. Katherine E. Finklestein, "Tempers Grow Shorter in Jury Room," *New York Times*, August 3, 2001, a.19.

152–53   On the right to have a jury in some types of civil cases but not in others: Fleming James, Jr., "Right to a Jury Trial in Civil Actions," 72 *Yale Law Journal* 655 (1963).

The Robertson Davies quotation is from his book *The Merry Heart* (New York: Viking, 1997), p. 195.

The *Washington Post* findings: Richard Morin and Dan Balz, "Americans Losing Trust in Each Other and Institutions," *Washington Post,* January 28, 1996, A1. The remainder of the *Post* series on how Americans view each other and their government appears in the January 29–31 and February 4, 1996, editions.

The Milton S. Eisenhower Foundation, in its 1998 report *The Millennium Breach,* concludes that "[t]he rich are getting richer, the poor are getting poorer, and minorities are suffering disproportionately." A more encouraging view of this country's ongoing communal values is Alan Wolfe, *One Nation, After All* (New York: Viking, 1998).

This country's share of the world's jury trials: Gerald Casper and Hans Zeisel, "Lay Judges in the German Criminal Courts," 1 *Journal of Legal Studies* 135, 135–36 (1972).

The jury besieged in Great Britain and Australia: Mark Findlay and Peter Duff, ed., *The Jury Under Attack* (London and Sydney: Butterworths, 1988).

CHAPTER IX: BETTER TRIALS

155–58 The continental systems:

Sybille Bedford, *The Faces of Justice* (New York: Simon and Schuster, 1961), is an engrossing account of continental trials by a polyglot observer.

John Merryman, *The Civil Law Tradition: An Introduction to the Legal Systems of Western Europe and Latin America*, 2d ed. (Stanford, Calif.: Stanford University Press, 1985), provides a scholarly summary.

Rudolf B. Schlesinger, "Comparative Criminal Procedure: A Plea for Utilizing Foreign Experience," 26 *Buffalo Law Review* 361 (1977), asks that we learn from the Europeans instead of continuing to ignore them.

John H. Langbein, *Torture and the Law of Proof* (Chicago: University of Chicago Press, 1977), describes the continental use of judicially supervised torture to gather evidence until about the end of the eighteenth century.

William Pizzi helpfully compares several European criminal justice systems to ours in *Trials Without Truth* (New York: New York University Press, 1999).

Professor Langbein's comment is from his article "The German Advantage in Civil Procedure," 52 *University of Chicago Law Review* 823, 866 (1985). Those who agree about "adversary tricksters" point to lawyer training manuals such as David Ball, *Theater Tips and Strategies for Jury Trials*, 2d ed. (National Institute for Trial Advocacy, 1997).

Because continental trials lack a single, focused occasion when the witnesses appear for questioning and the parties give their arguments, a trial may drag on for years. The Italian criminal system, for example, "is notoriously inefficient and slow." Alessandra Stanley, "3-Step Justice System: Conviction, Appeal, Escape," *New York Times,* May 23, 1998, A4.

On the crises of expense, delay, and ineffectiveness in continental as well as common law civil litigation, see Adrian A. S. Zuckerman, ed., *Civil Justice in Crisis* (New York: Oxford University Press, 1999).

On the history of American litigation, see generally Lawrence M. Friedman, *A History of American Law*, 2d ed. (New York: Simon & Schuster, 1985).

A good collection on the adversary system, including intelligent praise of it, is Stephan Landsman, *Readings on Adversarial Justice: The American Approach to Litigation* (St. Paul, Minn.: West Publishing Co., 1988). See also Stephen A. Saltzburg, "Lawyers, Clients, and the Adversary System," 37 *Mercer Law Review* 647 (1986); Stephan Landsman, *The Adversary System: A Description and Defense* (Washington, D.C.: American Enterprise Institute, 1984).

158–61   The case of the murdered Filipino union activists appears in the official reports only in regard to questions of jurisdiction: *Domingo v. Republic of the Philippines,* 808 F.2d 1349 (9th Cir. 1987), and 694 F. Supp. 782 (W.D. Wash. 1988).

Karl Popper's quotation is from *The Open Society and Its Enemies,* vol. 1 (London: Routledge & Kegan Paul, 1966), p. 158.

161   On reforming jury trials: Jeffrey Abramson, *We, the Jury*; Stephen Adler, *The Jury*; B. Michael Dann, chairman, *Jurors: The Power of Twelve* (Arizona Supreme Court Committee on More Effective Use of Juries, 1994); American Bar Association, *Charting a Future for the Civil Jury System* (Washington, D.C.: The Brookings Institution, 1992); B. Michael Dann, "Free the Jury," 23 *Litigation* 5 (Fall 1996); G. Thomas Munsterman, Paula L. Hannaford, and G. Marc Whitehead, ed., *Jury Trial Innovations* (Williamsburg, Va.: National Center for State Courts, 1997) (listing books, articles, and cases on the subject); Symposium, "Jury Reform: Making Juries Work," 32 *University of*

Michigan Journal of Law Reform (1999); *Enhancing the Jury System* (Chicago: American Judicature Society, 1999); Nancy J. King, ed., "The Jury: Research and Reform," 79 *Judicature* 5 (1996); Franklin Strier, *Reconstructing Justice: An Agenda for Trial Reform* (Chicago: University of Chicago Press, 1996).

161–63   On the evolution of democracy from direct participation to representative government, see Anthony Arblaster, *Democracy*, 2d ed. (Minneapolis: University of Minnesota Press, 1994).

Failures to report for jury duty are analyzed in Robert G. Boatright, "Why Citizens Don't Respond to Jury Summonses and What Courts Can Do About It," 82 *Judicature* 156 (1999). Based on a national survey and follow-up interviews in four courts, the author concludes: "Most citizens do wish to serve on juries, but are prevented from doing so by economic barriers. Many cannot take time off from work, and others have difficulty getting to the courthouse." The data are collected in a report by the American Judicature Society, *Improving Citizen Response to Jury Summonses* (1998).

On past and present failures to report for jury duty: Thomas L. Fowler, "Filling the Jury Box: Responding to Jury Duty Avoidance," 23 *North Carolina Central Law Journal* 1 (1997–1998); Nancy J. King, "Juror Delinquency in Criminal Trials in America, 1796–1996," 94 *Michigan Law Review* 2673 (1996).

The District of Columbia jury study is reported at "D.C. Jury Reform Project Recommends Bigger Juror Role, Fewer Peremptories," 66 *United States Law Week* 2517 (March 3, 1998).

Ten dollars a day in most Washington counties: Richard P. Guy, "From the Chief Justice: A Report to the Washington State Legislature" (January 2000), 4.

El Paso's success is reported in the *Dallas Morning News*, October 14, 2000.

The New York compliance program: Laura Pedersen, "Eight Million Stories in Dodge City (Jury Dodging, That Is)," *New York Times*, February 4, 2001, Section 14, p. 4.

"[T]he very cattle in the corrals": Mark Twain, *Roughing It* (Hartford, Conn.: American Publishing Company, 1872), 341.

164   Anthony Lewis's comment on jury selection is from his column "Mocking Justice," *New York Times,* December 12, 1994, A19.

165–68   On whether to abolish peremptory challenges, see Nancy S. Marder, "Beyond Gender: Peremptory Challenges and the Roles of the Jury," 73 *Texas Law Review* 1041 (1995); Morris B. Hoffman, "Abolish Peremptory Challenges," 82 *Judicature* 202 (1999); Robert G. Boatright, "The 21st Century American Jury," 83 *Judicature* 288 (2000); and G. Thomas Munsterman, "The Future of Peremptory Challenges," *The Court Manager #6* (1997).

"[A] sustained attack": Abramson, *We, the Jury,* 154.

A typical bit of trial lawyers' advice says, "You don't (and shouldn't) really want a 'fair' jury. You want jurors who seem predisposed to your side." Andrew T. Berry, "Selecting Jurors," 24 *Litigation* 8, 8 (Fall 1997).

Supportive of peremptories is James Gobert, *Justice, Democracy and the Jury* (Brookfield, Vt.: Ashgate Publishing Co., 1997).

The Ninth Circuit's comment on peremptory challenges is from *United States v. Annigoni,* 96 F.3d 1132, 1137 (9th Cir. 1996). Judge Motley's contrasting decision is *Minetos v. City University of New York,* 925 F. Supp. 177, 183 (S.D.N.Y. 1996).

On the futility of peremptory challenges: "A survey done in Chicago several years ago showed that a number of prosecutors and defenders had 'negative correlations' in challenging jurors in criminal trials. In other words, some defenders excused jurors who would have acquitted the defendant and kept those who voted to convict, while some of the prosecutors did the reverse." James W. McElhaney, "Trial Notebook," 24 *Litigation* 55, 56 (Fall 1997).

The $200 million yearly income for jury consultants is reported in Adler, *The Jury,* p. 85. But $400 million may be closer. See Franklin Strier and Donna Schestowski, "Profiling the Profilers: A Study of the Trial Consulting Profession, Its Impact on Trial Justice and What, If Anything, to Do About It," 1999 *Wisconsin Law Review* 441, 444–45.

The *Batson* complications began with *Batson v. Kentucky,* 476 U.S.

79 (1986). Justice Thurgood Marshall, dissenting, argued that the only practicable answer was to abolish peremptories.

Barbara Allen Babcock contends that abolishing peremptory challenges would sap public confidence in juries by shifting selection power from the parties to a remote, and necessarily fallible, judge; would require criminal defendants to submit their fates to jurors whom they fear and distrust; and would weaken the jury in unforeseeable ways. See her articles "Women's Rights and Jury Service," 61 *Cincinnati Law Review* 1139 (1993), and "In Defense of the Criminal Jury" in *Postmortem: The O. J. Simpson Case.*

168–69   The Supreme Court's ill-starred voyage to mini-juries and nonunanimous verdicts began with *Williams v. Florida,* 399 U.S. 78 (1970), and *Apodaca v. Oregon,* 406 U.S. 404 (1972), and stopped at six jurors in *Ballew v. Georgia,* 435 U.S. 223 (1978), and *Burch v. Louisiana,* 441 U.S. 130 (1979). The unfortunate results are described in Michael J. Saks, "The Smaller the Jury, the Greater the Unpredictability," 79 *Judicature* 263 (1996), and Richard S. Arnold, "Trial by Jury: The Constitutional Right to a Jury of Twelve in Civil Trials," 22 *Hofstra Law Review* 1 (1993).

Only two states, Louisiana and Oregon, have adopted nonunanimous verdicts in criminal cases. The other forty-eight and the federal courts require unanimity. More than thirty states accept nonunanimous, supermajority civil verdicts; the other American jurisdictions do not. J. Clark Kelso, "Final Report of the Blue Ribbon Commission on Jury System Improvement," 47 *Hastings Law Journal* 1433, 1494 (1996).

Arguments for accepting nonunanimous verdicts in both civil and criminal cases are presented in Jere W. Morehead, "A 'Modest' Proposal for Jury Reform: The Elimination of Required Unanimous Jury Verdicts," 46 *Kansas Law Review* 933 (1998).

A valuable compilation of articles and judicial opinions about jury size is J. Myron Jacobstein and Roy M. Mersky, ed., *Jury Size: Articles and Bibliography from the Literature of Law and the Social and Behavioral Sciences* (Littleton, Colo.: Fred B. Rothman & Co., 1998).

170   Justice O'Connor's quotation is from her article "Juries: They May Be Broken, But We Can Fix Them," 44 *Federal Lawyer* 20, 22 (1997).

A Los Angeles judge who had the lawyers make their full opening statements at the start of empanelment found that requests for hardship excusals were cut in half and some jurors even offered to call their employers to see if they could stay. Jacqueline A. Connor, "Jury Reform: Notes on the Arizona Seminar," 1 *Journal of Legal Advocacy and Practice* 25, 30 (1999).

172   Judge Rafeedie's quotation is from his article "Speedier Trials," 21 *Litigation* 6 (Fall 1994).

The federal rule confirming the judge's power to channel the trial toward finding the truth, and to avoid wasting time, is Federal Rule of Evidence 611(a).

173   Time budgets in civil cases are authorized by Rule 16(c)(4), Federal Rules of Civil Procedure.

173–74   On expert testimony and the problems of scientific evidence: John H. Langbein, "The German Advantage in Civil Procedure," 52 *University of Chicago Law Review* 823 (1985); Jack B. Weinstein, "Science and the Challenges of Expert Testimony in the Courtroom," 77 *Oregon Law Review* 1005 (1998).

The federal rule on neutral, court-appointed experts is Rule 706, Federal Rules of Evidence. The pros and cons of their use are discussed in Anthony Champagne, et al., "Are Court-Appointed Experts the Solution to the Problems of Expert Testimony?", 84 *Judicature* 178 (2001).

176   The Nevada attempted-murder instruction is one example of many given in Amira Elwork, Bruce D. Sales, and James J. Alfini, *Making Jury Instructions Understandable* (Charlottesville, Va.: The Michie Co., 1982). The translation into plain English is mine. See also Bethany K. Dumas, "Jury Trials: Lay Jurors, Pattern Jury Instructions, and Comprehension Issues," 67 *Tennessee Law Review* 701 (2000).

CHAPTER X: THE CHURCH AND THE STREETS

179   Ninety percent or more resolved without trial: Bureau of Justice Statistics, *Sourcebook of Criminal Justice Statistics 1996*, Kathleen Maguire

and Ann L. Pastore, ed. (Washington, D.C.: United States Department of Justice, 1996), pp. 448, 471; *Judicial Business of the United States Courts, Annual Report of the Director* (Washington, D.C.: Administrative Office of the United States Courts, 1998), pp. 136–254; Herbert M. Krizern, "Adjudication to Settlement: Shading in the Grey," 70 *Judicature* 161, 162–64 (1986).

180–81   On the undue costs of uncontrolled discovery: Roberta Katz, *Justice Matters: Rescuing the Legal System for the Twenty-First Century* (Seattle: Discovery Institute, 1997).

Discovery open to judicial supervision: Rules 26(6)(2) and 16(d) of the Federal Rules of Civil Procedure and Criminal Procedure, respectively, say so, and every state has comparable rules. Arizona's four-hour limit on depositions is at 16 *Arizona Revised Statutes,* Rules of Civil Procedure, Rule 30(d). A new federal Rule 30 uses seven hours as the maximum.

181–83   Jesus on settlement: Matthew 5:25.

Linda R. Singer, *Settling Disputes: Conflict Resolution in Business, Families, and the Legal System* (Boulder, Colo.: Westview Press, 1994), is a good summary of the origins and growth of the ADR movement, and of techniques that work. See also Rhonda McMillion, "Growing Acceptance for ADR," 82 *American Bar Association Journal* 106 (May 1996); David B. Lipsky and Ronald L. Seeber, "In Search of Control: The Corporate Embrace of ADR," 1 *University of Pennsylvania Journal of Labor and Employment Law* 133 (1998); Jack M. Sabatino, "ADR as 'Litigation Lite': Procedural and Evidentiary Norms Embedded Within Alternative Dispute Resolution," 47 *Emory Law Journal* 1289 (1998); and Dorothy W. Nelson, "ADR in the 21st Century: Opportunities and Challenges," 6 *Dispute Resolution Magazine* 3 (2000).

Arbitrations outnumbering court trials: Mark Curriden, "A Weapon Against Liability," *Dallas Morning News,* May 7, 2000, 25A.

Lincoln's "peacemaker" advice is quoted in "Fragment: Notes for a Law Lecture," in *The Collected Works of Abraham Lincoln,* vol. 2, Roy P. Basler, ed. (New Brunswick, N.J.: Rutgers University Press, 1953), p. 81.

183–84   On the need to extend mediation services to low- and middle-income people, see Jill Schachner Chanen, "Mediation for the Masses," 85 *American Bar Association Journal* 20 (July 1999).

Congress's recent statute is the Alternative Dispute Resolution Act of 1998, 28 U.S.C. §651 et seq.

The Kansas City federal mediation results are reported in Kent Snapp, "Five Years of Random Testing Shows Early ADR Successful," *Dispute Resolution Magazine* (Summer 1997).

The western Washington federal ADR program is codified at Local Rules W.D. Wash. CR 39.1, and the results are summarized in *Federal Bar Association Alternative Dispute Resolution Task Force Report* (Seattle: Federal Bar Association for the Western District of Washington, 1995).

The *kort geding* is described in Adrian A. S. Zuckerman, ed., *Civil Justice in Crisis* 34, 445–46.

185–87   On the controversy over plea bargaining: Robert E. Scott and William J. Stuntz, "Plea Bargaining as Contract," and "A Reply: Imperfect Bargains, Imperfect Trials, and Innocent Defendants," 101 *Yale Law Journal*, 1910 and 2011 (1992); Stephen J. Schulhofer, "Plea Bargaining as Disaster," id., 1929; Frank H. Easterbrook, "Plea Bargaining as Compromise," id., 1969; Albert W. Alschuler, "The Trial Judge's Role in Plea Bargaining," 76 *Columbia Law Review* 1059 (1976); and Donald G. Gifford, "Meaningful Reform of Plea Bargaining," 1983 *University of Illinois Law Review* 37.

On the settlement of criminal cases, see *United States v. Torres*, 999 F.2d 376 (9th Cir. 1993), permitting a judge other than the trial judge to help in the negotiations. Mandatory mediation, as a substitute for unsupervised plea bargaining, is recommended in Jennifer Smith, "Scrapping the Plea Bargain," 7 *Dispute Resolution Magazine* 19 (2000).

187   An early prediction of the "multi-door courthouse" is Frank E. A. Sander, "Varieties of Dispute Processing," 70 F.R.D. 111 (1976).

CHAPTER XI: LITIGATION IN THE TWENTY-FIRST CENTURY

189   A stimulating view of litigation's future is offered by the Colorado Judicial Department's long-range planning project, summarized in

Craig Boersma, "Vision 2020: Building a Strategic Plan for Colorado Courts," 22 *Colorado Lawyer* 11 (1993).

190–91   The American Bar Association section chairman's remarks: Robert N. Sayler, "Tigers at the Gates—The Justice System Approaches Melt-Down," 20 *Litigation* 1, 2 (Fall 1993).

A keen analysis of what the legal profession needs to do is Deborah L. Rhode, *In the Interests of Justice: Reforming the Legal Profession* (New York: Oxford University Press, 2000).

Critiques of the profession are collected in Richard L. Abel, ed., *Lawyers: A Critical Reader* (New York: The New Press, 1997). Lawyers' higher values and intangible rewards are discussed in Patrick J. Schiltz, "On Being a Happy, Healthy, and Ethical Member of an Unhappy, Unhealthy, and Unethical Profession," 52 *Vanderbilt Law Review* 871 (1999); and Michael Traynor, "The Pursuit of Happiness," 52 *Vanderbilt Law Review* 1025 (1999).

The Supreme Court's main decision on lawyer advertising and solicitation is *Bates v. State Bar of Arizona,* 43 U.S. 350 (1977). A typical account of the results is Nina Bernstein, "Battles over Lawyer Advertising Divide the Bar," *New York Times,* July 19, 1997, A1. A warning about lawyer advertising's effects on public confidence in the legal system is E. Vernon F. Glenn, "A Pox on Our House," 79 *American Bar Association Journal* 116 (August 1993). For the view that the public in fact gains from solicitation by lawyers because knowledge of legal rights is enhanced, see Monroe H. Freedman, *Lawyers' Ethics in an Adversary System* (Indianapolis: Bobbs-Merrill, 1975), pp. 113–25 (referring to "the professional obligation to chase ambulances").

On the gap between the legal profession's ideal of pro bono service and the reality that few lawyers live up to it, see Deborah L. Rhode, "Cultures of Commitment: Pro Bono for Lawyers and Law Students," 67 *Fordham Law Review* 2415 (1999).

On ethics and civility in litigation, see Austin Sarat, "Enactments of Professionalism: A Study of Judges' and Lawyers' Accounts of Ethics and Civility in Litigation," 67 *Fordham Law Review* 809 (1998); Victor H. Lott, Jr., "A State Bar President's Views on Professional Ethics,"

23 *Journal of the Legal Profession* 115 (1998/1999); Lawrence J. Fox, Nancy McCready Higgins, and Donald B. Hilliker, "Ethics: Beyond the Rules: Historical Preface," 67 *Fordham Law Review* 691 (1998).

A call for the profession to accept competition from nonlawyers is Deborah L. Rhode, "Meet Needs with Nonlawyers," 82 *American Bar Association Journal* 104 (January 1996). On the desirability of mandatory pro bono, see, by the same author, "Cultures of Commitment: Pro Bono for Lawyers and Law Students," 69 *Fordham Law Review* 2415 (1999).

192   The survey showing Americans' impressions of what percentage of government spending goes to the justice system is cited in Steven Keeva, "Demanding More Justice: Whether Americans Get What They Want from the Legal System Depends on Its Ability to Stretch Limited Resources," 80 *American Bar Association Journal* 46 (August 1994). The federal courts' share of the budget is reported in *The Judiciary Budget in Brief* (Washington: Administrative Office of the United States Courts, 2000), p. 1.

193   The pros and cons of racially conscious jury selection are discussed by Albert W. Alschuler and Randall L. Kennedy in "Equal Justice: Would Color-Conscious Jury Selection Help?" 81 *American Bar Association Journal* 36 (December 1995), and Nancy J. King, "Racial Jurymandering: Cancer or Cure? A Contemporary Review of Affirmative Action in Jury Selection," 68 *New York University Law Review* 707 (1993).